ONE DEAD INDIAN

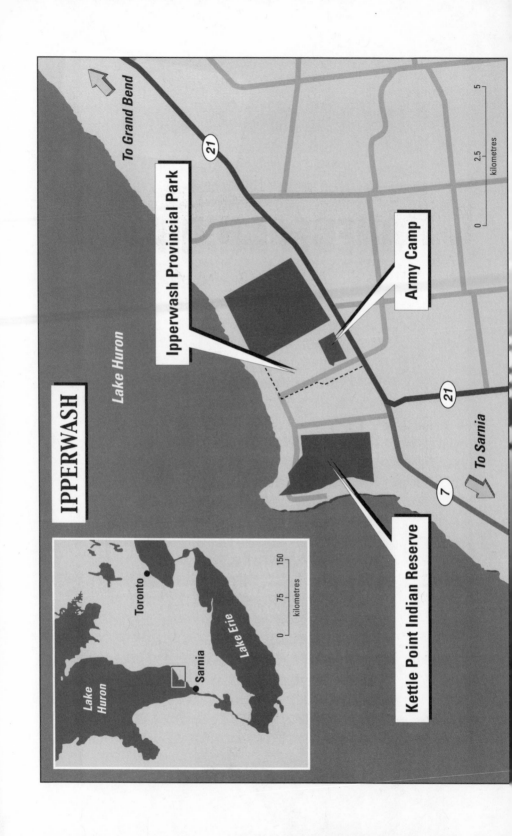

IPPERWASH

Lake Huron

To Grand Bend

21

Ipperwash Provincial Park

Army Camp

21

To Sarnia

7

Kettle Point Indian Reserve

0   2.5   5
kilometres

Lake Huron

Toronto

Lake Erie

Sarnia

0   75   150
kilometres

ONEDEADINDIAN

THE PREMIER, THE POLICE, AND THE IPPERWASH CRISIS

PETER EDWARDS

McCLELLAND & STEWART

Trade paperback edition with new preface and Afterword
published by McClelland & Stewart 2006
Cloth edition published by Stoddart Publishing Co. Ltd. 2001

Library and Archives Canada Cataloguing in Publication

Edwards, Peter, 1956-
One dead Indian : the premier, the police and the Ipperwash crisis / Peter Edwards.

Includes index.
ISBN 13: 978-0-7710-3047-5
ISBN 10: 0-7710-3047-9

1. Ipperwash Incident, Ont., 1993-. 2. Ojibwa Indians–Ontario–Ipperwash Provincial
Park Region–Claims. 3. Ojibwa Indians–Land tenure–Ontario–Ipperwash Provincial
Park Region. 4. Indians of North America–Canada–Government relations–1951-.
5. George, Dudley, 1957-1995. I. Title.

E99.C6E39 2003   323.1'1973   C2003-900159-8

We acknowledge the financial support of the Government of Canada through the Book
Publishing Industry Development Program and that of the Government of Ontario
through the Ontario Media Development Corporation's Ontario Book Initiative.
We further acknowledge the support of the Canada Council for the Arts and the
Ontario Arts Council for our publishing program.

Text design: Tannice Goddard
Map by CrowleArt Group

Printed and bound in Canada

This book is printed on acid-free paper that is
100% ancient forest friendly (100% post-consumer recycled)

McClelland & Stewart Ltd.
75 Sherbourne Street
Toronto, Ontario
M5A 2P9
www.mcclelland.com

2   3   4   5   09 08 07 06

To Barbara, James and Sarah, Amund and Pauline Hanson,
Winona and Kenneth Edwards, and John and Linda Findley.
For making me feel blessed

───⌒───

"A soft answer turneth away wrath:
but grievous words stir up anger."
— Proverbs 15:1

"Let the inquiry be held in broad daylight!"
— Emile Zola, J'accuse, January 13, 1898

"This government will not be seen as cooperating with the Indians."
— Aide in the Ontario Premier's Office, September 6, 1995

CONTENTS

PREFACE TO 2006 EDITION

I was sent by the *Toronto Star* to Ipperwash immediately after the shooting of Dudley George; I arrived there around 3:30 a.m. on September 7, 1995. Harold Levy and I have been covering the story ever since, often with Richard Brennan of the *Star*'s Queen's Park bureau. Since July 2004, I have covered the public inquiry of the Ipperwash violence in Forest, Ontario, about a twenty-minute drive from where Dudley George was killed. This printing of *One Dead Indian* comes after eighteen months of public hearings into the Ipperwash tragedy before Mr. Justice Sidney Linden. Our coverage of this story continues.

One Dead Indian is based on literally hundreds of hours of interviews and conversations involving the author and Harold Levy of the *Star*. Harold and I also attended key trials relating to the Ipperwash crisis. I consulted government records obtained under the Ontario Freedom of Information Act and the federal *Access to Information Act*, as well as extensive court transcripts and archival material, which includes transcripts of recorded conversations and statements given by police officers involved at Ipperwash. All conversations and scenes described in this book were drawn either from transcripts of conversations or the memories of people directly involved. The updated afterword was written after the testimony of ninety-four witnesses in the ongoing public inquiry into George's death.

ACKNOWLEDGEMENTS

Harold Levy was invaluable to me in the writing of this book, as well as in bringing the story out in the pages of the *Toronto Star*. We have discussed the case for hundreds, and perhaps thousands, of hours and Harold has constantly pressed for the full story to be told. It was a privilege and an adventure to work with him. His value to the project cannot be overstated.

Daphne Hart, my agent from the Helen Heller Agency, was her typical professional and cheerful self, finding a suitable home for this work, and then finding a suitable new home when the original publisher went out of business.

Editor Jennifer Glossop was excellent as usual, and I'm also grateful to Jim Gifford and Don Bastian of Stoddart for seeing the importance of a work on Ipperwash, and to Kathryn Dean for her exacting copy editing.

At McClelland & Stewart, I would like to thank Douglas Gibson, Pat Kennedy, Elizabeth Kribs, Doug Pepper, and Susan Renouf for their roles in keeping the book alive.

Dave Annis, Paul Archer, Alison Blackduck, Richard Brennan, Bruce Campion-Smith, Jim Coyle, Fred Edwards, Dave Ellis, Vian Ewart, Jonathan Ferguson, Warren Ferguson, John Ferri, Carol Goar, Emma Harries, Kate Harries, Fred Kuntz, Michele Landsberg, Caroline Mallan, Greg Smith, Steve Tustin, Ian Urquhart, Tom Walkom, and the entire *Toronto Star* library and switchboard all deserve thanks. Bruce Campion-Smith wrote eloquently about Ipperwash for years, and Fred Edwards (no relation to author) fought hard for the story at the *Star*, and neither of them grumbled when their names were thoughtlessly omitted from the original acknowledgements.

John Honderich of the *Toronto Star* has supported the story in the spirit of the *Star*'s founder, Joseph Atkinson.

Others in the media have also seen the profound value of the Ipperwash story, including Brent Barclay, Paul Barnsley, Rita Deverell, Gary Farmer, Rick Harp, Andrew Johnson, Jennifer Kawaja, Richard Mackie, Kirk Makin, Pam Matthews, Julia Sereny, Dan Smoke, Evan Solomon, Tim Southam, Maurice Switzer, Kevin Tierney, and Andrew Wreggitt. I feel extremely grateful to Sienna Films and Park Ex Pictures for capturing the spirit of the book on film and to CTV for airing a production in which all of the main characters are Native.

At Kettle and Stoney Points, I feel privileged to have met and talked with numerous residents, including Sam, Veronica, and Pam George, Nicholas Cottrelle, Gina and Judas George, Glenn and Bev George, and Ben Peugot.

Basil Alexander, Perry Chao, Murray Klippenstein, Delia Opekokew, Andrew Orkin, Gerry Phillips, Ian Scott, and Vilko Zbrogar helped me with their patience and intelligence.

Donald Avery, Elaine Bomberry, Robin Buyers, Diane Chester, Dennis Fox, Sheila Grantham, Nancy Johnson, Martin Long, Ann Pohl, Donna Smith, Romayne Smith Fullerton, Monica Virtue, Tommy White, Brian Young, and many others have also done much to build something positive out of a horrible situation. Although they aren't seeking praise, they deserve it nonetheless.

Mr. James French, formerly of Central Secondary School in London, Ontario, was the type of teacher every student should have. I can't thank him enough. I still benefit from his English classes, more than a quarter century after my graduation.

The staff at the Lambton Room in Wyoming helped me put the story in historical perspective. So did the late Clifford George, who always sent me away with a smile, even after telling stories that were enormously sad. A high point of my career was on September 20, 2004, when he called me "my good friend" at the public inquiry before Mr. Justice Sidney Linden into the night of violence that killed Dudley George.

Some of the better sources who worked with me and Harold Levy would prefer not to be mentioned here, and that is totally understandable. They know who they are and their courage is appreciated.

Peter Edwards
December 2005

1

A SHOT IN
THE DARK

911 Operator: "I think you need to speak to a police officer."
Aboriginal woman: "I can't. They're the ones doing the shooting."

The day before the riot squad marched on Ipperwash Provincial Park on the eastern shore of Lake Huron in southwestern Ontario, Cecil Bernard "Slippery" George had a feeling that something was going horribly wrong. On that day, Tuesday, September 5, 1995, the Kettle and Stony Point band councillor had been pulled over while driving on Highway 21 southeast of Sarnia. The Ontario Provincial Police officer had asked him all sorts of questions about the park and the occupiers. He'd replied that he knew almost all of them and he considered them good, peaceful people. As he spoke, he felt his words weren't making much of a difference. They weren't what the officer was hoping to hear.

Slippery's uneasy feeling only got worse as more police in squad cars kept appearing at Ipperwash throughout Tuesday and Wednesday, swelling their ranks with dozens of out-of-town officers around the military base and adjoining provincial park at Ipperwash. Just after suppertime on

Wednesday, Slippery went to the park to warn the Natives — especially his sister and eight-year-old nephew. He feared things might soon get violent. As a councillor from nearby Kettle Point, he held a position of some status, at least among the Native people, and he thought he could also act as an intermediary between the protestors and the police.

AS HE DROVE to the park at Stoney Point on Wednesday sometime around 10:00 p.m., Slippery noticed a familiar black pickup truck ahead of him in the darkness. The truck belonged to Gerald "Booper" George, also a band councillor from Kettle Point. Gerald had been pulled over by police at a checkpoint near the park.

"Don't go in there," Gerald warned Slippery.

If Gerald knew something, he wasn't letting on. Slippery ignored his advice and drove farther on down the road, where several Native people were standing against a fence, eager to see what was happening.

"There's trouble coming," Slippery warned them. "Somebody get the kids out."

No one seemed to take his advice, and the kids remained inside. He saw about fifteen Native people inside the park, just before the sun went down. Slippery crossed back over the fence and went home to get batteries for his walkie-talkie and his police radio scanner, which allowed him to listen in on police radio chatter. They should be of some use to his sister and the others inside the park, he thought.

As he drove back to the park, he turned on the police scanner. From what he heard, he guessed that the police were shutting down all the roads around the park and the nearby military base, attempting to seal them off. Despite the roadblocks, however, it wasn't tough for Slippery to sneak past the officers. His wife drove him down to the beach, and from there, it was an easy walk back into the picnic area.

There he found some of the younger Natives making a fire. They listened nervously to Slippery's description of dozens of police vehicles, including paddy wagons, heading toward them. By now, it looked as if there were about twenty-five Natives inside the park, including the women and kids. Slippery could see Anthony "Dudley" George, who would have a bullet in him before the night was over, and Dudley's cousins Warren and Judas George and Judas's sixteen-year-old son Nicholas. Some sticks and stones and pipes were piled up, but there were no guns. Judas had banned them from the park, knowing the Natives couldn't win a shootout with police, even if they wanted one. No one wanted to be a martyr.

While Slippery was talking to the Natives in the picnic grounds, the riot squad approached. This team of scouts and snipers was invisible to any but the most alert eye. They were from the Ontario Provincial Police's paramilitary Tactics and Rescue Unit (TRU), and this night their faces were hidden by camouflage greasepaint. One TRU sniper spotted what appeared to be a Native with a rifle by the side of the road. He also noted a reddish glow, like the aura that night-vision rifle scopes give off. The police scout immediately whispered into his radio: "CMU [Crowd Management Unit] be advised party on road may have a weapon in his hand. Check CMU person on the road does have a weapon, does have a weapon. Everybody move. Right, left, quick right, left, quick right, left, quick right, left, everybody quick right. Left."

Marksmen dropped to one knee and aimed their submachineguns, fingers on the triggers, waiting for the order to fire on the dark figure. A slight tug of one of their fingers and the man would be dead, never even aware that he had been a police target.

"Taken an aim. Taken an aim. . . . ," a sniper repeated.

"Confirm one man with weapon — long gun," another police scout replied.

Only one word — "fire" — now separated the man from death.

Seconds later, the potential target being none the wiser, the rifles were quietly lowered, unfired. It had all been a mistake. Constable Mark Beauchesne informed Acting Sergeant Ken Deane through the two-way radio linkup that the man in their sights didn't have a gun after all — just a walking stick. The suspicious red glow was not a laser gun sight but a lit cigarette. The man with the walking stick and the cigarette strolled off into the darkness, occasionally drawing on his smoke, unaware how close he had come to death.

The riot squad, also known as the Crowd Management Unit, continued its march up the sandy road toward the park and the remnants of a late-night picnic.

The Natives first saw the phalanx of officers when the police rounded a corner just outside the park entrance. It was an eerie sight. Under the three-quarter moon more than thirty officers in dark grey were marching upon them in tight ranks in what was known as a box formation. They looked more like robots or toy soldiers than men.

By the time the riot squad reached the park entrance, Constable Wilhelmus Bittner's eyes had adjusted to the moonlight, but as he neared the park, he couldn't see anything illegal or even particularly exciting — just several groups of Aboriginal families. It looked more like a loosely organized social event than anything illegal. Aside from the women and children and the elderly, most of whom appeared to be leaving, there were a few younger males there. They were likely the protestors who had occupied the park a couple of days before at the end of tourist season, saying it was on a sacred burial ground. It wasn't the job of Bittner or his fellow officers that night to talk or negotiate with the Natives or to hash over centuries of grievances between Native people and the Crown. It would have been hard to talk anyway, since Bittner and the others were wearing heavy helmets equipped with microphones, making it easy to talk to each other but next to impossible to communicate with anyone else. The peace officers wore body-armour from head to toe, including shin and elbow pads, and it went without saying that Bittner and the others knew they had not been sent to the park late that autumn night to chat.

The order went out on the officers' helmet radios for "shield chatter," and the riot squad began pounding on their Plexiglas shields with steel batons. It was an age-old tactic — noisy, intimidating, and notably popular with Zulu warriors. It still worked remarkably well. Some Natives responded by shooting back blasts of light from high-powered portable spotlights. When they caught the officers directly in the eyes, the effect was close to blinding. It was impossible for people on both sides of the park fence not to feel a surge of fear or adrenalin or a hybrid of both. This night was going to be seared into all of their memories.

When the riot squad could finally see the enemy, they didn't look human. They only appeared to be shadows, dark silhouettes against the moon. Moving potential targets.

In addition to the light beams, the Native protestors hurled epithets at the invaders.

"White trash!"

"This is our traditional land. Our forefathers were here before you!"

"Get back on the *Mayflower*!"

"Go back with the Pilgrims!"

"YOU DON'T NEED GUNS," Slippery shouted. "Leave the people alone in the park."

Now the officers were spread right across the road, up at the edge of the parking lot outside the park by the beach. This was something the riot squad had learned from English police — that if you stand too close together, you can't avoid projectiles and fire. Spread out and you're harder to hit and you look more intimidating.

"You're stealing our land!"

"Go back to England!"

"Get the fuck off our land!"

The police just stood there, pounding on their shields. Four or five Natives had moved outside the park fence now, and about ten or fifteen were still inside. Slippery kept yelling at the police to leave them alone.

Suddenly someone shouted "Punch out!" and "Go! Go! Go!" and the police charged forward, their steel clubs raised. Natives scrambled over the fence and into the parking lot. The parking lot was suddenly cleared of everyone but the riot squad officers.

Slippery jumped over the low fence as quickly as his heavy, middle-aged body would allow him and lumbered toward the police. If he was going to become a peacekeeper, he had to act now. He suspected that the police wanted to get into the park and club the Natives, then throw them all in jail. If he was to stop them, he had to do something right away.

"If you do this, you won't have our respect or any honour," Slippery shouted. "Our grandparents . . . are buried here on these lands," Slippery told them. "You'll never move the Aboriginal peoples from these lands."

Constable James Stirling of the riot squad could make out only some of Slippery's words. It sounded something like, "Kill us here. You killed our grandfathers. You fight with guns. We fight with courage."

Whatever Slippery said, it had no effect on the police. They were trained to ignore such yelling and just stood there, banging their shields with their batons, ready for the next order to charge.

Somewhere back in the riot squad ranks was a police dog, Niko, and his handler, Constable John Melnick. A black mongrel dog belonging to one of the Natives from inside the park heard it and ran forward toward the officers, hackles up, ready to take on the German shepherd. For an instant, it seemed that round one of the battle might be fought between the Indian dog and the police dog. Then a large officer in the middle of the riot squad reared back with a heavy boot and gave the black Indian dog a mighty kick. The mongrel scurried away, yelping.

The kick to the dog seemed to start something, like the clang of a bell at a boxing match. The tense standoff was over, replaced by something far uglier. Rocks and flaming pieces of wood and anything else the protestors could get their hands on were flung at the riot squad. Someone from the police ranks shouted out, "Go! Go! Go!" and the police charged a second time, flailing their steel batons while the Natives fought back with sticks and clubs and even a "No Parking" sign.

Slippery was now on his back. Someone kicked him in the head. Above him and all around him were forms that didn't look human; they were just dark shapes raining blows down on his body. He had no idea how many there were, just that they were everywhere, swarming him. It was awful and oddly fascinating. He was being beaten and yet soon he could no longer feel any pain. He felt only an odd, dull sensation, before everything went black. He lay face down, his mouth full of sand, and the blows kept coming. When the blackness lifted and he floated back into consciousness, he was still being beaten. "I give up," he called out to the dark strangers, thinking that he wouldn't even consider hitting an animal that way.

His voice was weak now, and seconds later, it stopped altogether, but he was still semiconscious. Now Slippery had the sensation of being dragged. His knees were scraped. Someone was yanking on his long braid, using it to haul him toward a paddy wagon. They were still beating on his legs. Then he was thrown into the paddy wagon, his hands and legs manacled. He drifted in semi-consciousness and thought he could hear things hitting the wagon, like hail on a tin roof. Were they shots? Stones? His imagination? Please, no one get hurt, he thought. Please, all get away. They've already got me.

Then he was moving. The vehicle pulled away. When it stopped, there was tugging on his body again, as he was carried from the paddy wagon into a brightly lit ambulance. Then the memories stopped, as he slipped further and further away from consciousness, like an empty boat pulled offshore by an irresistible current into a vast, bottomless pool of darkness. He couldn't hear it when the police told the ambulance workers that he wasn't really in too bad shape, or feel it when, on the way to the hospital, an ambulance worker felt for Slippery's pulse for a sign of life and found nothing.

SIXTEEN-YEAR-OLD Nicholas Cottrelle didn't know Slippery George well, but he had gone to school with Slippery's son. Slippery was a councillor from Kettle Point and Nicholas was a Stoney Pointer, and Kettle Pointers and Stoney Pointers didn't always get along so well — even though they knew that to much of the outside world, they were all seen as just Indians. Now, in the parking lot under the moonlight, Nicholas watched in horror as eight or ten police officers encircled Slippery, clubbing him with their batons and kicking him. It was like watching vultures in a feeding frenzy. Without a word being spoken, the police officers' fury strangely united Slippery and Nicholas. As Slippery was dragged out of sight by his hair, Nicholas decided he had to stop them, but he felt stunned and helpless.

Nicholas feared the councillor would die if the kicking and punching and clubbing continued much longer, but the Natives were easily outnumbered and the police were well equipped. Then suddenly a plan took form in his mind. Later, he described the ensuing moments this way: "I seen the bus running there. I just looked at the bus. It was there. Might as well be used. I jumped in." The black reserve dog that had been kicked and thirteen-year-old Leland George followed him into the bus.

Nicholas drove the bus against a dumpster, pushing it out of the way, then cut the wheel and hit the gas. Behind him was Dudley's second cousin, Warren George, driving a beat-up Chrysler New Yorker. He was also part of the rescue effort and followed close behind the schoolbus. For an instant Nicholas lost sight of Slippery, then he spotted him beside a prisoner van and drove across the sand toward him, passing within two and a half metres of some riot squad members, who stood their ground until the last instant, then leapt into a ditch for safety. Nicholas's father, Judas, saw about eight officers flee backwards and tumble into a ditch, along with a police dog, and later recalled thinking, "Oh, shit. These guys are supposed to be professionals and here they are, all tripping over each other. They just fell over like dominoes. Like the bus was nowhere near them. Maybe three or four feet."

Nicholas was more skilful behind the steering wheel than an average sixteen-year-old, as he had been driving that old bus for most of the summer. However, when he wheeled up to the police arrest wagon, the wagon's doors were closed and he knew there was nothing more he could do. Police were everywhere: behind the bushes and in two Chevy Suburbans and climbing out of the ditch. All the officers had pistols and about eight of those arms were pointed directly at him. At first, Nicholas froze, unable to shift the gears into reverse.

It was all strangely quiet inside the bus. Suddenly, the gears kicked in and the bus lurched backwards. A volley of bullets hit the schoolbus doors, then Nicholas heard the window behind him crack. He felt a sharp, stabbing pain in his back and his side as he drove the bus toward the park, crouched down as low in the seat as he could.

All the while, Leland had been holding tight to his frightened dog. He'd tried to cover his pet when the shooting started, lying over him on a bus seat. But when the shooting stopped, the mutt was limp and bloody, somehow shot dead in his owner's arms.

Warren George also made it back into the park, somehow untouched by the heavy police gunfire, although his New Yorker was now pockmarked with twenty bullet holes.

FROM HIS POST on the deck of the *H.H. Graham*, a thirty-five-foot OPP launch about a half to three-quarters of a mile off the Lake Huron shoreline, Senior Constable Randall Burch could hear the pop, pop, pop of the gunshots. Though there had been rumours that the Native protestors might bring reinforcements in from neighbouring communities, Burch could see nothing on the lake but waves. The only sounds he heard were those of police gunfire. Not wanting to be hit by a stray bullet, Burch pulled up anchor and headed farther out onto the dark lake.

FROM A TINY HILL overlooking the parking lot, Acting Sergeant Ken "Tex" Deane surveyed the battle, his German-engineered Heckler and Koch submachinegun gripped in his hands. It was as good a submachinegun as a police officer might hope to carry, a triumph of engineering, popular with the border police of the former East Germany and the elite paramilitary British Special Air Service (SAS) squad. When set on automatic, it could fire out some eight hundred bullets per minute, but that's not a lot for a submachinegun. It could propel each of those bullets at almost double the speed of sound — ripping through a body with about six times the force necessary to pierce human skin — but that's not particularly powerful for a modern submachinegun. What distinguished the Heckler and Koch in Deane's hands as a piece of state-of-the-art killing technology was its deadly accuracy — and special night-vision sights and a mounted flashlight meant bullets could be fired with surgical precision, even during this type of late-night duty. Acting Sergeant Deane set the gun on semiautomatic, which meant he could pop off an exploding hollow-tipped bullet every time his index finger gently tapped on the trigger.

Deane had a reputation for being cool under fire, but if he was tense that night as he stood on the tiny hill cradling his submachinegun, it was understandable. As a member of the Tactics and Rescue Unit, it was Deane's duty to protect his fellow officers in the riot squad as they stood in the wide-open parking lot. Before the march on the park began, he had been told that the Natives in the park had Russian assault rifles and Molotov cocktails. For some reason, the more vulnerable officers in the riot squad standing in the middle of the parking lot weren't given the same warning. That was odd, since they would have been clear, easy targets. By the time he reached the parking lot, Deane had already been on duty for more than sixteen hours, having reported for duty at dawn at the gathering spot for many of the officers — the nearby Pinery Park Meeting Centre. At that time, he was told that, the night before, three cruiser windows had been broken, that there had been reports of a large bonfire in the park, and that the Native protestors had shot off some 100 to 150 rounds of automatic gunfire.

By the time Deane also saw Dudley George, Deane had already tapped the trigger four times, as the protestors ran back into the park. Dudley was away from the bus on the roadway when Deane first saw him. So did Sergeant George Hebblethwaite, second-in-command of the riot squad. Hebblethwaite had squeezed off some rounds at a car that had left the park after the schoolbus, and his pistol was still out of his holster, but he wasn't alarmed by the sight of Dudley George, who was holding what appeared to be a stick, not a rifle.

Dudley George was about fifteen feet from the park entrance when Deane pumped out a volley of three shots at him. Somehow he missed altogether with the first blast and just grazed Dudley on the leg with the second. He touched the trigger a third time, and finally a bullet found its mark.

Dudley George dropped to his knees, muttering to a nearby Native, Robert "Burger" Isaac, "Robert, I think I'm hit."

Dudley gestured toward his shoulder, but Isaac had a sick feeling that the bullet had hit closer to his friend's heart.

THE POLICE WERE CLIMBING back up out of the ditch where they had fallen. A muzzle flash seemed to be pointed directly at the protestors.

"Holy fuck, let's get the hell out of here," Judas shouted.

Judas George was standing near the bus when he turned to see Dudley being dragged back into the park. He was concerned, but he also had his own son, Nicholas, to worry about. He ran to the front of the bus to guide Nicholas back, as airport ground workers do, through a gate barely wide enough for the bus. The vehicle rammed the same dumpster it had hit on the way out, and Judas and a couple of others had to tip the heavy metal container three times to get it out of the way.

As they struggled with the dumpster at the edge of the park, a police officer walked up to the bus and popped off another volley at Nicholas. The bus brushed against a post, then rumbled back inside.

As Nicholas got out of the vehicle, he could see some Natives dragging another protestor, Buck Doxtator, by the arms and legs, and he thought Buck looked beat up pretty good.

"You're hurt, Buck," Nicholas said.

"Yeah, yeah, we're okay."

"Come. Come here," Judas ordered, then lifted up his son's shirt. "You're shot."

Nicholas reached back to feel his shirt. It was drenched in blood.

There was a police roadblock nearby and Judas and his wife Gina drove over to it, seeking help from the same group that had shot Nicholas. Gina jumped out of the car and ran toward the officers, screaming out for an ambulance for her son.

"Put your hands in the air and get on the ground," an officer ordered.

"I'm not armed. Nobody here is armed. And you people opened fire. And my son was shot and you'd better get him an ambulance now."

"Get on the ground!"

Three rifles were pointed at Gina.

"I'm not getting on the ground for anybody."

Realizing Gina wasn't going to budge until her son was cared for, an officer walked forward, saying, "Why should you get an ambulance?"

That's when Judas appeared, all six-foot-four of him, bellowing, "Get her a goddamn ambulance."

The guns were out again, but now Gina was shouting, "My son, he's sixteen years old. Now you better get him a damn ambulance."

An officer pointed a gun at her head. An ambulance arrived at the roadblock, but police wouldn't let it through, so Judas and Gina drove Nicholas to the roadblock, where they were ordered out of their car. This time Gina agreed to lie face down on the pavement with Judas, as Nicholas was loaded into the ambulance.

Judas and Gina weren't allowed to go with their son in the ambulance.

When it finally drove away, they walked slowly back to the park entrance where the fighting had taken place. As they came to the sandy area where Dudley George and their son Nicholas had been shot, all was strangely silent and peaceful, the way it normally was, with the wind blowing through the tall trees and the gentle sound of the waves of Lake Huron lapping against the shore. It had always been such a restful place and the sounds of the wind and waves were oddly soothing again. Judas and Gina saw no one there now under the pines and willows — not even any members of the OPP squad who had so badly wanted to control the land just an hour or so before, badly enough to fight to the death over it.

MELVA GEORGE WAS one of the Native people inside the park that night. She was Dudley George's aunt, a descendant of the family of the great war chief Tecumseh, a seventy-one-year-old great-grandmother, and the recipient of a citizenship award from the governor general of Canada. She was used to solving problems and getting respect. When the fighting and shooting began that night, she and her daughter Marcia Simon drove as quickly as they could out of the park, looking for help, though they were not sure how they would find it.

They stopped at McPherson's Restaurant a few minutes up the road, where there were outdoor payphones, and Marcia called 911.

A cruiser pulled up and Melva was ordered to raise her arms, but she had trouble doing so because she had arthritis. Her arms and shoulders would hurt for months afterwards. The officers slapped handcuffs on her and pushed her into the back of a cruiser.

Meanwhile, Marcia was still on the payphone, trying to explain something she didn't really understand herself.

"I think you need to talk to a policeman," the operator said.

"I can't," Marcia replied. "They're the ones doing the shooting."

DUDLEY GEORGE LAY LIMP like a wet rag as his fellow protestors scooped him up and drove him back inside the park, but the car they were driving was in no shape to handle highway speeds. Instead, they'd get Dudley's brother Pierre to put the wounded man in his 1977 Chevrolet Impala and take him to the hospital in Strathroy. The car was rusty and had a cracked wind-shield, but there was no time to wait for an ambulance. The Impala was a reserve, or "res," car. It wasn't licensed and had cost only fifty dollars, but it was better than nothing and considerably better than the car that had brought Dudley into the park.

Dudley's arms and legs flapped grotesquely as he was loaded into the Impala. His tiny sister Carolyn "Cully," shocked and stunned, was pushed into the front seat by a Native woman who shouted, "Go! Just take him! Just go!"

IN THE BACKSEAT of the Impala with Dudley was a fourteen-year-old friend, J.T.

J.T. pressed his hands against Dudley's chest to try to stem the bleeding from a gaping hole. The blood was warm and sticky, but it wasn't coming out too hard. Unbeknownst to the teenager, Dudley's life was pouring from a torn artery and he was literally bleeding to death inside as his chest cavity filled up with blood. J.T. couldn't stop that, no matter how hard he pressed his hands on Dudley.

For a while, Pierre felt a strange sense of calm as he guided the rusty Impala along the backroads through Northville and toward Thedford and along the Forest-Arkona Line. Then the car hit a pothole and a tire blew. Panic surged through him. Light from a farmhouse shone like a beacon of hope, and Pierre pulled in and pounded on the door. A man answered, dressed only in underwear.

"I need an ambulance right now, man! My brother's got a gunshot wound to his chest!"

The near-naked farmer was so nervous he couldn't dial 911. He could see steam or smoke coming out from under the hood of the Impala. He hollered at his wife to come and make the phone call for him. Then they gave Pierre a blanket, two diapers, and some ice cubes. Pierre bolted from the house, ran to the car, and pulled up Dudley's shirt. He could see just a little puncture wound. He put his head to Dudley's chest and felt his brother's heart still beating. It wasn't fast or strong, but it was still beating, though when Pierre talked to him, Dudley said nothing.

"Dudley, we're going to help you," Pierre promised, but there was still no reply.

Pierre could hear rubber tearing off the rim as he pulled down the road, and then the banging and bumping of metal against the pavement. Still there was no sign of police cars or ambulances. He stopped at the corner at Watford, sure that an ambulance must be on the way. How could they not find them? There were only two roads into Strathroy, and the police had to know they were going to the hospital there. But they were alone in the dark. Pierre pushed his foot to the floor again, now frantic, barely able to keep the Impala on the road.

THE 911 CALL from the farmhouse went out at 11:31 p.m., just after the Impala sped away. The farmer's wife told the ambulance dispatcher that a man and woman had left and she didn't know where they were heading. An ambulance was dispatched in hopes of catching up to the car with the Indians and the flat tire.

Once they got to Strathroy, Pierre had no problem finding his way to the hospital, because that's where his little boy Lakota had been born.

There seemed to be police everywhere as they pulled up to Emergency.

"Look at the cops!" Pierre said. "What do we do? What do we do?"

"They know where we're going," Carolyn replied. "Don't even stop. Just wait till we get there. They're going to grab us anyway."

Pierre slammed the Impala into park and ran around to the back to get Dudley, but never reached his brother. Someone grabbed him from behind and swung him till his face was flat against the brick wall of the emergency ramp.

"You're under arrest for attempted murder," a police officer said.

"Are you crazy? That's my brother in there!"

As his face was pressed against the bricks, Pierre could see two female officers wrestling Carolyn down and handcuffing her.

"What did we do?" Pierre asked. "Who the hell am I supposed to have tried to murder?"

"They just told us to hold you."

"Who the hell is they?"

The officer stopped answering questions and began reading Pierre his rights.

Carolyn called out for the police to bring a stretcher, but no one replied. "Bring a fuckin' stretcher!" she screamed again.

Pierre looked back at Dudley, who was finally lying on a stretcher now, his arms flopping limply down. Why wasn't Dudley inside yet? What was taking them so long? Couldn't they see his brother was dying?

THERE WOULD NORMALLY have been just one doctor working late that night at the tiny Strathroy-Middlesex General Hospital. However, general surgeon Dr. Elizabeth Saettler was still there, cleaning up some paperwork in her office before beginning a ten-day holiday the next day. Shortly before midnight, she heard a call over the public address system for a cardiac arrest and went out to assist Dr. Alison Marr, the physician on call.

The Code 6 emergency call wasn't a complete surprise. At 11:15 p.m., the police had called in an alert that something might be happening at Ipperwash Park that night. At 11:50 p.m., there was another telephone call, saying that two gunshot victims were on the way. The patients arrived in reverse order of the seriousness of their injuries: Nicholas Cottrelle shortly after midnight, Cecil Bernard "Slippery" George minutes later, and then Dudley George at 12:08 a.m.

The only wound visible on Dudley George was a small puncture in the left superclavical region, near the base of his neck, but there was no heart activity and no blood pressure, and there were no other vital signs of life. There was a small hole in the upper left portion of his T-shirt just at the hem line; there were no exit wounds on his back. He had been hit by a hollow-tipped "mushroom" bullet, designed to expand instantly upon contact with flesh, creating a small explosion inside his body. Mushroom bullets are commonly used on farms for killing pests. The one that caused the massive damage to Dudley was still inside him.

The doctors needed some clues — and quickly — so they could treat him. Surely the people who'd brought him in could help out, so Dr. Saettler dispatched a nurse to find them. The police didn't tell the nurse that Pierre and Carolyn were in squad cars, heading for jail. The nurse was only told that they had left, which message she relayed to a puzzled Dr. Saettler. It struck her as odd that they would leave so quickly, since normally victims' families are anxious for any news. However, the doctor had a life-and-death problem in front of her and no time to dwell on the vagaries of human nature.

While the nurse was out searching in vain for Pierre and Carolyn, two intravenous lines were hooked into Dudley, an endotracheal tube was inserted, and external cardiopulmonary resuscitation was attempted. Still, Dudley had no pulse, and his pupils remained dilated and nonreactive to light. When doctors listened for any activity in his heart, they heard nothing. The ECG strip offered not even a flicker of hope; its monitor revealed only a straight, flat line.

The conclusion was obvious and inescapable; they just had to make it official. When Dr. Marr declared Dudley George dead at 12:20 a.m. on September 7, she had no way of knowing the short, stocky man in the T-shirt, running shoes, and jeans tied with a rope belt was taking a place in history. He was the only Aboriginal person killed by a police officer in a land claims dispute in Canada in the twentieth century.

THE DOCTORS COULD STILL help Dudley's second cousin, Cecil Bernard "Slippery" George. His body was a mass of bruises and cuts. His face was puffy and bruised, and he was tender all over, especially in his rib cage and abdomen. Confused and unable to explain what had happened, he tried to ask whether anyone else had been hurt or killed. When she heard his slurred speech, Saettler feared he had suffered a serious head injury. She couldn't smell alcohol on him, but asked anyway if he had been drinking. Slippery replied that in fact he abstained from alcohol and added that he was a band councillor from Kettle Point. As he spoke, she noted that the ugly bruising on his right forearm was consistent with a person trying to ward off a blow.

"Move your hand. Open your eyes," the nurses said. The commands were repeated three or four times before he did anything, and even when he finally responded, Slippery was still clearly in a deep fog.

"Is anybody hurt? Is anybody hurt?" he would ask, and then drift away, out of the conversation and consciousness altogether.

Slippery recovered enough to mumble that he had been kicked in the stomach some time before. He then talked about regretting having been there, although he didn't say where "there" was or what had happened. He muttered something about not intending any violence. From his utterances, Dr. Saettler got the impression that he thought he could somehow have prevented a problem, although he didn't say exactly what that problem was or how he might have prevented it.

The nurses asked him where he was, and he mumbled, incorrectly, "Sarnia Hospital."

"How did this happen?" the doctors kept asking. "Did you fall? Were you shot? How did this happen to you?"

"I was in the wrong place at the wrong time," he said, then added there were no guns involved.

Finally, he talked about being in a fight but he wouldn't say with whom. That explained the twenty-eight blunt-force trauma wounds all over his body. It was clear he hadn't been beaten just with fists, since the long, thin wounds on his back were consistent with being repeatedly struck with some force. The only thing he could remember, Slippery said cryptically, was seeing seven stars.

Did that mean he'd been punched seven times? Dr. Marr asked.

No, he replied. He just remembered seven stars.

Some time later that morning, he was able to see his reflection in a mirror, and he was sickened by what he saw. "First of all, I seen a broken heart," he later recalled. "Not my heart, but my people. Then I seen black eyes, a swollen lip, swollen arms."

That morning, Slippery George learned that he'd been charged with assault.

Slippery seemed to be genuinely trying to cooperate with the doctors and nurses; he was just unable to do so very well. So with Dudley dead and Slippery incoherent, it fell upon young Nicholas Cottrelle to explain what had happened that night.

NICHOLAS HAD BEEN CONSCIOUS when he was brought to hospital at 12:05 a.m. He was lying strapped down on a stretcher with a neck collar on. He complained of pain in both sides. Despite the injuries, however, he was fairly calm, and he was moved out of the operating room into a cubicle outside in the hall shortly after Slippery was brought in.

Hovering in the background near each of the Native patients — even Dudley after his death — were at least two OPP guards, scanning the halls for intruders and listening in for bits of conversation.

Nurses listened to Nicholas's chest with a stethoscope to make sure there were no crackles in the base of his lungs, which would suggest a life-threatening internal injury. They heard nothing. He could move his toes and hands, so their fears about paralysis were also quickly calmed.

When he had seen Slippery and Dudley wheeled in, obviously in far worse shape, the teenager didn't say much, but appeared to registered nurse Kay Powell to be terrified. Despite his clear discomfort, Nicholas spoke only when he was spoken to and struck the nurse as a pleasant, civil young man.

Years later, when he was a young father at the age of twenty-one, Nicholas would still be unable to shake the horror of that night. "I would hear them," he recalled. "They checked his pulse and said there was nothing they could do — he was gone. It's really hard to explain the feeling that comes with that experience. I felt later I had aged five years in one week. It's constantly there. It's nothing I'll ever forget."

Once it was apparent that he wasn't too badly hurt, Nicholas asked if he could go home, but he was told he should probably wait twenty-four hours. Doctors still weren't sure there wasn't a bullet somewhere in him. Besides, he learned later, he was about to be charged with attempted murder.

A little later, Nicholas overheard that Dudley's family had been told Dudley had died, and he became extremely saddened.

At about 3:00 a.m. he was questioned by Constable Caroline Kennedy.

Q. "Where are you hurt?"
A. "My back."

Q. "Where are you from?"

A. "Living at Stoney Point."

Q. "How did you get hurt?"

A. "I got shot."

Q. "Where?"

A. "One grazed me. The other's still in me. A specialist is coming to look for it."

Q. "Where were you?"

A. "Just standing around."

Q. "Why did you get shot? What were you doing?"

A. "Just standing around."

Q. "Were you with anyone?"

A. "No."

Q. "Anyone else get hurt?"

A. "Yeah, the guy downstairs got shot in the chest and he is dead. George, my cousin."

Then Nicholas closed his eyes and appeared to fall asleep, effectively ending the police questioning.

THE LATE-NIGHT TELEPHONE CALLER didn't identify herself and her name didn't matter anyway to Dudley's brother, Maynard "Sam" George. "Dudley got shot," she told Sam. "They took him to hospital." Sam called to his wife, Veronica, and brother Ron, then hobbled as quickly as he could on a broken leg to his car. The three drove as fast as they could to Strathroy-Middlesex General Hospital.

The roads were clear and the drive through the darkness took only about thirty minutes, but it felt as if it would never end. All the way to Strathroy, Sam kept pushing his worst fears away, but they kept flooding back. His little brother Dudley couldn't be dead. Once Sam saw him at the hospital, Dudley would explain what had happened. It would all make sense then. Dudley was always joking, always happy-go-lucky, and maybe he would even make a little joke of it. Dudley couldn't be involved in anything tragic. He couldn't be dead. Sam kept his foot on the gas pedal.

Police were everywhere at the hospital, but a nurse or a nun — Sam couldn't remember which — had been waiting for Sam to arrive. She ushered him in quickly, directing him to a little room. Sam felt a horrible chill. He knew what the little room was for. It was where they took you before they told you the worst. Sam felt some of his own life rush away. His darkest fears were confirmed: Dudley had gone to be with the Creator.

Shock and anger and sadness hit him all at the same time. There was also an overpowering need to look at Dudley. Maybe, just maybe, it wasn't Dudley who had died. Maybe it was someone else who just looked like Dudley. Dudley wasn't that distinctive looking. Maybe Dudley was somewhere else and would come bounding back into Sam's life, teasing him about the big scare. That would be just like Dudley. He loved jokes, the crazier the better. He would get a laugh out of this one.

Nursing supervisor Glenna Ladell led Sam into a room in the emergency ward to see a small man with an ugly gash in his left shoulder. It was Dudley. There was another awful rush of emotions as Sam realized that his little brother, once the liveliest member of a family of twelve, with countless cousins, the one who could never stop smiling, no matter what the problem, had died alone. When he'd drawn his final breath, there wasn't one family member near him to say goodbye.

Dudley's sister Pam was crying inside Room 9, while Sam showed no tears, although he was torn by emotion. They burned sweetgrass over their brother's body in a purification ceremony around 1:00 a.m. Two police officers stood guard outside the room, but the nursing supervisor didn't watch, out of respect for them. Meanwhile, other OPP patrolled the streets of Strathroy, concerned that other Natives might be preparing to enter the hospital, scoop up the body, and race away with it to perform burial rites. Dudley was dead, but the battle over him was just beginning.

After Sam and Pam burned the sweetgrass, Dr. Gary William Perkin, a southwestern Ontario coroner, took stock of the damage to Dudley's body, which included fractures of the approximate seventh, eighth, and ninth ribs on the left side, a cracked collar bone, and two large fragments of presumed bullet lying in the subcutaneous soft tissues. As Dudley lay in the morgue, a police officer applied ink to his lifeless fingers to make a set of fingerprints.

SOMEONE AT THE HOSPITAL told Sam that he might want to go and see his brother Pierre and sister Carolyn. They were each sitting alone in cells in the Strathroy jail, charged with attempted murder.

Pierre was distraught. He'd called his cousin, Ron George, a lawyer nicknamed "Spike." Ron George had once made the newspapers as the first Aboriginal OPP officer to reach the rank of inspector. He then made the news again as the first Aboriginal person to set up a law practice at Kettle and Stony Point.

Pierre also asked if someone at the jail could call the hospital to see how Dudley was doing. They refused. That terrible night, Pierre tried banging on the walls of the Strathroy town jail to establish contact with Carolyn, as if that would somehow make things a bit better, but she couldn't hear him. Again, he asked a guard in the jail to tell him how Dudley was, and again there was no answer.

Cell 1 at Strathroy jail was Carolyn's own private hell. There she sobbed alone and asked herself how the events could have escalated so wildly. Carolyn tried to explain to officers the next day that she was hypoglycemic and that she had to eat her meals on time to regulate her blood sugar, but when her jailhouse meal arrived, it was greasy fast food. She was feeling faint and tried to explain to one police officer about her medical condition.

"I have to eat properly," she said.

"It looks like you're eating well enough to me," he replied.

The police wanted Pierre to sign a statement, but his lawyer, Spike George, refused. The attempted murder charges against Pierre and Carolyn were dropped the next day, hours after Dudley was pronounced dead and his body was zipped into a body bag and moved to London. Pierre and Carolyn didn't expect an apology and didn't get one. A detective told them as they were released, "You know, if you guys would have cooperated, you would have been out sooner."

"Cooperated in what?" Pierre asked. "I didn't do nothing. All I did was I brought my brother to the hospital because you guys killed him."

THE STORY WAS on the radio news by the time Sam finally drove home. The way police told things, the officers had been defending themselves when they'd killed Dudley, and who could blame them for that? Sam heard on the radio that the police had returned fire only after Natives in a schoolbus had tried to run them down and shot at them from the vehicle. Sam knew this couldn't be true. Dudley didn't own guns. He was never good with them or even particularly interested in them. He had once tried to use a gun and had broken it. No one liked to hunt with Dudley because he scared the animals away with his constant chatter and joking. Now he was being portrayed in the media as some kind of crazed gunman and murderer. It was as if they were killing Dudley again; first his body, then his reputation. For his brother Sam, the world seemed to have spun off its axis. "It was just a complete turn, a spin, that's still revolving," he said years later.

KETTLE AND STONY POINT CHIEF Tom Bressette knew the little red dots of light on his head were something to fear. Bressette had served with the Canadian military overseas and knew the little red spots were from the high-tech sights of rifles trained on him from someone out in the darkness that night. In a fraction of a second, there could be bullets and blood everywhere the little red dots were now.

"Don't move," Bressette told the friends in his car just outside Ipperwash Park. A police officer dressed in commando gear appeared from the darkness at the intersection near Stoney Point.

"What's in your hand?" the stranger asked.

"It's only a cell phone."

"Put it down."

Bressette slowly lowered the cell phone. A shotgun was pointed at his face.

The sun still hadn't come up after the shootings, and the chief felt he had to get inside the park. He knew he wasn't a popular man amongst the Stoney Pointers, but he felt he had to get inside anyway. In an odd way, the violence had pulled the two communities together, at least for a while. He had an awful feeling that more violence was to come soon. It didn't feel like an isolated incident.

"Our elders were fleeing the community," Bressette said later. "They were afraid the army would come back with the police and kill them." So

Bressette cut through backroads to try to get into Stoney Point, although he wasn't quite sure what he would do once he got there. At an intersection near the park, he was waved down by police officers and his drive toward the park was over. He returned to Kettle Point, where he heard an inaccurate report shortly afterwards that both Dudley George and Councillor Slippery George had been killed. Charles Fox, Grand Chief of the Nishnawbe–Aski Nation of Northern Ontario, and Ovide Mercredi, grand chief of the Assembly of First Nations, were now on their way, and Bressette waited for them as his band members worried that the horrible night might soon get far worse, with even more bloodshed.

AFTER THE SHOOTING, some Natives built a bonfire in the middle of Highway 21 at Kettle Point, a ten-minute drive from the occupation at the park near Stoney Point. Most were neighbours, not protestors. Someone pushed wood into a four-foot pile across the roadway with a backhoe, then set the roadblock on fire, presenting a wall of flames to any police who might drive toward Kettle Point from Stoney Point. When media started arriving from the other direction — heading toward Ipperwash on Highway 21 — in the middle of the night, the Natives at the burning roadblock had to make a quick decision about what to do with the sudden presence of white strangers with cameras and notepads and questions. It was quickly decided it would be best to allow them to stay, and to put them at the front of the crowd — the reasoning being that white police would be loath to fire upon other whites, especially ones from powerful media outlets. When the cameras weren't around, and it was just Natives and white OPP officers in the darkness, that was when it was time to really worry. One Kettle Point woman said, "That's when the police and whoever can do what they want."

No weapons were visible to the reporters and camera people. The Native people at the fire were scared and confused, not hostile, and sought comfort, not firearms or revenge. Asked if they were armed that night, one Native man who sometimes worked as a hunting guide looked a *Toronto Star* reporter directly in the eyes and asked, "Don't you think we could have hit something?"

Premier Mike Harris's name was mentioned frequently by those around the roadblock fire, and never in a good way. It was all very personal, as the Natives told it. If their opinions were to be believed, it was as though Harris was behind the police operation that night. To a white outsider, it sounded a little paranoid, even if the outsider wasn't particularly fond of the government. It's a basic understanding in a democracy that police keep a professional distance from politicians. It has to be this way. Otherwise, police would soon find themselves ordered to crack down on the political rivals of whoever is in office, as happens in Third World police states. That would be the certain death of democracy.

Kettle Pointers nervously told the reporters a wild story about low-flying surveillance helicopters and a big police boat spying on them from offshore and police snipers opening fire with machineguns and riot troops charging unarmed Natives, many of whom were women and children. Cell phones didn't work well here, and suspicious Natives said that was because police were deliberately scrambling their signals. Soon, there was even a report of a military invasion coming, with massive armoured personnel carriers rumbling into the normally sleepy rural area. There were also stories of spies in their midst.

It was a little overwhelming for the newly arrived press. Up to that point, few of them had had much idea of where the tiny communities of Kettle Point and Stoney Point were, and most of them had no knowledge of the tensions that had simmered there for centuries. The Natives seemed to be sincere, but to out-of-town reporters, the stories sounded more than a little far-fetched.

The conversation kept coming back to Premier Mike Harris, as if he personally had to answer for the death that night. The police hadn't acted like this before Harris and his Tories had been voted into power less than three months earlier, and that couldn't be just a coincidence, the Native people reasoned. "Somebody took an order from somebody and we lost our cousin because of this," said Gail Bressette of Kettle Point. She'd left the park shortly before the killing and said, "I just had a really bad feeling when I left." There was a brief argument about whether the police or the government were to blame, and it was settled when one woman said the discussion was just splitting hairs. "They [the police] are the government. We can never trust the police." Many people said that no one could feel safe in their homes until they had answers for the night's violence. "We want to know why this happened," a mother said. "My kids are at home and they're scared."

The mood shifted from fear to sadness whenever Dudley George was mentioned. Nobody referred to him by his real name, Anthony. They just called him Dudley. It seemed so bizarre that anyone was shot, but Dudley . . . ? He seemed such an unlikely victim, capable of laughing anything off, and now he was dead. He wasn't a terrorist or leader but Dudley the joker. "He was just a human being like everybody else walking around," one Kettle Point woman said. "You don't shoot people like dogs."

There was also sad talk about Slippery George getting a fearsome beating when the police charged, and concern that his might be the second death from the violence that night. "He's pretty bad," said Robert Isaac, who'd held Dudley in the sand after he was hit by the fatal bullet. "I hope he's not crippled for life . . . It's hard to explain. They didn't bring no papers, just clubs and guns and shields. Fifty rounds — rapid fire — right into the crowd."

At one point in the night, someone threw a string of firecrackers behind the half-dozen or so reporters, and the pop, pop, pop sounded just like the report of a machinegun. There wasn't panic, just annoyed smiles. One couldn't help but wonder if the police could hear it also, from wherever they were now.

MIKE HARRIS WAS three hours away in Toronto as the Natives from Kettle Point and Stoney Point were blaming him for the bloodshed. The night of the shooting, he was celebrating his election victory in Toronto at the stately York Club, described by James FitzGerald of *Canadian Business* as "that magnificently aloof Romanesque relic of the robber baron era."

The York had once been the mansion of George Gooderham, president of the largest distillery in the British Empire. That night, the brick and stone former manor home was the site of a congratulatory dinner hosted by the *Financial Post* newspaper, where the newly elected premier shared a head table with *Post* editor Diane Francis; Conrad Black, president of Hollinger Inc.; Ted and Loretta Rogers of Rogers Communications Inc.; Fredrik Eaton, CEO of Eaton's of Canada, Inc.; Paul Godfrey, president and CEO of the *Toronto Sun*; and Douglas Knight, president and CEO of the *Financial Post*.

After grace was offered by Lionel Schipper, chairman of the *Financial Post*, the guests dined on a seven-course meal that included smoked fillet of mountain rainbow trout, chilled vichyssoise, black Angus roast tenderloin, and cold pear and juniper berry soufflé. The evening was capped when Francis presented the premier with a framed and autographed copy of her May 6, 1995, *Financial Post* column with the headline, "Mike Harris and his Tories will win the Ontario election."

The dinner wound down at 9:40 p.m., just about the time when the riot squad and OPP snipers were ready to march down onto the park.

LOOKING TOUGH WITH NATIVES made some political sense to Mike Harris. In Quebec, Premier Robert Bourassa had lost power as Liberal leader in 1994, and some commentators said he suffered in part because some voters saw him as weak in the 1990 standoff with the Mohawks at Oka. (That crisis represented a nightly humiliation on the national news, and it had dragged on for almost three months.)

Harris might be many things, but he wasn't soft on Native issues. While drumming up support as Opposition leader, he spoke to a small gathering of tourism businesspeople at Elmhirst's Resort on Rice Lake near Peterborough. "There's a whole notion of guilt," he said, "because Native people haven't fully adapted from the reservations [reserves] to being full partners in this economy. We can't let that guilt preclude us from reaching a common sense solution."

In June 1995, Harris won a landslide election to defeat the incumbent NDP and exuberantly told reporters, "We are going to implement changes. . . . Some people may not want those changes." Among the proposed changes which some people might not have wanted were these: scrapping employment equity, which would have called upon employers to draw up plans setting targets for hiring women, visible minorities, people with disabilities, and Native people.

JUST AS HARRIS set foot in the Premier's Office to discuss the transition of power with Rae, a television camera person knocked a large plaster bust of Agnes Macphail, a hero of outgoing New Democrat Premier Bob Rae, off its stand. It shattered into pieces in the hallway. There are those who would argue that the crash was merciful, since Macphail, the first woman elected to the legislature and to the House of Commons, would not have wanted to be around to see what was going to happen next.

2

THE NEUTRAL
NATION

"They were an individualistic, free people,
each of whom considered himself equal to the others."
— JESUIT PRIEST'S DESCRIPTION OF THE EARLY PEOPLE OF KETTLE POINT

Aboriginal people had lived and died for some ten thousand years in the area along Lake Huron where Dudley George was shot dead. When Samuel de Champlain, the father of New France, arrived in a birchbark canoe at the mouth of the French River on nearby Georgian Bay in the summer of 1615, he found a rich and complex Native culture.

The early Kettle Point economy thrived because of the bubbles of flint and obsidian that oozed up through the granite along Lake Huron's shoreline. This stone looked as if it was still liquid, as it had been thousands of years earlier when it was forced up through a volcanic vent, but it was actually extremely hard. This made it perfect for arrowheads, tomahawks, knives, and drills. The rich Kettle Point flint deposits came in black and red and even a rare white variety; all invaluable for both trade and defence.

Champlain noted that the tribe that controlled these flint beds was not at war with either the Hurons to the north or the Iroquois to the east, whereas the Hurons and Iroquois themselves were bitter enemies, battling for control of the new fur-trading routes. No one knew exactly why the Native people of Kettle Point so valued their neutrality. Perhaps their non-partisan tendencies were encouraged by the Native belief that natural resources like the shoreline flint beds were gifts of the Great Spirit to all peoples, and not something to be hoarded by one group. The neighbouring Hurons to the north had called the shoreline dwellers "Attawandarons," meaning "peoples of a slightly different language," but the Jesuits chose to call them the Neutrals.

SOON AFTER THE VISIT from Champlain, the Lake Huron Natives found themselves in regular contact with traders, who wanted their furs, and priests, who sought nothing less than their souls. In 1620, Father Joseph de la Roche Daillon, a Franciscan friar, arrived in what was the area's first Christianizing effort. He was first looked upon favourably: as one of the fathers wrote, "The pretext of trade made everything easy." What the friar found was a land of mysteries and surprises as well as beauty and rich farmland — a land where, after thunderstorms, gas deposits escaping from stone sometimes caused otherworldly light shows in the night sky over Lake Huron. Like other Iroquoian tribes, the Neutrals communally grew corn, squash, beans and other vegetables, as well as tobacco for trade. "The earth gives good grain [corn], more than is needed," wrote Daillon in 1627.

HOWEVER, THINGS SOURED after the Hurons told the Attawandarons negative stories about the French, and three months after his arrival, Daillon left temporarily, wary of the tensions. The Hurons were afraid that the priests might convince the Attawandarons to cut them out as middlemen in their dealings with the French. They also blamed the blackrobes for recurring smallpox epidemics and crop failures. Some even suspected the priests of spying for the rival Iroquois.

The Jesuits were a hardy lot, however, and Fathers Jean de Brébeuf and Joseph Marie Chaumonot were back with a plan to work in five villages, including a place called St. François, on the shores of Lake Huron between what are now Sarnia and Grand Bend — likely near what is now Kettle Point. They arrived in November of 1640 after a gruelling eight-hundred-mile canoe trip from Trois-Rivières and arrived on Lake Huron just in time for a particularly harsh winter. Snowbound, Brébeuf spent much of his time putting together a grammar book and dictionary in the Neutral dialect so that he could better communicate with these Aboriginal people, whom he loved as his brothers and sisters under Christ.

The early Jesuits were clearly impressed with the culture they found, which was in many ways superior to what they had left behind in Europe. As Father Jérôme Lalemant wrote, "I can say with truth that, as regards to intelligence, they are in no ways inferior to Europeans. . . . I would never have believed that, without instruction, nature could have supplied a most ready and vigorous eloquence, which I have admired in many Hurons; or more clear sightedness in affairs, or a more discreet management in things to which they are accustomed."

The priests often noted the Native people's strong affection within families, especially toward children. Babies were wrapped in soft moss, down, or fur, and paintings or beads were attached to cradles to amuse them. At night, infants slept in the highest, warmest parts of a lodge, with young animals or birds as pets.

THE JESUITS ALSO NOTED that the Neutrals made a point of passing on their history to their children orally, and there was a strong sense of continuity between past and future generations. This included relaying meticulous rules of social etiquette, which placed a heavy emphasis on generosity. Gifts were frequently given to show affection, share a hunt, cement friendships and alliances, and to conclude peace meetings. Doors were opened to strangers and help was expected — and given — in times of sickness and trouble.

Gifts were also a way of smoothing over wrongdoing — even murder. Champlain noted that "as to punishments, they employ none, nor positive commands either, but everything they do is by entreaty of the elders, and by dint of speeches and remonstrances they accomplish something, and in no other way." When a murder was committed, the goal wasn't punishment, but rather restitution. A council ruled on the number of presents that should be given to the victim's family or village or tribe by the guilty person or by his or her village or tribe. This was done to stop blood feuds. Shame was considered punishment enough for a murderer.

THE NEUTRALS BELIEVED in a Creator, whose world was filled with spirits that influenced all of their activities, great and small. Spirits lived in the sky and wind, in all animals, birds, and fish, and in trees and stones. Dances and ceremonies were done to appease and honour spirits, and the Kettle Point Natives might deposit presents on rocks or throw tobacco in streams to keep the many spirits around them happy. They believed the sky was the giver of life, controlling rain, winds, the sun, and all growth.

The priests were particularly struck by the marked devotion the Neutrals showed their dead. Bodies were painted and carried "to the burying ground only at the very latest moment possible when decomposition [had] rendered them insupportable; for this reason, the dead bodies often [remained] during the entire winter in their cabins." Every ten or twelve years, there was a Feast of the Dead, when bones of the dead were placed in a ceremonial pit in an elaborate ceremony that lasted for several days and in which several villages took part. Donors were often impoverished by presenting valuable possessions like furs, beads, tools, and food for the use of the souls.

The end for the Neutrals came at the hands of the Iroquois, and it was their customary generosity that sealed their fate. The Iroquois were infuriated to hear reports that the Neutrals were taking pity on the Hurons and giving them refuge in their houses to escape the Iroquois.

The Iroquois had acquired modern rifles by bartering furs with Dutch and English traders in Albany and turned their new-found firepower upon the Neutrals, including an attack near the Kettle Point flint beds. Some of the Neutrals were said to have been burned at the stake, while others were forcibly incorporated into the fighting forces of the Five Nations. Several of the Kettle Point warriors were buried where they fell, while there was a graveyard for bodies of leaders just to the east of Kettle Point under a hill.

The once-prosperous Kettle Point Natives were now on the run. "Famine pursues these poor fugitives everywhere," Jesuit historian François Du Creux wrote of the Neutrals, "and compels them to scatter through the woods and over the more remote lakes and rivers, to find some relief from the misery that keeps pace with them and causes them to die." The victorious Iroquois moved on from the Ipperwash area after their victory, while the surviving Neutrals were driven west and south and assimilated into other tribes. Some even resettled, eventually, in Iroquois territory.

MORE THAN A century later, and hundreds of miles to the south, there were tensions that would profoundly affect the Kettle Point area. In 1782, American General Daniel Brodhead ordered Colonel David Williamson to teach the Natives on the Tuscarawa and Sandusky rivers of Ohio a bitter lesson in revenge for Iroquois attacks on White settlements around Fort Pitt.

Williamson took 160 American militiamen to the village of Gnadenhutten, east of present-day Columbus, and there he found hungry Delawares nervously gathering corn in what had become a war zone. Delawares were easier targets than Iroquois, since they were devout Moravian Christians and Pacifists. Williamson and his soldiers told them they would escort them to food and safety. Instead they were "bound and charged with being warriors, murderers, enemies and thieves," writes Peter Schmalz in *The Ojibwa of Southern Ontario*, since they had in their possession horses and tools used by whites but not usually owned by Natives. They were ordered into the mission and missionary's house in Gnadenhutten and systematically clubbed to death from behind with a cooper's mallet, and then scalped.

The mass execution completed, the buildings were burned to the ground, the scalped bodies still inside, a symbolic mutilation of both body and soul. Years later, the Nazis would do the same to Jews — murder them and then burn the bodies in their synagogues — a cruel mockery of their religion and the power of their God to protect them. Only two Delawares somehow managed to feign death and escape.

Moravians are pacifists, so the remaining Moravian Natives and the now guilt-ridden missionaries who had struggled to convert them fled to the British-controlled area that would later become Canada. Many of them settled in the area of southwestern Ontario now known as Moraviantown — not far from Ipperwash.

THE GREAT SHAWNEE war chief Tecumseh was born near Gnadenhutten in the Ohio Valley around 1768, the son of the powerful war chief Pucksinwah. When Tecumseh was just eleven, his older brother Chiksika, then twenty-three, lectured him with these words: "When a white man kills an Indian in a fair fight it is called honorable, but when an Indian kills a white man in a fair fight it is called murder. . . . When an Indian is killed it is a great loss which leaves a gap in our people and a sorrow in our heart; when a white is killed, three or four others step up to take his place and there is no end to it. The white man seeks to conquer nature, to bend it to his will and use it wastefully. . . . The whole white race is a monster who is always hungry and what he eats is land."

Two of Tecumseh's nephews later moved to Kettle Point, as part of the wave of refugees who fled north after the American War of Independence. The two nephews had been orphaned when American soldiers killed their father, and their mother died in later skirmishes. Known in Canada as "Oshawanoo," meaning "from the south," they looked for their relatives the Waupegas, or Johnstons, and made the Ipperwash area their home. As Beattie Greenbird, a Kettle Point chief and direct descendant, wrote in 1934, they "pitched their teepees at the mouth of the Shawanoo creek that runs parallel to the southern end of Kettle Point named after the Oshawanoo." There they stayed until word came from the south that they too were needed on the battlefield.

THE WAR OF 1812 gave Tecumseh an opportunity to join with the British in a common front against the hated Americans. To this end, the war chief went north to enlist the help of his relatives in the Kettle and Stoney Point area — including Oshawanoo, who left his wife and daughter at Kettle Point and joined his brother Sheegnobike and uncle Tecumseh in battle. To enlist Native help, the British promised them pensions, and 160 acres of tax-exempt land outside their "own reservations."

Tecumseh found a friend and respected ally in British Major-General Isaac Brock, the commander-in-chief of British western military operations. When Brock was shot dead in 1812 at Queenston Heights while defending the Niagara Peninsula, Tecumseh was isolated, stuck with

Brock's replacement, General Henry Procter. Overcautious, arrogant, and extremely mistrustful of Natives, Procter led Tecumseh to moan at least once publicly that he thought the man was better suited to petticoats than a soldier's uniform.

Things came to a head outside Windsor in the Amherstburg municipal town hall, on September 15, 1813, when Procter announced that he would flee an impending American invasion, burning Fort Pitt and withdrawing a short distance to the Thames River. Tecumseh couldn't contain his sarcasm as he spoke against what he saw as a cowardly plan: "You always told us you would never draw your foot off British ground, but now, Father, we see that you are drawing back and we are sorry to see our father doing so without seeing the enemy. We must compare our father's conduct to a fat dog that carries its tail on its back but, when affrighted, drops it between his legs and runs off."

The chief continued, but his words now shifted from caustic mocking to something resembling a plea: "Father, you have got the arms and ammunition which our great father sent to his children. If you have an idea of going away, give them to us and you may go and welcome! For us, our lives are in the hands of the Great Spirit. We are determined to defend our lands and, if it be Her will, we wish to leave our bones upon them."

By September 20, 1813, Tecumseh had given up trying to stiffen Procter's spine and told his supporters, "I see ahead no glory, no victory, only pain and suffering, despair and ultimate defeat. What was once our dream to do and what we might once have done is now no longer possible to us. I have seen it! We are at last finished and must soon, like the leaves of this season, blow away and scatter before the powerful wind of the Americans. I now relieve you of your vows and promises and advise you to take your warriors and go home while there is yet time."

Some of the chiefs took his advice and left, while others stayed, including Oshawanoo, now war chief of the Chippewa, and his younger brother, Sheegnobike — Tecumseh's nephews who had moved as orphans to Kettle Point years before. Without consulting Tecumseh, Procter fled again on October 4, 1813. The Native leader had about two hundred warriors with him that day when the enemy finally appeared — in the form of a thousand mounted Kentuckians. Tecumseh's men had destroyed a bridge over McGregor's Creek, south of the Thames River near Chatham, and were able to hold the invaders off in a two-hour gunfight in which Tecumseh's left arm was hit by a bullet.

That night, as fighting cooled down, Tecumseh got word that Procter was resting near the Moravian Indian town, where the Delawares had settled after the massacre at Gnadenhutten. Tecumseh then rattled his supporters with predictions of his own death at the hands of the oncoming Kentucky militia, commanded by William Henry Harrison, a future president of the United States. Tecumseh again told them that he would respect them if they chose to return to their homes, since near-certain defeat awaited those who ventured onto the battlefield.

That said, Tecumseh removed everything he wore that denoted his rank — a large medal bearing the likeness of King George III, a pair of bracelets, a bear-claw necklace, and his two-feathered headband — and passed out his treasured possessions to his supporters. Then Tecumseh handed his flintlock and ramrod to Wasegoboah (whose name aptly meant Stand Firm), who had been beside him since he'd been a young teenager. "Wasegoboah," he said, "if it is possible for you to do so, keep close to me when we engage in our battle tomorrow. When you see me fall, fight your way to my side and strike my body four times with this rod. If you will do so, I will then arise and, with my life renewed and charmed against further harm, will lead you to victory. But should I fall, and this cannot be done, then retreat at once, for further fighting will be useless."

"As for me," Tecumseh continued, "I keep only my war club, which my brother Chiksika gave to me when I was a boy and with which I have slain many enemies. I have but one ambition remaining — that I may be with Harrison face-to-face tomorrow and let the last victim of this club be him."

Tecumseh died in the battle the next day — October 5, 1813, shot dead, some say, by a private from Kentucky, who screamed in glee, "I've killed one damned yaller Indian booger!" Another version of Tecumseh's death came from a retired British officer, who maintained that Tecumseh was shot in the back by the British. Completing the possibilities, Chief Beattie Greenbird of Kettle Point maintained that the story passed down in his family was that Tecumseh was shot in the back by a Native, a traitor within his own ranks.

Whatever the case, at the instant Tecumseh was shot, Wasegoboah was too far from the chief to tap him with the rod and so, as Tecumseh had instructed, a cry went out for the Natives to retreat, which they did. Sorely outnumbered and now leaderless, there was no point in losing more Native lives that day.

Hours before Tecumseh died, Greenbird said, he warned his braves that he had a sick feeling about the promises made so freely by the British when the British needed their help. It would be easier to win on the battlefield than to collect on the promises in peacetime, he said. "The promises made to you by these British are not on record. You often see a dog shunned by all people. Some day you will be in the same way. [You] will be like a small dog barking at a lion."

His words could have been taken as a prophecy of what would happen at Stoney Point nearly two centuries later.

YEARS AFTER THE great warrior's death, a little girl picking wild plums on St. Anne's Island near Walpole Island saw an old Native man performing a medicine ceremony over a grave. When she asked about it, the old man told her that this was the grave of the great war chief Tecumseh. The man should have known what he was talking about, since he was Tecumseh's nephew, Chief Oshawanoo, the one who had helped remove Tecumseh's body from the battlefield by the Thames River.

There were others in the Wallaceburg area near Chatham who had also heard the rumours that Tecumseh's body was buried in an area of the St. Anne's Island shoreline called "Dark Bend." Occasionally, boaters saw Chief Oshawanoo beating on a drum and chanting alone by a small fire there, and sometimes the old warrior would throw something into the fire to make it flare up suddenly, and then the chanting and drumming would resume.

Natives would sometimes tell of how, sometime around 1860, Chief Oshawanoo had moved the bones of Tecumseh from woods near Tilbury to St. Anne's Island, where Oshawanoo now lived, and that Oshawanoo had requested that his body be buried seven feet to the west of Tecumseh's grave. The old chief, who dressed partially in buckskin and partially in white man's clothing, walked with a limp from an injury suffered in the finals days of the War of 1812 and was now said to keep a Union Jack at one end of the grave and a cross at the other, always freshly painted white. It was said that only Oshawanoo visited the grave, as other Natives were warned away by a mysterious "dance of the ghost lights," while white settlers never settled on the tiny island, perhaps scared off by superstition.

Chief Oshawanoo was long dead when, in 1910, a Dr. Mitchell of Wallaceburg, the Indian physician at Walpole Island, heard the story of Tecumseh's grave from a Native person and couldn't resist the urge to dig it up. Sometime that May, the doctor and a party of Wallaceburg residents measured seven feet east of Oshawanoo's grave and then began shovelling soil. If anyone had tried to dig up the remains of Tecumseh's ally, Major-General Brock, there would have been enormous public outrage and certainly criminal charges. However, Native burial grounds were not protected by the same laws that applied to non-Native cemeteries — not even the graves of great Native heroes. What the doctor and his friends were doing was not considered to be grave robbing or illegal; it was simply an adventure. Not long after they began digging, they did find bones, laid on an oak plank, under birchbark and a pine board, which was now very much decayed. They also found a skull, now in two pieces, and a black stone pipe. Several photographs were taken of the bones as they lay in the ground, while the pipe soon vanished. Their digging completed, the doctor's team proudly posed for photographs, which were published in a local newspaper, along with a write-up of their expedition.

Natives were mortified when they heard that the remains had been removed. Three days later, after a walk of about nine miles into town, prominent members of the Walpole band showed up at the doctor's door in Wallaceburg and collected the bones. The Walpole chief moved them to his home, with the vow that they would never again be disturbed by anyone, whoever they might be. Then, quietly, the bones were returned once again, in an unmarked grave, to Mother Earth.

3

"FALLING FAST"

*"In the War of 1812, the British Government called
on them to come to their aid and they did so."*
— FROM A LETTER WRITTEN ON MAY 20, 1881, FROM
NATIVES AT STONEY POINT TO PRIME MINISTER JOHN A. MACDONALD

The totem Chief Joshua Wawanosh drew on the treaty looked a little like an inverted U, an elegant piece of calligraphy with a wing on the top, easily conjuring up an image of a bird in flight. It was a simple, flowing imprint and it appeared atop the totems of seventeen lesser chiefs, whose distinctive markings brought to mind images of turtles and birds and other creatures, all of whom the Natives believed were invested with vibrant spirits. In later years, Native people would mark their signatures on documents with unsure X's, but, on July 10, 1827, the imprint Chief Wawanosh gave for his name was strong and graceful and confident, like the man himself. He drew this distinctive totem at a conference table in Amherstburg outside Windsor, the same spot where, fourteen years earlier, Tecumseh had erupted in anger over what he considered to be the cowardice and duplicity of General Procter.

Now, Chief Wawanosh and the lesser chiefs, who represented 440 Chippewas in southwestern Ontario, were at the conference table to address the problem of white "squatters" living throughout the area. When the treaty was concluded, His Majesty George IV had acquired some 2,200,000 acres of prime land, including all of Perth, most of Lambton and Huron, and parts of Middlesex, Oxford, Waterloo, and Wellington counties. The Kettle and Stoney Point reserves, then known as the St. Clair Reserve and Sauble Reserve, were established in what is now Bosanquet Township, with a mere 5,000 acres between them. The act also set up reserves at Walpole and Sarnia. The combined area of the Native lands was 25,000 acres, a tiny amount compared to the 2,200,000 acres acquired by the Crown. For all of this land, the Natives obtained a promise that the Crown committed itself to pay "the sum of one thousand and one hundred pounds of lawful money of Upper Canada in goods at the prices in goods usually paid for the time being for such goods in the city of Montreal, in the Province of Lower Canada; provided always."

IN 1827, WHEN Chief Wawanosh and the other chiefs made their totems on the treaty at Amherstburg, it was with the understanding that they had reached a deal that would bring payments annually and forever. Upon completing the deal, Chief Wawanosh thanked the Great Spirit for white men, and then said, "Do my young men good." However, it is worth noting that the government negotiators did not seem so optimistic about the fate of Native people. They made a point of stating that the Crown wouldn't have to keep paying the same amount if the Native population decreased. No thought was given to what would happen if the Native population should actually increase. Native people weren't expected to prosper and over the years, most did not, but contrary to the predictions of many, they didn't die out either.

In 1833, the Potawatomi of Wisconsin were pushed off their old lands by western American expansion. Some moved to Kansas, some lingered in Wisconsin, and others moved to Canada. This last group included Dudley George's ancestor George Manidoka, a Potawatomi chief whose name came from "Manitou," meaning the Great Creator, and Manidoka's wife, Charlotte Shinoot. When he moved to Canada in about 1836, Manidoka took on the surname George after the British king. Dudley George's family are direct descendants of Manidoka and Shinoot, one of four recorded families to settle in the Kettle and Stoney Point area that year.

The new arrivals at the Kettle and Stoney Point reserves found a home of often spectacular beauty. Six-thousand-year-old pristine sand dunes rose up along the shores of Lake Huron. Farther inland, pine, cedar, cherry-wood, whitewood, and oak savanna could be found, with open hollows and meadows, where deer could often be seen grazing among clumps of long grass, shrubs, and brightly coloured herbs. Near those open areas were forests so thick that settlers had to crane their necks to see the sky. Not surprisingly, the Chippewa considered parts of the land especially sacred and used them for burial grounds.

NATIVES LIKE DUDLEY GEORGE'S ancestors were valuable to the British as allies during war, but when things settled down, they were seen as a problem. The April 29, 1837, issue of the *Penny Magazine* of the Society for the Diffusion of Useful Knowledge described the "Chippeway" of southwestern Ontario alongside offerings of pseudo-scientific opinions regarding the makeup and function of the wings and tails of hummingbirds, falcons, and pigeons. The "Chippeway" were treated as just another interesting species of regional wildlife by the magazine, which stated, "Whatever definition we may give of the word 'civilization,' there can be no dispute that the life of the North American Indian does not come within it. His habits and customs, his state of precarious existence, his alternate indolence and violent activity, are altogether averse to the improvement of [the] permanent happiness of man. Still we cannot but feel a deep interest in the history of so remarkable a race, who, generally speaking, cannot or will not amalgamate with Europeans, and who are falling fast before their power or their vices."

Like the Jesuits centuries before, the writer noted that the Natives of Kettle and Stoney Point had an intense interest in their dead. The author seemed a little surprised that First Nations people could mourn their dead as intensely as they did, noting that "they commonly evince a strong affection for their offspring, and bewail for a length of time of the loss of their relations."

NATIVE PEOPLE WERE basically seen by representatives of the Crown as people who must be changed and made white, or at least more white. Missionaries clearly had a better chance of converting the Natives now that they were all confined to one place, and in 1864, the Reverend Thomas Hurlburt, Methodist missionary to Sarnia and Kettle and Stoney Point, wrote in the *Lambton County Gazeteer and General Business Directory* that religion made sense from a monetary as well as a spiritual standpoint. "This is the easiest and cheapest way to dispose of the Indians of North America; for they must be disposed of in one of three ways; killed in war or by drink or Christianized by missionaries and thus made useful members of society."

The reverend continued: "Having been in the mission among the Indians for the past 35 years, and having lived and labored among them in that capacity, I am acquainted with most of the tribes from Texas to the Hudson's Bay territory, as well as in Canada, I have taken pains to gather the statistics of various Indian wars — the Florida, Black Hawks and others, and I find it requires $25,000 to dispose of an Indian by war, in addition to one white man being killed for every Indian. To dispose of them by drink I found by the statistics of those tribes who had large annuities, and consequently drunk much, that it required about $2,000 to kill an Indian by whiskey.

"In taking the statistics of our own Indian missions, I find it requires about $200 to Christianize and civilize an Indian, and train him twenty years, and thus give him a chance for both his life and that which is to come. Thus it is seen that it requires as much to kill an Indian in war as would Christianize 125, and train them twenty years. It requires as much to kill an Indian by whiskey as would Christianize and save ten. There are 125,000 Indians in British North America."

A HANDWRITTEN REPORT, written on August 27, 1881, was marked "Confidential," and sent directly to Canada's first prime minister, Sir John A.

Macdonald, from his agent A. Dingman of Strathroy, the town where Dudley George would be pronounced dead in hospital more than a century later. The secret report noted the Crown's obligation to look out for the Native people's interests. Dingman sadly noted that there was wholesale plundering of the Natives on the Kettle and Stoney Point reserves by nearby white businesspeople and farmers.

A key villain of the report was a Mr. A.L. Smith, who years before had bought a failed timber mill from the Canada Company. Areas of land populated by whites had long since been stripped of valuable timber "and there is now absolutely no place from which it is practicable to get logs with which to stock the mill except they come off the Indian Reserves. It is situated in such an out-of-the-way place that any person so disposed could easily get logs off the Reserves and few people would be aware of the fact unless they were specially interested in finding it out. . . . If the object was to plunder the Reserves of timber no better place could be found than the spot where the mill is situated."

Dingman was clearly shocked by wholesale and ongoing theft of trees from the Stoney Point Reserve and the debilitating effect this had on the people of Stoney Point. He informed the prime minister that Smith had been stealing from Native lands for years, getting away with the crime because, Dingman reported, "Mr. Smith represented himself, and was understood to be, the forest bailiff of the then Indian Agent, Mr. Robt. Mackenzie."

The problem was that there was no such title as forest bailiff. What made this particularly troubling, Dingman continued, was that some of the trees were being taken as part of a scam involving the construction of a church at Stoney Point. The Natives, many of whom were newly converted to Christianity, badly wanted a new church of their own. The deal was that they would get some boards back to build the house of worship, but "never a board was used on the church. This process was repeated time and time again until fully $5,000 worth of timber was cut and sawed into timber, but not one board went towards building the church." There still were trees at Stoney Point, Dingman noted, "but one more winter like last winter of unrestricted plundering and there would not be much left. . . ."

Ironically, the Natives had no lumber for fences of their own, although their wood was used in fences for farms for miles around the reserves. The Native farmers had problems beyond a lack of fences, Dingman noted, writing that "the land is a series of swamps, lakelets and barren sand hills, of almost no value for agricultural or grazing purposes." This bleak situation was worsened because outsiders cutting timber often left rotting logs lying on the reserve, creating a fire hazard.

Even then, Dingman noted, the residents of Kettle Point Reserve were better off than their neighbours at Stoney Point. "In Kettle Point the Indians are more comfortably situated than on the Sarnia and Stoney Point Reserves. This Reserve [Kettle Point] contains 2,448 acres, about one-quarter of which is good land." He noted the cabins and horses and pigs owned by Native families, like the Georges, Shahwanos, Bressettes, Pewashs, and Shawkences, and he mentioned that Chief Isaac Shahwano said he was a descendant of Tecumseh. "It is worthy of note," he continued, "that those Indians who are really industrious and wish to make improvements, want the Reserve surveyed so that they can know where their land is, and can build their fences in the proper places. At present, one Indian claims a piece of land here, and another there, and the utmost confusion prevails."

SOME OF THE Stoney Pointers still preferred to live in traditional wigwams, he noted, and some had relatives in Kettle Point. Dingman visited a Stoney Point man named Solomon Crow, who lived with his wife "in a little log cabin with a bark wigwam attached as a sort of kitchen." He told a sad tale — that all of his children except for a daughter had died and Dingman noted that his land was sandy and unfit for farming. "He says he is destitute of everything, has been suffering for a long time and thinks the Government should do something for him now, because when he was young and strong he served them and fought for them in 1812; he is a Methodist and a Non-Treaty Indian."

These Natives had been waiting more than half a century for promises from the Crown to be kept regarding their service in wartime. It was a refrain that had been sounded before them, and which would continue on in future generations. The complaint of broken wartime promises remained constant in the tiny community of Stoney Point, with only the names of the people and the wars changing.

Canada's wily first Prime Minister did find a solution to the problem of the stolen timber. In the end, the timber interests won out, as Treaty no. 242 of 1885 stated that the Natives had given the federal government permission to sell their timber rights "upon such terms as the Government of the Dominion of Canada may deem most conducive to our welfare." For this, Ottawa would receive some $2,000 for its efforts, plus another deduction of the "usual proportion for expenses of management." Whatever money was left was to be placed in an account for the Natives, with interest money paid to them and their descendants.

For the Stoney Pointers like Solomon Crow, receiving payment clearly wasn't as good as retaining their original timber preserves. The amount they received wasn't even close to restitution for all that had been stolen. There also was no mention of any charges being laid against the men who had so boldly stolen from the Natives for years or any probe of the government corruption or incompetence that made this possible. But it was something, and for the struggling people of Stoney Point, that was better than continuing to be robbed outright.

PRIVATE ROBERT FRANKLIN was in a muddy fox hole in France, when during a lull in the shelling from German artillery, he let his mind drift ahead to a day sometime off in the future when the gunfire and bloodshed would stop and he would finally return home to his Alnick tribe, near Peterborough, Ontario. As he sat below ground in the trench, across the Atlantic Ocean from his home, he was buoyed by reports of the efforts back in Canada to win Native people the right to vote in provincial and federal elections.

The private began writing a letter to his friend, Chief Daniel Whetung, with the words, "Somewhere in France, November 1917," and continued to tell Whetung that he had recently been thinking a lot about how wonderful it would be if all Native people had the right to vote. Now, amidst publicity about the Aboriginal contribution to the war effort, there was a move to extend the franchise to Canada's original inhabitants, and it seemed possible that Franklin's hopes might be realized. "You quite understand how humiliating it is to be held as a ward of the Government and firmly believe it will prove to be a great advantage to our Indians of Ontario," Franklin wrote. "I am writing this from a dugout behind the firing line and my companion is a Six Nation Indian from Brantford by the name of Jake Jakobs. Although we speak different languages he expresses the same views as I do. We can speak English good enough to understand one another so at night after our day's work is over we discuss the franchise question, while Fritz is dropping his bombs on us."

In 1917, F.W. Jacobs, president of the Grand Indian Council of Ontario, used the Native participation in the war effort to press for the right to vote outside reserves. "We Indians, like all humanity, are endowed with the same instincts, same capabilities, and it only remains for the Government to give us a chance to develop those qualities."

Such words often found a sympathetic response during wartime, but once the battles were over, memories of Natives fighting shoulder-to-shoulder with other Canadians in defence of Britain soon faded, just as they had after the American War of Independence and the War of 1812. The wartime contribution of volunteers like Private Franklin were but a distant memory in 1927, when a group of Lambton County land speculators eyed fast dollars in a land swap of reserve property along Lake Huron. Now it was the businesspeople with powerful friends in Ottawa, not the Kaiser in Germany, who were a threat to the Native lands.

Bribes of five dollars were offered to band members who voted to surrender some 33 acres of lush parkland along the Lake Huron shoreline to developers. Another payment of ten dollars was promised, if a vote to surrender the land was passed by council. That was big money at the time, especially on the reserves. The land was at Kettle Point and the Kettle and Stoney Point bands had separate chiefs, but despite this, the vote — and bribes that went with it — was opened up to men of both bands. The Kettle Pointers didn't like it, but their voices were muffled by the sound of money changing hands. Not surprisingly, the vote passed.

The land was bought for $85 an acre. Then about half of it was immediately resold for $300 an acre under a pre-existing deal. That meant that the Kettle Point band got some $7,706.20 for the land, half of which fetched an immediate price of $13,200.

The federal government had a protective obligation to the Aboriginals, but the Indian agents looked the other way as the speculators turned their fast and tidy profit. It would take seventy years before the Indian Claims Commission would rule that Ottawa had cheated the Natives of their prime beachfront property, and by that time, cottagers would have occupied it for a couple of generations and considered it their own. Instead of helping the Native people, Ottawa was creating disharmony between the Stoney and Kettle Point bands, while causing the Native people to lose faith in the government that was supposed to protect them.

THE GREAT DEPRESSION WAS winding down when, in 1936, the impoverished Native people of Stoney Point lost more of their land. The Province of Ontario bought 108 acres of land sold the previous year to private interests to create Ipperwash Provincial Park. In the summer of 1937, workers in the new park found human remains showing evidence of a Native burial ground close to where Dudley George was shot dead decades later. The band council then asked that this grave land be fenced off, and the requests were approved in at least four letters signed by officials from various federal and provincial government agencies. It wasn't a major issue in their view. A fenced-off gravesite took relatively little room. It represented only a couple of days of work and it would cost the government very little.

However, despite the seemingly unanimous Native and government approval, nothing happened. There was a big rush to get the park ready and the fence was apparently simply lost in the shuffle. Nothing was put up around the graves, and tourists were soon playing horseshoes and having picnics in that sacred area. The Natives quietly waited for the new set of promises to be kept.

There were rumblings of yet another world war overseas when, in 1938, the Department of National Defence set up the Pinehill Camp military training facility a few kilometres from Stoney Point on leased land near the town of Thedford. That meant lucrative contracts for nearby businesses for supplying fruit, vegetables, eggs, bread, ice, oil, and canned goods and for providing garbage removal. However, the base had no running water, and a decision was made to close it in 1940, as the military said it did not want to bear the cost of building a water pipeline from the lake. Townspeople scrambled to win it back. On April 17, 1941, the Thedford village council passed a resolution stating that "the lands known as Pinehill Camp be offered for use as a military camp without charge for the duration of the war, and that the site is well located for such purpose."

The free land offer was relayed to Ross W. Gray, West Lambton member of Parliament and chief whip for Mackenzie King's Liberal government in Ottawa. The military base had given him the role of deciding whom to recommend for service contracts at the base, and this had become a wonderful way to reward party faithful. In spite of all the benefits, the free land offer was declined by the Department of National Defence, which replied, "It would cost too much money to provide an adequate water supply system to Pinehill unless it was to be a permanent base and that the provision of a permanent base is in abeyance for the duration of the war."

Ottawa still needed a military training facility, however, and local merchants continued to crave the business it would provide. Stoney Point was a gorgeous site, right on Lake Huron, with water running through it, while Thedford was a couple of miles inland. What's more, the political fallout would be negligible if the military took over that area, since the Natives of Stoney Point didn't have the vote anyway. Native lands were also considered nonproductive, in spite of the fact that Native people depended on their farms for food. And so, on February 9, 1942, the Secretary of Indian Affairs wrote the local Indian agent that it was urgently important for the government to obtain Stoney Point for the base. It would be put to a vote, as required under the *Indian Act*. However, this was merely a formality, since, the letter continued, Ottawa was "prepared to use the War Measures Act if the Indians refused a Surrender."

Not wasting any time, the military had the land appraised in March 1942 at $15 per acre, the price paid for land deals between Native band members. Since that was considerably less than market value for neighbouring lands off the reserves, the federal official responsible suggested that they be "discreet" with this appraisal, as they wanted to prevent the Natives from "making comparisons and hatching up all kinds of funny ideas about comparative values it may be well to avoid."

The Stoney Point band got their chance to vote about the future of their land on April 1, 1942. They were asked to give up their houses and farms and all 2,211 acres of their land for a one-time payment of $50,000. It was a far cry from the treaty signed by Chief Wawanosh back in 1827, which called for payments from the Crown annually and forever. Band members who were overseas fighting for Canada did not have the right to vote on the land surrender and some of those soldiers did not even hear about it until much later. Despite promises that the interests of the band would not suffer and land would be returned to the Natives when the war was over, the Stoney Pointers voted to keep their homes, rejecting the surrender by an overwhelming 59–13 vote. A counter-suggestion by the Natives that the land be leased to Ottawa was quickly dismissed, even though it would have given the military its base for the duration of the war.

Two weeks later, on April 14, 1942, Ottawa forced things, sowing the seeds that would grow into a full-blown crisis half a century later with the Ipperwash standoff and shooting. The federal government passed an order-in-council calling for appropriation of the Stoney Point Reserve, despite the clear message of the surrender vote. In effect, the Natives were being told that they were free to vote any way they chose, as long as they chose exactly what Ottawa wanted. Now, despite their men fighting overseas and despite serious doubts in the federal Department of Justice of the legality of taking lands without a successful surrender vote by the Natives, the people of Stoney Point were stripped of their homes under the *War Measures Act* as if they were enemy aliens. Ottawa did pay the $50,000 in compensation, but Stoney Pointers complained that almost all the money went to the Kettle Point band and not themselves, increasing tensions between the neighbouring communities.

It was the duty of the Department of Indian Affairs and Indian agents to look out for the welfare of Aboriginal people, but they did not seem at all alarmed by the loss of the Stoney Point land. The move made it easier for their officials to deal with the Natives, packing them closer together. The displacement of the eighteen Stoney Point families from their homes was, in the words of the federal Indian agent, a wonderful opportunity to gather a "few straggling Indians" and transfer them to the neighbouring Kettle Point Reserve. The Stoney Point and Kettle Point bands were merged into one band, with only one chief. And as a final insult, Ottawa imposed a revised spelling of "Stoney" Point to "Stony Point" on its communications to the band. Exactly why they changed the spelling wasn't clear. Stoney Point resident Clifford George heard it was because there was another "Stoney Point" near Windsor, and the new spelling made it easier for bureaucrats to tell the two communities apart. Whatever the reason, the people of Stoney Point clung defiantly to the original spelling. Having lost their homes and their land, they were not so quick to give up this tiny piece of their identity.

Among the "few straggling Indians" who were uprooted from their lands on Thanksgiving weekend 1942 to make way for the Canadian Forces Base at Ipperwash (CFB Ipperwash) was Reginald Ransford "Nug" George. Only sixteen at the time, he was the younger brother of one of the soldiers fighting overseas. He would later become the father of Anthony "Dudley" George.

PEARL GEORGE WAS NOT directly related to Dudley George's family, although the two families shared the same wartime experience. On Thanksgiving weekend 1942, she was twenty-one years old and working in her large family garden at Stoney Point, as she often did. "I was working in the field," she recalled. "When we came home, our house was up on jacks and our two log cabins were gone. They didn't tell us anything." She had been born at Stoney Point, she had grown up there, and she expected one day to be buried there. Now, strangers were loading her frame home onto a truck to haul it to the Kettle Point Reserve down Highway 21. "They never even let us know they were coming so we could pack up the little things. A lot of things were broken. They moved us to Kettle Point, to a swamp."

The nearby farmhouse built by Levi Johnson was not put on blocks and moved to Kettle Point. It was the only brick home at Stoney Point, a testament to Johnson's status. He had been a descendant of Tecumseh's nephew Oshawanoo, and the grandfather of three young men now fighting overseas in World War II. Johnson had died in the 1919 influenza epidemic, so he wasn't there to defend the home he had built. When federal agents came to the solid house of his widow on Thanksgiving weekend 1942, they quickly decided that the brick structure was too heavy and difficult to move, so instead they bulldozed it flat. Mrs. Johnson was given a smaller wood frame house at Kettle Point, which cost $175. Also levelled was the small frame church at Stoney Point. Anyone visiting the community for the first time after that Thanksgiving weekend would have found little trace of the people who had lived there, apart from the grave markers in a little area nested back under the tall pines — and soon many of the headstones in that cemetery would also be levelled.

The Stoney Pointers were relocated onto small sites at Kettle Point, where they lost their rights to graze cattle, hunt, or gather wood without the permission of the Kettle Point people. One of their houses was placed on four large stones, directly over a swamp. Pearl George would have eight children at Kettle Point, three of whom died from illness. She couldn't help but feel they might have survived if the family had been allowed to stay at Stoney Point. "Some of the children couldn't stand the water, and got diarrhea and they passed on."

One of Pearl George's sons, Maynard, grew up at Kettle Point feeling like a refugee. "It was sort of like in Bosnia where they put two different ethnic groups together. They did not allocate us good wood or housing. We could not become members of the band council or get any work on the reserve."

LEVI JOHNSON'S GRANDSON, Ken George, a distant elder cousin of Dudley George, was overseas fighting when he read the news in a letter that his home and the rest of Stoney Point had been taken by the military. He was reassured that the move was only temporary. "I received a letter from my father telling me that our home was destroyed, and our land was confiscated by the government for war purposes," he later recalled. "He also wrote that the officials told him it was for only till the war was over. When finally the war was ended in Europe, I began to wonder, 'Where will I go home to?'"

He had enlisted with his younger brothers Clifford and Clarence, and three other young men from the reserve's dozen families. Clifford George didn't know much about Nazis when, as a twenty-one-year-old, he volunteered for action. However, he did know that army life meant free room and board for as long as the fighting continued and as long as he stayed alive. He was proud that, when he was growing up, Stoney Pointers hunted, fished, worked on area farms, sold firewood, and "got through the deepest depression without any government assistance. We knew what hunger was, but so did everyone else in the 1930s. White people were no better off. We were self-sufficient."

Clifford soon found himself in the thick of the action, stationed as an anti-aircraft gunner on the southern coast of England and helping shoot down a Luftwaffe bomber in England in 1943. When the Allies invaded Europe, Clifford survived the carnage of a major tank battle in France in 1944. There wasn't even a tree left standing when the firing stopped. During the last winter of the war, he was a prisoner of war in northern Italy, fearing he might starve to death. Sometimes, he was able to cope with the gnawing hunger by thinking about Stoney Point and his plans to settle there with his British war bride, Agnes. The two had met when Agnes was visiting her aunt and uncle in Brighton, and they had stayed in communication through letters as Clifford marched into Europe.

Clifford George considered himself a fortunate man when he returned to Canada after the war, with Agnes on his arm and a half-dozen medals on his chest. Fellow volunteers, Lloyd Bressette of Stoney Point and Herman Thomas of Kettle Point, didn't return, killed on battlefields in France. Clifford's brother Clarence was shot in the back but recovered. His other brother Ken suffered severely from what was called "battle fatigue." Ken arrived back at Stoney Point, expecting to surprise his family, but instead saw that the entire old community was levelled and the land was off limits because it was now the property of the Crown and managed by the Department of National Defence. His family and their home were gone, and he didn't know what to do or where to go, feeling confused and alone. He spent that night sleeping in a ditch. The next morning, he was able to collect his thoughts and he recalled the letter from his father, in which he'd been told that the family home was taken, although it was to be returned immediately after the war. Then he walked two and a half miles up the road to Kettle Point, to stay with his grandmother until he could get his life back on track.

"I came home to nothing," Clifford George later recalled. "I'll never forget the feeling I had when I first went there [to Stoney Point] and couldn't find my mother's grave. They had removed the headstones and there were bullet holes and trenches dug. They could only do that to an Indian. That would never happen to white people." While overseas, Clifford George had become convinced of the rightness of the Allied effort to stop the Nazis. "We all became proud Canadians and proud soldiers," he later said. But, at the same time his parents' homeland was being bulldozed by the Canadian government he was defending.

Clifford had told his war bride, Agnes, that they would be able to farm on the reserve, but when they told their plans to the Indian agent, he said, "'You're not bringing that white woman on this Godforsaken reserve which will never see hydro or water or working toilets like she's used to,'" Clifford recalled. "'In town, that's where you belong.'" The Indian agent said he would help Clifford come up with the down payment on a small house in the largely white community of Forest. Clifford had heard that returning veterans were generally getting $5,500 in resettlement money from Veterans' Affairs, while Native people were supposed to deal with Indian Affairs and were getting just $2,200 each. "We're only half as good, I guess," Clifford later said. Clifford received $400 for the down payment, and that was the last soldier resettlement money he ever saw.

A couple of months later, he got what was called his "blue card" in the mail, entitling him to vote and buy alcohol but stripping him of his Indian status. It was called an "enfranchisement card," but Clifford couldn't help feeling he was losing something precious. "That was the first time I was told that I wasn't an Indian any more. That I had sold my rights for $400."

Aboriginal people still didn't have the right to vote in Canada, and when Clifford George went for a drink at the Legion Hall in the nearby town of Forest, he felt he was still seen as an Indian and an outsider, not as a victorious Canadian soldier. The George brothers had been written up in the Goderich newspaper as heroes, and they were among the troops that had held the last Canadian line in northern Italy against a Nazi onslaught, but such heroics didn't seem to count for much anymore at the Legion, so Clifford soon stopped going. Perhaps worse, he had to ask permission from the Department of National Defence — for whom he had fought overseas — when he wanted to visit family graves inside the new military base. "I came back to find the real enemy was here," Clifford George said years later.

IN OTTAWA, THE *Transitional Powers Act* was passed to allow for an orderly transition to conditions of peace and to replace the *War Measures Act*. On May 31, 1946, things looked hopeful for the Stoney Pointers when the advanced infantry training centre at Ipperwash was closed and the Departments of National Affairs and Indian Affairs began corresponding on returning lands to the Natives. But what happened next was . . . nothing. The *Transitional Powers Act* expired on December 31, 1946, never having been used to return the old Stoney Point lands at Camp Ipperwash. At the same time, however, the act was not used to give the Department of National Defence authority to extend its hold on Stoney Point. Yet despite its shaky legal ground, the Department of National Defence went ahead and established a permanent military base at Ipperwash, ignoring its own promises and the wishes of decorated veterans like Clifford George. Instead they promised a few of them jobs as groundskeepers on the new base.

"I had no place to go. I couldn't find a job," Clifford George said. "That's why I went back in the army in 1950 for Korea. There was discrimination against us [Natives]. Sure, some of us hit the drink pretty bad when we got back, but we were all classified just the same as a bunch of drunks."

At the time, there were no welfare or social assistance programs on reserves, only charity. Native people who had lost their farms drifted to outlying white communities. Clifford's brother Ken could peek through the fence around the military base and see the married officer's quarters where his family home had once stood. Then he would wonder exactly why he had risked his life fighting overseas. "The government had taken everything, and suddenly I knew what it was to belong nowhere."

MRS. OPAL DALE WAS called as soon as the bones were found. The wife of the park superintendent at Ipperwash Provincial Park, she was inside her house when, in late April 24, 1950, park worker Owen Burley called her outside. Beyond the willow trees and between the pumphouse and her home, the wind had blown away some light sand, revealing what appeared to be human bones. She saw no sign of a coffin or leg bones, but there was clearly an upper torso, arms, and a head, so she snapped two photographs of the discovery for scientists to study. When the photos were developed, she gave them this caption: "a skeleton unearthed at Ipperwash where the bathhouse now stands."

The skull, and probably also the lower jaw, were sent on to archaeologist Wilfrid Jury of the University of Western Ontario. It was a curious find, but not a surprising one, since park workers, anthropologists, and Native people already knew that there were burial grounds there in the park.

4

"DUDLEY'S PLACE"

*"The Chippewas of Kettle Point have repeatedly requested the return
of these lands which are needed to enable the Band to improve its
economic and social position. Time has not altered the Indians' view that
they were wronged by the forcible taking of their reserve in 1942."*
— JEAN CHRÉTIEN IN 1972, WHEN HE WAS INDIAN AFFAIRS MINISTER

Anthony O'Brien George was born on March 17, 1957, the eighth of ten
children, fifteen years after his family's land at Stoney Point had been taken.
The birth was at Sarnia General Hospital, as his mother, Geneviève
"Jenny," and his father, Reg "Nug," were among the Stoney Pointers who
had moved to the Sarnia Reserve after their community was destroyed to
make way for the military base. His Irish-sounding first and second names
were chosen because of his St. Patrick's Day birth, but he was soon
nicknamed Dudley, because he loved to laugh at Saturday morning TV
cartoons showing the well-meaning but bumbling Mountie Dudley
Do-Right, who often rode his horse backwards. The nickname stuck, as did
his sense of humour.

He was always happy-go-lucky and loved to swim in a creek at the reserve, not bothered by the frogs and snakes sharing the water. Teachers found him cheerful and bright, and he once came home and proudly announced that he had won a spelling bee. However, by the time he was just seven, it was clear there were also problems. He was sniffing gas, finding cheap escape by pouring it into a bag and inhaling the fumes. Soon he was drinking as well.

When Dudley was eight, his father decided it was time to return to the Stoney Point area. The base still stood where their home had once been, so the Georges moved to Kettle Point, just up Highway 21 from their old place. "He thought it was time to go home," Dudley's older brother Sam said. "He wanted to bring us back to the community." Less than two weeks after the move, the homecoming was ruined when the George children stepped off the schoolbus to find the family home had been levelled by fire.

Such loss was sadly familiar for Natives of his generation, as many grew up in homes that were little better than fire traps. And water supplies on reserves were often so inadequate that it wasn't worth a fire department's time to respond to a call.

After the fire, the children were temporarily put in the care of aunts and uncles as their father rebuilt the house. When Dudley was twelve, his eldest sister Karen was killed in a car crash, and the grieving hadn't stopped when fire struck again in the family house. This time, there was one room left inhabitable — the kitchen. That was where the ten George family members now ate and slept. They had no running water, sleeping was tough, and it was impossible for everyone to eat together. Schoolwork was out of the question. The thought of privacy was laughable.

When Dudley was fourteen, his mother died and his father struggled to raise the children alone while working as a transport driver. He often worked twelve-hour shifts, taking 3:00 a.m. to 3:00 p.m. runs driving a chemical tanker to the Niagara region. While he was considered a good father, it was tough to provide for his family, and there were long hours away from home.

Dudley George grew up among the new and peculiar tensions that had arisen between the Kettle and Stoney Pointers. Some Kettle Point residents saw their new, transplanted neighbours as visitors who just wouldn't go away, while Stoney Pointers often complained they were taunted by their Kettle Point neighbours, who nicknamed them DPs — short for displaced persons. Schoolyard battles between children from the two communities were common. Crowding at Kettle Point, especially with the postwar baby boom, was a problem for both groups, and many young people moved off the reserve to nearby, mostly white, communities like Sarnia.

After the death of his mother, Dudley took refuge in TV watching; it became both his passion and his escape. He joined the Banana Splits Club, named for a children's program, and became briefly known as Brother Banana around the reserve. He had a route for selling *TV Guide* at Kettle Point and was such a sharp television watcher that he won a T-shirt in a contest for spotting TV bloopers.

Dudley wasn't much of a fighter, but he did get into trouble. When he was seventeen, he was one of a group of teens who set fire to a warehouse in a lumberyard in the nearby community of Forest. The building burned to the ground, with damage estimated at two hundred thousand dollars. He was the only Native in the group, and the police investigation ended after he pleaded guilty to arson. As Jack Aubry noted in an excellent profile on Dudley George in the *Ottawa Citizen*, James R. Marshall, his principal at North Lambton Secondary School, urged the court to give him a second chance, telling the judge that he was honest and reliable and hard working. "I believe in this young man," he said.

The judge took a hard line instead, sentencing Dudley to twenty-one months in jail. And so, with only a grade ten education, Dudley's full-time schooling was over, although he would later try a few upgrading courses. For a while, he lived at home again, doing odd jobs around the reserve and spending time with his father, in those precious hours when Reg, Sr., wasn't on the road.

When Dudley was twenty-three, his closest brother, David, committed suicide after his son was stillborn. Dudley broke down at the funeral, where he was a pallbearer. Then he simply disappeared for a couple of weeks, and when he reappeared, he could never bring himself to talk about the pain. He wasn't alone in having to deal with such tragedy: the suicide rate among

Canadian Aboriginals at the time was consistently five to six times the national average.

Dudley had grown up hearing stories of how on Thanksgiving weekend back in 1942, his father's family had been kicked off their traditional lands to make way for the military base. And people remembered the sacred burial ground that now lay inside the park amidst the oak savannah and the pines. To Dudley, Stoney Point seemed to be a better, almost mythical place, where he might feel whole again.

AS DUDLEY WAS growing up, letters were still occasionally being written back and forth in Ottawa, from one government department to another, about how it might be a good idea to give the Stoney Point land back to the Native people. In 1972, Indian Affairs Minister Jean Chrétien sounded truly sympathetic when he wrote to the minister of national defence:

> Since 1946 our respective Departments have been corresponding on the subject of the return of some 2,200 acres comprising Canadian Forces Base Camp Ipperwash which was appropriated in 1942 by the Department of National Defence under the War Measures Act. . . .
>
> The Chippewas of Kettle Point have repeatedly requested the return of these lands which are needed to enable the Band to improve its economic and social position. Time has not altered the Indians' view that they were wronged by the forcible taking of their reserve in 1942. Moreover, it was their understanding that the land was to have been returned to them at the end of hostilities.
>
> With cuts in the Canadian Forces Bases indicated it seems to me that this is an appropriate time to reconsider this matter and I would appreciate having advice as to your Department's plans for Camp Ipperwash. The transfer of this land to the administration and control of this Department so that it could be returned to reserve status would be of great importance to the Kettle Point Indians and would remove a major source of dissatisfaction with the manner in which the Federal Government have dealt with this reserve.

Despite Chrétien's entreaty, nothing was done, and the Stoney Pointers remained barred from their original home.

Some members of the community expressed frustrations about the burial grounds in adjoining Ipperwash Provincial Park, but in 1972, after a series of archaeological test digs in the area, the Ontario government said there was no basis for any Aboriginal claim about graves inside the park. The government-commissioned study sounded very scientific. Somehow, official memories were lost about the bones that had been found by park workers and all of the government letters back in the 1930s, when everyone seemed to agree that fencing off the graves was a simple, cheap, and proper thing to do. The author of the new study also seemed unaware of the discovery of bones by the park superintendent's wife in 1950.

IN THE AUTUMN OF 1985, Dudley's father began losing weight and experiencing a pain that repeated trips to the doctor and painkillers couldn't extinguish. By the time it was diagnosed as cancer of the pancreas, he had little time left to live, and his family moved back into his home to be with him. Dudley knew he should sit with his father, but he couldn't. Facing the death of his one remaining parent was simply too much, and so Dudley wasn't present when, on April 13, 1986, his father died in his bedroom, surrounded by his family. The funeral was so large that it had to be held in the Kettle Point Community Centre.

Dudley began drifting even more, hitch-hiking around Lambton County, where friends always seemed quick to give him a ride, knowing he'd be pleasant company and full of chatter and jokes. After his father's death, Dudley frequently showed up at the doors of friends and family unannounced, looking to spend the night. He didn't seem like a candidate for marriage himself, calling weddings "hangings," but he did love family life and especially enjoyed looking after his nieces and nephew. Soon, he was nicknamed Uncle Buck, for the sweet, funny, gruff character played by John Candy in the movie of the same name.

Dudley George finally went back to Stoney Point in 1990, as a pallbearer at the funeral of his uncle, Daniel George, Sr. Daniel was the husband of Dudley's Aunt Melva, the Anglican minister who witnessed the shooting at Ipperwash five years later. Dudley's uncle was returning home in a casket, but it was a homecoming nonetheless and a watershed event for Dudley and other Stoney Pointers. Finally, someone had returned to the old community. Hopefully, the rest of the Stoney Pointers would not have to wait until after their last breath before they returned home.

THAT SUMMER, THE MOHAWKS of the Iroquois Confederacy were locked in an armed standoff at Oka, Quebec. They had set up a blockade to prevent the town from expanding a golf course onto a sacred burial ground. When about one hundred police stormed the Mohawk blockade, someone shot Corporal Marcel Lemay, a Quebec provincial police tactical squad officer. Corporal Lemay died.

The seventy-eight-day Oka standoff was played out daily in the national news. Natives from the Ipperwash area watched with great interest and decided to get involved as peacekeepers and healers, not as fighters. Bruce Elijah of the nearby Oneida band went to Oka to act as a peacekeeper and spiritual advisor.

When the Oka crisis finally ended, the most famous of the Mohawk Warriors, Ronald Cross (known better by his *nom de guerre*, "Lasagna"), quietly took time out with the Oneida near Ipperwash and received traditional Native treatment for his alcohol and cocaine dependencies. Bruce Elijah's mother gave Lasagna a hard look when he arrived in the Oneida community, then joked, "This is Lasagna? He's not that big. In the news, he looked big. I bet even I could whip him."

IN 1980, OTTAWA paid the Kettle and Stony Point band $2.5 million in partial compensation for the base, and there was a promise the land would be returned once military exercises were completed. Stoney Pointers grumbled that the money only went into the hands of Kettle Pointers, increasing tensions between the two communities.

By 1992, half a century after the land at Stoney Point had been taken over by the Department of National Defence, it still looked as though the Stoney Pointers might win their land claim through paperwork, not violence. In March 1992, the Standing Committee on Aboriginal People (now Aboriginal Affairs) tabled a report recommending that Ottawa return the Camp Ipperwash lands to the Stoney Pointers. A month later, members of the Kettle and Stony Point band followed up on the report by serving the Department of National Defence with an "eviction notice," giving it ninety days to evacuate.

Among the one hundred people who showed up outside Camp Ipperwash in the cold rain the day the eviction notice was read were a few members of the National Association of Japanese Canadians. Spokesperson Van Hori said they could relate to Stoney Pointers because many in their group had had their land expropriated during World War II. "It took us forty-six years to get an apology and some kind of compensation. . . . These people are still waiting." Demonstrator Cathy George didn't want just compensation and an apology. She wanted the land back. "My Dad is buried there and they don't even let us in to visit his grave," she said sadly. "We have to sneak in to visit. . . . and the cemetery is in a deplorable state."

In August 1992, the Department of National Defence replied that there was a continuing need to retain the Camp Ipperwash lands, but agreed to consult with First Nations people. It was now just a few months short of a half-century since the land had been taken.

ON MAY 27, 1993, something finally snapped. A group of Natives calling themselves the Stoney Point First Nation simply marched into the east end of the military base and refused to leave. They said they were doing a "reoc-cupation" of their lands and called the reclaimed land *Aushoodaana Anjibaajig*, or "resting place." As in the case of Ipperwash Provincial Park, there was a Native cemetery in the military base, but the Natives were reclaiming the entire base — their former community — not just the bur-ial ground.

Among the ranks of the protestors was Dudley George. Now well into his thirties, he had finally found a purpose for his life. When Dudley tried to explain why he was joining the demonstrators, he said he was "doing it for Dad." He also liked to mention how his mother would brag that he had an inner compass, like a true Chippewa. He would often say that, at Ipperwash, he had finally found his way home.

The protestors had no running water or electricity or phones, and no alcohol was allowed on the property. They simply lived alongside the soldiers of Canadian Forces Base Ipperwash, each side doing their best to ignore the presence of the other. Native children played soccer and chased their dogs and learned to fish in tiny ponds beside abandoned tanks as military personnel in greasepaint drove about in jeeps.

Dudley moved into an area of the military base along Highway 21, living alone in a trailer some friends had bought for him for four hundred dollars. (It had been surplus from a Sarnia construction site.) Dudley's closest neighbour was his distant cousin, war veteran Clifford George, who lived in a tiny cabin made from wood he'd managed to scrounge from around the area. Clifford put up a sign reading "Uncle Cliff's Cabin" on his new home, while Dudley painted one for his trailer which read "Dudley's Place." "That made him happy — the first home he'd ever owned," Clifford later recalled.

The Stoney Pointers pitched tents and lean-tos and parked trailers on fields and rifle and grenade ranges. The community was quickly home to about one hundred people, with another fifty frequently dropping by for visits, including guests from the Six Nations Reserve at Brantford and from the United States. Outside groups like the Canadian Auto Workers (CAW) began showing interest, supplying timber for homes and generators for electricity. The men hunted deer in a cull in nearby Rondeau Provincial Park, while some of the women prepared traditional bread, called *gungin*, over open flames. Others just bought their provisions in supermarkets in nearby Forest and Kettle Point.

Clifford George was nothing less than euphoric. "This is the first time in fifty years, since before the war, that we've all been together so close. We're finally back together again, and that's why we have such a good relationship. . . . I'm back to stay. They'll have to carry me off and they better lock me up because the minute they let me loose, I'll come back again."

For his part, Dudley George was also happier than he had been in memory. Glenn George, a second cousin and a direct descendant of Tecumseh's family, would tell Dudley about Native ways. Dudley loved to hear the history. He also delighted in irritating the soldiers and the police, dropping his pants and mooning them, throwing tomatoes, or standing in the middle of the road and making them drive around him. When Dudley did drive, it was often in a res car with "Pig Fucker" painted on the side. He wasn't dangerous but he wasn't quiet either. It was impossible not to notice Dudley, especially when he was in a crowd, heckling the military. "It [words] really rolled out of him, when he was with the guys," Clifford said.

A chief and council were elected, just as they had been in times past, and within a month of the "reoccupation," the Stoney Pointers' first permanent building went up. It was easy to see from Highway 21 — a tiny, nondenominational wooden church, replacing the house of worship that had been bulldozed flat in 1942. Nearby, a peace tree was planted over a traditional stone axe, a symbolic attempt to bring together Stoney Pointers who held traditional beliefs with those who were Christian. Janet Cloud, a resident of Stoney Point, told Paul Morden of the *Sarnia Observer*: "The people believe that the right thing to do is to honour God for all He does for us."

THE IDEA WAS SIMPLE, as clever ideas often are. The plan would test the Native ownership of surrounding lands, and it might also put a few dollars in their pockets. In July 1993, Clifford George, then seventy-three; Derrick John George, thirty-two; and Martin Glen Kewageshig, twenty-six, set up a makeshift toll booth on Matheson Drive leading to Lake Huron and began charging occupants of vehicles five dollars to get to the beach. They simply stood by the road and asked visitors to pay the money. People walking to the shoreline were billed one dollar.

Not everyone paid or thought the idea was amusing or clever, and within a few hours, the three men were behind bars, charged with mischief. For Clifford George, the arrest came before any money actually reached his hands, although he estimates ten dollars or fifteen dollars were collected. "We just held our hands out," Clifford recalled. "I never as much as asked anybody."

The men went to jail on a Saturday, and the next Monday they were handcuffed together and led up three flights of stairs, into court, where they were told they could gain bail, but only if they agreed to stay away from the disputed land. Clifford George and the two younger men refused, so they were sent back down the stairs in handcuffs to their cells. The next day, after three days in custody, Stoney Pointers were worried about Clifford's health. There were several dozen supporters in bail court when Clifford and the two others appeared in the blue clothing of prisoners, handcuffed together again. This time, they agreed to new bail conditions worked out by their lawyer, Ron George. Supporters cried and cheered in the courtroom and in a nearby courthouse lobby as the men walked free after agreeing to cease toll collection for the time being as a goodwill gesture. There was a hero's banquet that night, but Clifford tried to shrug off the applause. "I'm no hero," he told the press. "I'm just an old bugger who pulled off a crazy stunt."

It was the first time in a half-century that Clifford had been behind bars. The previous time was when he had been a prisoner of war in World War II, after being captured by German soldiers in northern Italy. However, he appeared none the worse emotionally for his time in jail; instead he spoke of how he had recently found an inner harmony that had been missing for many years. "I have never enjoyed life so much. I'm at peace with the world. . . . We only want our land."

TENSIONS GOT WORSE as the summer wore on. The military remained cooped up in their low buildings, and plans had to be made to bus some 1,500 cadets around southwestern Ontario to complete training that would otherwise have been done at Ipperwash. At nights, now, the Stoney Pointers complained about low-flying helicopters swooping over their tents and trailers. "Sometimes they flew so low they raised dust," Clifford George complained. "They scare the kids and old people. I'm all in favour of laying of charges of harassment against the military."

On August 23, 1993, some of the Natives used portable searchlights to light up a Bell 212 helicopter from the ground during a late-night, low-level reconnaissance over Camp Ipperwash. The aircraft's crew turned on its landing lights to keep oriented. Inside the helicopter, the high-beam lighting from the ground was followed by an odd "tick" sound in the tail section. Someone in the helicopter joked about how they might have been shot at, and this seemed pretty funny until they landed at London, Ontario, checked the aircraft, and found a bullet hole. If the shot had hit the helicopter in its fuel tanks, hydraulic lines, or tail rotor, all five people on board might have been killed in a crash. Ironically, the squadron had just returned from a peacekeeping mission in a war zone in Somalia, where, to their knowledge, they had not been fired upon.

By 2:00 a.m., the OPP had sealed off the camp and were allowing no one to enter. All vehicles leaving were searched. However, after scouring the area for nine hours, all the police found was a flare gun, a pellet gun, and several rounds of ammunition.

The military defended the helicopter's "routine reconnaissance mission," with Major Brian Hay saying the flights were intended as safety exercises, to ensure that unattended campfires didn't spread and the occupiers didn't stray into areas of the base where there might be live ammunition or hand grenades. "As long as there are people there who have no legal right to be there or knowledge of military objects that might be there, the flights will continue," Hay vowed. But whoever pulled the trigger was never caught.

THREE WEEKS LATER, on September 12, 1993, some of the Stoney Point people occupying the former military base felt they needed to do something dramatic to press for their rights. The helicopter story had received broad coverage in the media and now the Native protestors were being called terrorists — not ridiculously patient people who had been cheated of lands.

And so Clifford George put on his war medals and another Stoney Pointer, Maynard George, stuck a sign on the back of his sister's car that read "Amos 9:15," referring to a Bible quotation which says, "'I will plant them upon their own ground; never again shall they be plucked from the land I have given them, say I, the Lord, your God.'" Then they began a three-week walk to Ottawa with about thirty others to press the government to recognize their treaty rights to Stoney Point, which they had been promised forever for their use and enjoyment, when Chief Wawanosh signed the treaty of 1827. Clifford was too old to do much walking. Instead he provided support by driving alongside the walkers in his Hyundai and by taking walkers for washroom breaks and snacks. The walk was covered sporadically in the media and perhaps this attention hit a nerve. In February 1994, in the federal budget speech, the government in Ottawa announced it would negotiate the return of the Camp Ipperwash lands to Aboriginal people. Exactly when it would be returned, however, still remained unclear.

IN 1995, TWO SUMMERS after the "reoccupation" of the Camp Ipperwash fields and artillery ranges, the Stoney Pointers and the military were still uneasily coexisting at the base. Some decided that three generations of waiting was enough. On July 29, 1995, a few Stoney Pointers boarded a rundown yellow schoolbus and crashed through the door of a hall in the base. The military, which had said it was still in the midst of turning the base over voluntarily, left to avoid further confrontation. As occupations go, it was spectacularly peaceful. A week after the main camp was taken, on August 4, 1995, military technicians were helping the Native occupiers learn the day-to-day operations of the base, so that equipment wouldn't be damaged. Soon Native people had contracts with the federal government to cut lawns and generally maintain the base for $10 an hour. After waiting and negotiating and pleading and praying for more than half a century, taking back their homeland was remarkably simple in the end. They just drove an old yellow schoolbus inside and refused to leave.

THE STORY COULDN'T have been considered too shocking. It ran on page 19 in the August 23, 1995, edition of the *Forest Standard*, a local weekly newspaper with a paid circulation of 3,839, which covered, among other communities, the Township of Bosanquet, where Kettle and Stoney Points are located. Occupying more prominent pages in that issue were a picture of area fruit growers proudly holding baskets of peaches, some salmon derby fishing contest winners, and news that the Sheppard family of Pinawa, Manitoba, had recently visited relatives in Thedford.

Readers who made it past these news items to page 19 found the story under the headline, "Sunday Incident." It indicated that there were some disputes between non-Natives and Natives in which the Natives resorted to confrontational tactics — but there was no massive outbreak of violence.

CONFRONTATION AT ARMY BEACH BRINGS CALL FOR ACTION AT COUNCIL
An altercation involving natives and non-natives at the army camp beach Sunday night, presented a disturbing picture for Bosanquet councillors Monday.

A Port Franks woman who witnessed the alleged attack said she couldn't sleep after watching the incident and decided to attend council Monday to demand action be taken.

The woman said . . . [a family with four young children] had beached their boat on the shore, a common practice on summer afternoons, and had set up their cooler and beach umbrellas on the sand, just as other boaters had done all along the waterfront.

About six adult native males had driven down the beach and stopped where the family was sitting and apparently told them to leave.

The woman told council that the men had taken the family's cooler and umbrella and put it in their car. The mother had retrieved the cooler when the confrontation seemed to escalate and the husband intervened in the scuffle.

She told council the four young children were screaming as the altercation occurred. The family escaped to their boat and got away as a jet skier distracted the male natives. Before they left a glass bottle was thrown at the boat she told council.

. . .

Coun. Bill Graham said this violent confrontation isn't the first time council has heard warnings about potential problems.

"I think it's time we initiated a meeting of those concerned and say we've had enough."

The woman's story led to a call to Lambton MPP Marcel Beaubien's office, resulting in a meeting arranged the next day (Aug. 22) to discuss the issue.

. . .

In a follow-up in the August 30 edition of the *Forest Standard*, Kettle Point councillor Gerald "Booper" George weighed in on the picnic basket issue with a letter to the editor, which slammed the Stoney Pointers. He wrote:

> When I read your article last week about the natives that harassed the family on the Camp Ipperwash Beach it made me very angry. I am a councillor for the Kettle & Stony Point First Nation. I am glad these Army Camp Indians call themselves separate from my First Nation because I would not want any of my fellow band members to act like animals and give my home a bad name.
>
> I do not refer to these jerks as Stony Pointers either because my grandparents were Stony Pointers, also my mother and uncles are as well and I am sure that they never acted this way.
>
> Therefore I will not insult my relatives by calling the people at CFB Ipperwash, Stony Pointers.
>
> When the army pulled out of Camp Ipperwash, the actions that followed reminded me of the L.A. Riots.
>
> The army camp Indians have strained relations between Kettle & Stony Point and the surrounding communities. We all do not act like the army camp Indians, so please do not think that all Chippewas act this way,
>
> *Gerald C. George*
> *Councillor*
> *Kettle & Stony Point.*

Gerald "Booper" George wasn't the only Native person who viewed the Stoney Pointers suspiciously. Unbeknownst to them, there was a genuine spy in their midst, feeding information for money to both the federal spy agency, the Canadian Security Intelligence Service (CSIS), and the Ontario Provincial Police.

JIM MOSES' INVOLVEMENT in the Ipperwash affair began with a strange telephone call in 1994 from an officer at CSIS, who arranged for a meeting in the library in downtown St. Catharines, in the Niagara Peninsula. Before that afternoon, Moses had never met the earnest, nondescript white man. But the officer had apparently heard of Moses because of Moses' work in journalism, as a contributor to both Native publications and mainstream outlets, including helping with research on Native issues with the CBC TV newsmagazine *the fifth estate*. The caller wanted everything he could get from Moses on any involvement at Stoney Point of the militant Mohawk Warrior Society of eastern Ontario and western Quebec. "They had not a clue about the situation on the Indian reserves," Moses later said. "That's why they latched onto me."

Moses had his own reasons for wanting the spying job. Mohawk Warriors are traditionally protectors of their people and peacekeepers, but since the Oka standoff in Quebec, some drug traffickers and arms runners on Iroquois reserves were now calling themselves Mohawk Warriors. Moses, an Iroquois originally from the Six Nations Reserve near Brantford, Ontario, wanted to make sure that the bogus "Mohawk Warriors" did not gain a foothold in southwestern Ontario. He said he considered it nothing less than his duty to spy against them. If the police and government were willing to pay him a little for this information, so much the better. He said the OPP paid him less than two thousand dollars for two and a half years of spying on Native groups, while CSIS paid between four hundred dollars and eight hundred dollars monthly, but he often had to pester them to pay up. "I don't think I've double-crossed anybody," Moses later said. "I think I've reminded them [the OPP and CSIS] of their jobs and their responsibilities." Moses went to Stoney Point, joined in with the people at the base — including Dudley George — and asked as many questions as he could without drawing attention to himself. He was particularly interested in illegal guns and drugs. It was to his advantage to report some wrongdoing, since that might mean more work and money, but he simply couldn't find anything. He reported back to the police and CSIS with his findings, or lack of findings. In May 1995, he added that he had heard that the Natives intended to occupy Ipperwash Provincial Park at the end of the 1995 Labour Day weekend, a plan that was already widely known in the area, since the protestors had announced it to the police themselves.

Moses didn't get to know Dudley George well, but Dudley was so talkative he was impossible to miss. Moses considered him a joker, not a fighter or a leader, and never saw him with a gun or any other weapon.

In fact, Moses never saw any of the Stoney Point Natives with guns. "Dudley was a happy-go-lucky, friendly guy," Moses later said. He spoke of his death with sadness. "I was sick. I felt empty . . . ," he said. "It was totally unnecessary."

ACTING SUPERINTENDENT John Carson of the OPP didn't panic easily. He knew Ipperwash as well as or better than other senior OPP officers, since he'd been the incident commander on the CFB Ipperwash occupation since 1993. Before that, he'd been a staff-sergeant at the nearby Forest detachment. He knew enough not to get overly excited about dramatic pronouncements of occupations — especially ones that were planned for a time when the park would be mostly empty anyway. Back in May 1993, Carson was at the Forest OPP detachment when a group of Natives, led by Carl George, delivered a document saying they were going to take over the military base at Ipperwash because they were tired of waiting for Ottawa to act. They were polite and up front, so it was no surprise when, later that month, Stoney Pointers cut the base's main lock, opened a fence, and proceeded to set up campsites on firing and training ranges alongside Highway 21 at the east end of the base. Carson noted that the military never did get a court injunction so they could legally order the Natives out.

When the Natives also moved into the built-up area of the base on July 29, 1995, after crashing the schoolbus through the military hall, there were minor confrontations as some protestors told sun-lovers they weren't welcome any longer on the army beach in front of the Department of National Defence property, which they had enjoyed for years. This banning of non-Natives wasn't absolute. The joke was that it cost one case of beer to get into the park, and two to get out, but not everyone thought it was funny.

Jim Moses wasn't the only spy keeping an eye on the Stoney Pointers. Throughout the summer, the OPP had officers posing as tourists on the park beach, making sure things didn't get out of hand. And as Labour Day approached, the OPP also put two undercover operators into the park, posing as campers. The undercover campers were referred to as "badgers" by the force and operated out of a trailer and a mobile home. What they saw wasn't too fearsome. Non-Natives kept going on the beach, despite warnings from the Stoney Pointers and the occasional five-dollar beach fee.

But since the Stoney Pointers were still boasting that Ipperwash Provincial Park would soon belong to them, on August 29, Carson met with Superintendent Anthony Parkin, Acting Sergeant Ken "Tex" Deane of the OPP's paramilitary unit (the Tactics and Rescue Unit (TRU)), and with Carson's superior, Chief Superintendent Chris Coles from A Division, which covered the Southwestern Region of Ontario. They met in Coles' office in London, Ontario. The point of the meeting was to map out contingency plans. The next day, Carson met with half a dozen key officers, including Deane, Sergeant Brad Seltzer from the Chatham training unit, and Sergeant Stan Korosec from the Emergency Response Team (ERT). (The ERT was trained to deal with hostile crowds and hostage takings, but its presence would not be considered as ominous as that of the Tactics and Rescue Unit, whose original mandate was to combat terrorism.) The OPP was not going to be caught off guard by whatever the Natives had planned.

At that time, it was impossible for anyone reading newspapers or watching the news to be unaware of a tense standoff at Gustafsen Lake, British Columbia, where armed Natives had taken over a ranch from a private citizen. The communities of Stoney Point and Gustafsen Lake were separated by two mountain ranges and were more than 4,300 kilometres apart (roughly two and a half times the distance from London, England, to Leningrad). Furthermore, there was no connection between the Gustafsen Lake incident and what was going on at Ipperwash, except that they both involved people with Native blood. Still, television news brought the B.C. standoff into Ontario homes and made the tensions seem much closer and much more threatening.

There were also ugly reports reaching Carson's desk of Natives going onto dunes adjacent to the park and yelling at campers, "Fuck off," "This land's our land," and "You're gonna be paying us next year to use this park." It wasn't an armed confrontation like the protest in British Columbia and it wasn't even violent, but it did put a damper on some summer fun.

The police crisis group met on the Friday before Labour Day 1995, to go over their strategy. They knew the Natives planned to enter the park in a few days — after the tourists left — so the OPP planned to approach the

Natives then to tell them that the park was closed and that they were trespassing. Meanwhile, they would keep some Emergency Response Team
(ERT) members in the park as "badgers" to watch the Stoney Pointers,
while other team members would be posted around the perimeter of the
park to keep more Natives from coming in. A trailer was brought in to be
used for communications, and maps of the area were posted on its wall,
along with a message in large letters, clearly spelling out the goal of the
operation: to settle things peacefully.

5

PROJECT
MAPLE

"Let everybody know we are ... being gentlemanly about this."
— OPP Acting Superintendent John Carson in September 4, 1995, police log

MONDAY, SEPTEMBER 4, 1995 — LABOUR DAY

Acting Superintendent John Carson couldn't have been too surprised when he got the call at 7:40 p.m. on Monday, September 4, saying the Natives had moved into the park. After all, since the previous May, they'd been saying they would do just that. While technically an occupation, it lacked drama. One local reporter ventured down to the park early in the evening, then left, bored.

The park had officially closed at 6:00 p.m. that day, since it was Labour Day. At 7:30 p.m., twenty minutes before sunset, a Native protestor cut a hole in a wire fence surrounding the park. It was peeled back, and a few old cars were driven into the park and across a dusty roadway. With that, Ipperwash Provincial Park was officially occupied.

Within a couple of hours, more protestors from Kettle and Stoney Point had joined the original dozen, increasing the numbers to about thirty-five.

Among them was Dudley George. Even if there had been news cameras there to record the event — and there were none — it would not have made for dramatic television.

Acting Detective Staff Sergeant Mark Wright and Acting Superintendent John Carson spoke on the phone at 9:40 p.m. Carson stressed that he didn't want things to get hostile between the police and the Native protestors. His plan was to wait until the Natives refused to leave, then go for a court injunction. Without that injunction, it would be difficult to prove that the occupation was illegal. "We may be forced to control outside," Carson said, according to a summary of his comments prepared by another officer. "We can . . . have [a] press release [prepared] for around 6 a.m. [We can] take control of area before media advised."

The undercover police campers, or "badgers," were still hiding in the park, eyeing the protestors from a distance. They described what they saw as "very disorganized." Gustafsen Lake it wasn't. So far, it wasn't even as dramatic as the picnic basket incident.

However, when uniformed officers arrived in cruisers at the park's perimeter, things got ugly fast. Some of the protestors dented three cruisers and smashed their windows with a hockey stick and rocks, and someone tossed a flare in the general direction of a police officer. Protestors set bonfires in the park, and police later told investigators from the province's Special Investigations Unit that they heard rapid gunfire near one. The Natives, however, later said it was just firecrackers.

Carson figured there wasn't much point in trying to talk that night. Perhaps the protestors would be more cooperative by daylight. Demonstrations tend to fizzle with time, and there was no rush to do anything in the dark. Carson therefore moved the mobile police command post about a kilometre away from the park, on East Parkway Drive. The command post didn't look threatening, as it was in a van painted to look like a St. John Ambulance vehicle. At 9:56 p.m., inside the corral of police vehicles there, Carson distributed the police master plan, code-named Project Maple, for dealing with the Ipperwash occupation.

The project's primary objective — as stated in bold capital letters on the second page — was "to contain and negotiate a peaceful resolution."

To that end, the comprehensive plan called for a team of thirteen negotiators and three backups to be on call around the clock. Local ambulances
were to be placed on alert, as were Corrections Canada caged buses.
Information was provided on rooms for more than two hundred police
officers in the Forest and Grand Bend areas near Ipperwash. "Members
should plan to stay for at least one week (accomodation [sic] and meals
provided)," the document said. Arrest teams were to consist of a male and
female officer (as the plan said "we can expect arrests will include both
men, women and children"), and band lists from the nearby Walpole,
Kettle Point, Saugeen, and Oneida First Nations were to be consulted to
help identify any Natives arrested. The arena in nearby Forest was to be
used as an arrest centre, and the Legion Hall in Forest was set aside as a
media centre. Polaroid cameras were to be available on each police vehicle
used in arrests, and two OPP officers were to videotape any arrests so the
police couldn't be wrongly accused of brutality. As the document said,
"This will help both co-oborative [sic] evidence for criminal court and
protection in civil litigation."

"Let everybody know we are doing the best and we are being gentlemanly about this," Carson told other OPP officers at 10:46 p.m.,
according to a police log from the command post.

Carson didn't have to be reminded that this wasn't just the occupation
of an empty park, but also a live political minefield, federally, provincially,
municipally, and even between the people of Kettle and Stoney Points. It
was too big a deal to be kept quiet. At 10:55 p.m., MP Rosemarie Ur
(Lambton-Middlesex) called. Carson told her that the Native protestors
were in the park and assured her that adequate resources were being used
and that they were working with the Ministry of Natural Resources. The
occupation was also of interest to the provincial government at Queen's
Park in Toronto. Still, it clearly wasn't an Oka or Gustafsen Lake situation,
as the Natives appeared to be unarmed. According to a provincial Cabinet
briefing note, the Stoney Pointers were carrying "no visible weapons," and
the takeover of the park was nonviolent.

Shortly before midnight, Carson requested that two negotiators be ready
for the next day and that another negotiator be placed on standby. Project

Maple was about talking, not bullets. That was the way the OPP had handled such protests, at least until now.

TUESDAY, SEPTEMBER 5, 1995

Acting Superintendent Carson was still on the job at 1:27 a.m. as Monday turned into Tuesday and the park occupation entered its second day. He warned fellow officers that they could expect media to be everywhere. That part would be just like Gustafsen Lake. He cautioned officers: "Don't speak about this anywhere, coffee shops etc., a lot of planning went into this. . . . We want to do this right."

By 2:20 in the morning, two St. John Ambulance members had signed in. Nobody was hurt, but Carson wasn't taking any chances. He wanted them there on standby anyway.

IT WAS CALM at dawn on Tuesday morning at the mobile command post. In a 7:40 a.m. briefing, Carson reminded fellow officers that all they wanted to do was to contain the area. "Today we have to access everything," Carson said. "Just control the area. We don't want to be ambushed."

Next, he called Kettle and Stony Point Chief Tom Bressette. A heavy-set, slow-talking man who had served with the military overseas in Germany, Bressette said he didn't support the Stoney Pointers, who constantly undermined his authority to speak for all Native people in the area. When Carson hung up, he felt Bressette was on side. "He feels they should be dealt with," Carson noted. Things seemed well under control now. The police were acting, but not endangering lives. The park occupiers seemed calm. There was no real threat to neighbouring cottagers. At 8:27 a.m., a police scribe wrote in an official police log: "We are trying to contain it, objective to contain and resolve it peacefully. No one in community is in any danger, as we have adequate [police] services present."

There were actually more than adequate police services, even if the situation somehow escalated. The OPP had also arranged with the Canadian military to borrow armoured personnel carriers, and another had been secured through GM Diesel in London, Ontario. The factory had a special arrangement with the London police force to lend it carriers in times of crisis, and now the London police, under Chief Julian Fantino, had agreed to lend one to the OPP. At 8:34 a.m., an OPP officer was cautioned to "keep the gun vehicles out of sight." By now, police technicians had installed special phone lines and equipment to scramble Native phone communications, while public relations staff were put on alert.

At that time, according to an OPP log, local rookie Tory MPP Marcel Beaubien was on the scene. Beaubien, former chair of the Petrolia Police Services Board, wasn't content with phone contact alone. He loved to watch the police in action. A local Bosanquet municipal politician suggested that someone declare a state of emergency, but Carson gently replied that things were well under control. No lives were in danger, and the press wasn't even particularly interested. There was a massive police presence and no indications from any of their surveillance that the Natives had any weapons.

When, at 9:02 a.m., Carson asked if there had been any incidents during the night, Acting Detective Staff Sergeant Mark Wright replied that some of the demonstrators had dropped their pants and mooned police officers.

By 9:25 a.m., police were drawing up warrants for three Natives for smashing the cruiser windows and throwing the flare in the general direction of a police officer on Monday night, when the occupation began. Meanwhile, Beaubien was making it clear he wasn't going to go away or take a backseat. Also, at 9:25 on Tuesday morning, Beaubien's name appeared again in police notes, along with that of an officer involved in the operation; "S/Sgt. [Wade] Lacroix has been in contact with Marcel Beaubien, local member of Parliament. He is updating the premier on the situation."

It was clear from the police notes that the OPP knew they were being intensely watched by high-placed politicians in Queen's Park. Other police notes recorded that morning stated: "Carson updated Chief [Supt. Chris] Coles that Marcel Beaubien has contacted the Premier."

DOWN AT THE PARK that morning, park superintendent Les Kobayashi tried to serve the Stoney Pointers with a written notice to leave, and as the police had anticipated, the protestors refused to take it. With that, legal officials for the Ministry of Natural Resources started preparation for a court injunction to order them to leave. Without that injunction, it was uncertain that the occupation of the park was technically law breaking. The meeting between the Stoney Pointers and Kobayashi wasn't cordial, but it wasn't hostile either. The park superintendent actually gave the Natives a key to the main building, figuring that then they wouldn't damage the buildings by breaking in. Ironically, Kobayashi was a Canadian of Japanese descent, and his family had lost property and possessions on Canada's west coast to the Canadian government during World War II under the same *War Measures Act* that had been used to take Stoney Point.

AMONG GOVERNMENT WORKERS and the press gallery at Queen's Park in Toronto, Debbie Hutton had a reputation for getting her way, and Premier Mike Harris's way. Just twenty-nine years old and a member of the premier's inner circle, Hutton had begun working with Harris as an office go-fer when she was twenty-two, back when Harris was in the wilderness years of Opposition. Working for Harris was the only full-time adult job she'd ever held, and now that her party had finally won power, Hutton demanded respect. She bore the impressive title of "executive assistant, issues management" for the premier.

At eleven o'clock that Tuesday morning, Hutton was at a meeting in the Ontario Native Affairs Secretariat Green Boardroom — Suite 1009 above The Atrium on Bay mall near Queen's Park. The secret meeting was for the Emergency Planning for Aboriginal Issues Interministerial Committee, a group that the NDP government had set up four years earlier. There were twenty people present, including senior representatives of the Ontario Native Affairs Secretariat; the Ministry of the Solicitor General, which was responsible for policing; the Ministry of the Attorney General, which was responsible for Crown attorneys; the Ministry of Natural Resources; the Ontario Provincial Police; and OPP Superintendent Ron Fox, who had been seconded to the Ministry of the Solicitor General as a special advisor on First Nations Issues. Three more Ministry of Natural Resources personnel were also able to take part through a teleconferencing hookup. True to form, Hutton wasn't the least bit intimidated.

The meeting was chaired by Julie Jai, the head of the Native Affairs Secretariat. Like Hutton, Jai was a small woman, but unlike Hutton, she did not call attention to herself, preferring to handle things in a nonconfrontational way. She had been a member of the left-leaning Law Union, which sought to make laws work for the disadvantaged, not simply for the moneyed and the well connected. People who had known Jai for years couldn't recall ever having heard her raise her voice. In short, her approach was very different from that of Hutton.

The bureaucrats at the meeting made note of the Native argument that part of Ipperwash Provincial Park was on a burial ground — but one official from the Ministry of Natural Resources suggested that there was no evidence of the existence of that gravesite in the park. He was obviously unaware of the considerable evidence to the contrary, including at least four provincial and federal government letters and decades of work by archaeologists Wilfrid and Elsie Jury of the University of Western Ontario. He added that it would be very expensive to conduct a study to prove the existence of a burial ground, and he doubted that the people of Stoney and Kettle Points could afford to go this route.

According to meeting minutes, it was noted that there was no evidence of firearms in the park, despite the intensive surveillance of the Native protestors. There was also no confirmation that noises in the park at night had been made by automatic weapons. Some buildings had, however, been entered, and public statements about break-and-enter could be useful in the future as "damage control," an official noted ominously. It didn't seem to matter that the Natives had been given a key to the main building.

It was noted that the Ministry of Natural Resources could make eight to ten media relations people ready, and it was made clear they should "stick to the script." It was also explained that Minister of Natural Resources Chris Hodgson was not happy with being seen as the minister in charge of the situation. A note from the meeting states, "Hodgson does not want to carry it longer." Interest from the very top level of government was recorded, as one note stated, "Premier [sic] office — any way to confirm gunfire."

A background synopsis of the conflict prepared for the secret meeting stated that "The Stoney Pointers are a dissident group from the Kettle and

Stoney Point First Nation who are not recognized as an independent band under the Indian Act." This summary was debatable at best, because it ignored the fact that the Stoney Pointers and Kettle Pointers had separate survey numbers with Indian Affairs and that they had lived separately, with separate chiefs, before the federal government had forced them to amalgamate. The two groups were living together now only because of the relocation of 1942, which both sides had considered temporary. The meeting concluded with the interministerial committee's recommendation that the government seek an injunction against the Stoney Pointers and with this statement: "The province will take steps to remove the occupiers ASAP." Exactly how that would be done was left unexplained.

AS THE MEETING WAS being held in downtown Toronto, Acting Detective Staff Sergeant Mark Wright was arranging for aerial support to go along with the armoured personnel carriers from GM Diesel and the offshore police boats. The Natives would be covered by land, air, and sea, by day and by night. Two helicopters were flown in so police could videotape the protestors with night lenses. At that point, according to one police estimate, the number of Native protestors in the park had dwindled to just nine, including two women and three children, and still none of them had been seen with guns.

THE OPP'S PARAMILITARY Tactics and Rescue Unit (TRU) team was now due by 7:00 p.m., but Sergeant Brad Seltzer made it clear he still thought there was room for talk and suggested that they try using a Native negotiator. An obvious candidate was Ron "Spike" George, a lawyer on the reserve, a former OPP officer, and the first Native to reach the rank of inspector. He was also a cousin of Dudley George. For reasons left unexplained, no one called him. Meanwhile, police notes for that evening give a terse account of what the officers saw happening from the park:

14:08:   Insp. [and Acting Superintendent John] Carson discussing visit to the park with Sgt. Seltzer. Sgt. Seltzer advises that he concurs with D/Sgt. Wright's observations that the first nations people are very

disorganized and nervous. He says we shouldn't do anything until
we know what's involved.

16:07: D/Sgt Wright suggests that 8 officers be put on highway #21 as a
fear first nations may be bolder tonight. Insp. Carson stated that if
the first nations get lippy, don't take too much. If they become
pushy, arrest them and get them out of there. D/Sgt. Richardson
states that 100 arrest packages have been prepared.

16:45: Insp. Carson reports that the military will be releasing a couple of
vehicles to us. . . . The military is prepared to train two teams.

16:45: Insp. Carson updated Chief Coles that Marcel Beaubien has contacted the Premier. There is to be a press release by the solicitor
general stating that this is not an Indian issue, it is a MNR and
provincial issue.

17:08: Insp. Linton [Inspector Dale Linton] advised Insp. Carson that he
had talked to [Kettle and Stony Point Chief] Tom Bressette earlier
in the day and that he has a concern about the cottages at the end
of the outer drive. Also that he feels that Pinery park [beside
Ipperwash Provincial Park] may be next.

At about 6:00 p.m. on Tuesday, the last of the campers who weren't part of
the protest quietly exited the park. They were OPP Constables Bryan Gast
of Petrolia and Mark Dew, the police "badgers" who had been spying on
the park occupiers. They still hadn't seen any guns in the hands of the
Native protestors.

MEANWHILE, BETWEEN VISITS to the mobile police command post, Conservative backbencher Marcel Beaubien was working on a press release to be
distributed on official government letterhead. It referred to Gerald
"Booper" George's letter to the editor in the August 30 edition of the *Forest
Standard*. Beaubien wrote: "A councillor from the Kettle and Stony Point
Band stated in a local newspaper recently, 'The army camp Indians have
strained relations between Kettle and Stony Point and the surrounding
communities. We all do not act like the army camp Indians, so please do
not think that all Chippewas act this way.'"

"This councillor is right," Beaubien continued. "We are not dealing with your decent native citizen, we are dealing with thugs. [The incident of thuggishness he was referring to was the attempted theft of the picnic basket.]

"Are we to assume as law abiding and tax paying citizens, that we have a legal system, in this province and in this country, that it [sic] two-tiered. Do we have a double standard with enforcement of the law?

"Enough is enough. Where is the leadership from not only the provincial officials, but the federal officials and from First Nations itself. [sic] How can we negotiate with irresponsible, law breaking dissidents. [sic] We must come to our senses and take back control before something irreparable happens. As citizens of this country, we have a responsibility to be law abiding, reasonable people. This should apply to all who live here."

In his release, Beaubien neglected to mention that there had been no attempt to negotiate yet. Beaubien also omitted to mention that so far, the Native protestors' move into the park had not been ruled illegal. What's more, if the Natives could make an argument that they had a burial ground there, the courts might conclude that they were well within their rights. As for Beaubien's question about whether there was a double standard influencing law enforcement in Canada, that was something the Natives themselves would soon be asking.

IN THEORY, THERE ARE strict rules governing the use of weapons of war belonging to the Canadian military against Canadian citizens. The *National Defence Act* states that the Canadian military cannot be called out "in aid of the civil power" unless there is "a riot or disturbance of the peace, beyond the powers of the civil authorities to suppress, prevent or deal with and requiring that service, occurs, or is, in the opinion of an attorney general, considered as likely to occur."

Police notes from September 5, 1995, make it clear that there was no riot or out-of-control disturbance of the peace at Ipperwash Provincial Park. The police had also found nothing in the conduct of the Native protestors to suggest a riot was about to occur. Neither their Native and police

spies nor intense surveillance had revealed any weapons. The only dangerous buildup of force in the park was on the police side, and that was still
escalating. The worst disturbance so far was the denting of three police
cars, the smashing of their windows, and the tossing of a flare in the general direction of a police officer. These actions, while regrettable, were
almost a day old that Tuesday when the OPP called on the Canadian Forces
for military equipment to confront the Stoney Pointers. Since then, the
worst offence perpetrated by any Native people was the mooning of police
officers.

That Wednesday, the Canadian military dispatched Captain Doug
Smith to act as a liaison officer with police. Both the police and the military knew they were walking a fine line, since legislation clearly states that,
at the federal level, decisions to use the Canadian military against
Canadians must be considered by the minister of national defence in con-
sultation with the rest of the federal Cabinet. At Ipperwash, all the police
requests for help from the military were informal, but there is no doubt
that the requests were made.

The possibility that the OPP would need to turn to the military for help
at Ipperwash had already been considered and given a cuddly code word:
"Panda." A confidential memo, dated September 1, 1995, was circulated
through Toronto; Petawawa; London, Ontario; St. Hubert, Quebec; and
Department of National Defence headquarters in Ottawa. It read as follows: "Panda is code word given . . . to the OPP wrt [with respect to] the
current sit [situation] in the Ipperwash Park and surrounding areas. This
msg [message] will serve to tie together and formalize the events, that to
date, have taken place by voice comms [communications]."

All the same, the military wanted to hang in the background, as an
undated Department of National Defence document, stamped "SECRET"
states:

MISSION: On order, LFCA [Canadian military's Land Forces Central Area
in North York] wil sp [support] law enforcement operations in the IPPER-
WASH area. . . . EXECUTION. . . . Concept of Ops [operations].

(1) It is the aim of DND [Department of National Defence] to remain at "arms length" and not to become directly involved in law enforcement operations. The intent of Comd LFCA [the Canadian military's Land Forces Central Area in North York] is to avoid direct involvement by providing resources and advice to the OPP which will enable them to successfully accomplish their mission. Concurrently, LFCA [Land Forces Central Area] will ensure that prudent preparations are completed at all Levels . . . is prepared to assist LEAs [law enforcement agencies] if so ordered.

A secret memo from the London detachment to regional headquarters in Toronto suggested that the military believed the OPP were planning to take action. It also showed that the military fully knew that they didn't have permission to directly aid the police. After describing preparations for the provision of armoured personnel carriers, the memo stated:

. . .

6. OPP are cognizant that no auth [authorization] for direct sp [support] in their operation has been formally received by me or approved by DND [Department of National Defence]. Regardless of the support approval process, my experience tells me that such rehearsals are invaluable.

7. While I understand your predicament of attempting to get this approval, from my perspective, I also know that the turtle can only make progress when he sticks out his neck.

WEDNESDAY, SEPTEMBER 6, 1995

The Ontario Provincial Police knew that the most important battle at Ipperwash wasn't on the sands of the actual park, but over the television and radio airwaves and in the newspapers. So OPP Inspector Dale Linton began on Wednesday, September 6, 1995 — the final day of Dudley George's life — with a 6:01 a.m. briefing of media relations officer Doug Babbit. There Babbit was told that three police vehicles had been damaged by rocks and that there were reports that people had heard what sounded like fifty to one hundred gunshots. However, no one had yet actually seen a gun in the hands of any Native protestor inside the park, and no one had even really investigated the report of gunshots.

By 8:11 a.m., Acting Superintendent John Carson asked Acting Detective Staff Sergeant Kent Skinner of the OPP's paramilitary Tactics and Rescue Unit if he had a big canister of pepper spray with him, then noted that some new weapons — expandable steel batons — might be used on the Natives. By 8:50 a.m., Carson put out a message that he needed fifty-seven of the new batons, giving police more than four of the specialized clubs for the dozen or so men, women, and Native children who had originally crept through the gap in the fence to occupy the park.

INSIDE THE ARMY CAMP, Stoney Point protestor Judas George was jarred awake at about eight in the morning by a loud banging on the door of the barracks he now called home. It was Robert "Burger" Isaac from nearby Walpole, and he was really wound up.

"Quick, come on!" Robert said. "Everybody get down to the park 'cause the cops are coming."

Robert went on to tell a story about Dudley and a youth named J.T. and threats from police. The Native protestors said that the police had shouted racial slurs, and that several police were calling out at Dudley, saying, "Dudley, you are going to be the first," "Come on over to this side of the fence, Dudley!", "Come on over, Dudley. Come on over. Welcome to Canada!", and "You want to be the first?"

"Fuck off!" yelled a few of the Natives.

"They said there was about twenty OPP officers all decked out in their riot gear, laying belly-on-the-ground, with all of their guns pointed at them," Judas later recalled. "That's when Dudley received his threat — 'You're going to be the first.'"

Judas was immediately concerned when he heard the names of Dudley and J.T., because he considered them both peaceful and vulnerable. J.T. was an adolescent from Kettle Point and Dudley was a joker, not a fighter.

"Go wake everybody else up," Judas told Robert.

Judas knew that there were plenty of OPP in the area and he took

Robert's story to be evidence that police roadblocks were going up around Ipperwash.

Judas wasn't sure what strategy the officers were following. Were the OPP testing them, trying to find out how long it took the Stoney Pointers to get from the army base to the park? And what did it mean that Dudley would be the first?

The men went with Robert Isaac to the park, but by the time they got there, the OPP were long gone. Dudley didn't seem too worried when he was asked about the incident, but he did say, "I'm going to be the first that gets shot if they come in."

Dudley George's family had warned him to be careful, but it still all seemed to be a joke to him. Even the appearance of more and more police around the park didn't appear to rattle him. "Dudley always maintained that they wouldn't shoot our people," his brother Sam said later.

After saying he'd be the first to get shot, Dudley reversed his position and said there wasn't anything to worry about. The police knew who was in the park, so they must have understood there was no need for dramatic action. He also thought the police had an instrument inside the low-flying helicopters that sensed the exact location of individual body masses. With all that equipment, the police had to know there were children in the park. They weren't going to *attack*. The police, Dudley said, "don't shoot people who aren't armed. All we've got here are sticks, and they know it."

The police officers in the park didn't appear particularly edgy either. One officer talked with World War II veteran Clifford George about buying some of his wood carvings, while another listened as one of the Natives talked about sweetgrass — how it is a sacred substance that was used after a house was cleaned, to purify it, and that it came from swamps and wasn't smoked. As they chatted, Dudley watched from a distance, unsuccessfully trying to get another Native protestor's all-terrain vehicle to work.

By 10:02 a.m., the police started the paperwork to get a warrant for Dudley George for mischief and possession of stolen property. Nowhere in the papers did anyone state exactly what the stolen property was.

At 10:06 a.m., one Native OPP constable said, "It's time for an arrest, show them it's a big plan happening. Show them that we have a plan. . . .

It may encourage them to talk because if one of their people is gone arrested they may talk."

There was another reference to the incident involving Dudley in OPP notes from that morning. Corroborating the Native version of events, Dudley was reported to be, apparently, in his typically carefree frame of mind when police saw him at 10:19 on the last morning of his life. Police notes said officers received a report that picnic tables were blocking a public beach, so they "Went in . . . and loaded tables. They identified Dudley George, sitting on a picnic table, [and he] turned and waved when we arrived."

Later that morning, the Native protestors saw OPP officers escorting residents of a brick cottage beside the park to their van and helping them load a big-screen TV into the van. If something's going to happen, it's going to happen soon, Judas thought. Judas made it clear they didn't want anybody smoking pot or drinking. Everybody should have a clear head. By now, it was ten or eleven in the morning. It was a sunny day and everyone was relaxed, even with the excitement the OPP were providing. Some of the women and children had a picnic, but when a surveillance helicopter buzzed down low over them, food was blown from the tables.

RECORDS OF THAT DAY suggest that Acting Superintendent Carson was getting a bigger headache from politicians than from the Native protestors. MPP Marcel Beaubien fired off a harsh letter to Bill King in the Premier's Office, attaching a letter from "a respectable, responsible, tax paying, law abiding lawyer in my riding. Bill, as we said during the campaign, 'local solutions to local problems.' I am prepared to go along with Minister [of Natural Resources Chris] Hodgson's proposal in dealing with this situation but please remember local constituents also understand the situation we are faced with very well."

The letter from the "respectable, responsible" lawyer opened this way: "I am extremely upset by events unfolding at Ipperwash Provincial Park. It is the first place my parents took me camping. . . . Now the park is occupied by natives. Hooligans is a better word, for there is no respect for the law. . . . I do not want to see the provincial government back down in the face of lawlessness. Under trespass law, the occupiers can be arrested. This should be done immediately. . . . The time to act, and act decisively, is now. If people are hurt, so be it — the laws must be enforced to be respected. . . . If illegal acts are tolerated, they spread. The end result is anarchy. People begin to perceive the government cannot protect them and their interests — they begin to take steps to protect themselves. These steps can lead to tragic consequences. . . ."

Ironically, the lawyer was unwittingly echoing the frustrations of the Native people themselves, who had been waiting for about half a century for the Canadian government to grant them their legal right to return to the reserve at Stoney Point and to have the burial ground in the park fenced off. It was the perfect moment for peaceful negotiations. Instead, this lawyer went on to say: "The Conservative government had a large law and order plank in its platform — I want to see it live up to its election promises and my expectations. I want to see Ipperwash Provincial Park remain in the public domain, and I want the law enforced to see that it does."

IT WAS EASY to tell the bureaucrats from the representatives of the Premier's Office when the Emergency Planning Committee met again in downtown Toronto above The Atrium on Bay mall. They were in the Green Board-room again — Suite 1009. The bureaucrats were the ones with the stunned looks on their faces. Julie Jai, head of the Ontario Native Affairs Secretariat, who was once more chairing the meeting, said gently she was not sure the government had the legal right to force the Natives out of the park. "Are you sure that we have strong legal grounds?" asked Jai.

Such caution seemed lost on the representatives from the Premier's Office. Debbie Hutton made it clear that Harris was the boss. A written record of that meeting notes that Hutton said Harris wanted the protestors out of the park and "nothing else." Minutes of the meeting also state that police had "been asked to remove" the Stoney Pointers and that there would be no negotiation of their claims over the land.

The role of speaking for the OPP was left to Superintendent Ron Fox, a reasoned and intelligent man. Technically, he was working with the

Ministry of the Solicitor General now on a secondment, and he found himself trying to explain concepts that should have been painfully clear to any police recruit of average intelligence.

"This is ridiculous," a representative from the Premier's Office complained. "Why are we treating them [the Stoney Pointers in the park] any differently?"

"We're not 100 per cent certain that they don't have a land claim," a bureaucrat replied.

Fox came right to the point. "We're not treating them any differently," he said. "We all want to avoid an Oka situation. It's very important that we keep them calm. If someone was holed up in a house with guns, this is exactly what we'd do."

"Why can't we just order the police to go in and get them out?" asked a frustrated aide from the Premier's Office.

"Because the police are not the government's army," Fox replied.

There was increasing heat from Queen's Park to do something and to do something fast. The newly elected Harris government did not want to be seen as dawdling or ineffective, and that's how they felt the RCMP looked in the Gustafsen Lake standoff. The Gustafsen Lake protest had been on the nightly news for a month, with the protestors opening fire on police and forest workers. In the end, patience and negotiation won out, and the rebels finally surrendered, with no loss of life on either side.

Perception and optics are as important as, or even more important than, reality in the world of politics, and the Harris people wanted to be seen as quick and decisive and tough. In handwritten notes from the meeting, these words appear by Hutton's name: "want to be seen as actioning."

In notes from the meeting, under the heading "Next Steps," it was clear that Acting Superintendent John Carson's plan to negotiate a peaceful settlement was in peril. "It was noted," the record said, "that there will be no 'negotiations' with the Stoney Pointers regarding their claim to ownership of the land, and that the goal of any discussions would be removal of the occupiers from the park."

The notes also indicate that the Stoney Pointers had used picnic tables as barricades and had entered park buildings. Then they continued, "An aerial surveillance of Ipperwash Provincial Park will be conducted today to determine the extent of the damage done to MNR's equipment and facilities, what the Stoney Pointers are doing with MNR's equipment, and whether the Stoney Pointers have any weapons."

Under "Ministers' Directives," the following appeared:

MNR: The Minister wants to act as quickly as possible to avoid further damage and to curtail any escalation of the situation.

MAG [the Ministry of the Attorney General]: The Minister agrees that application will be made for an injunction.

SGC [the Ministry of the Solicitor General]: As a matter of protocol, the SGC will not involve itself in the day-to-day operations of the OPP. The OPP will exercise its discretion regarding how to proceed in removing the Stoney Pointers from the Park and the laying of appropriate charges.

While this seemed moderate and peaceful, the next paragraph appeared to reverse directions, saying, "Police have been asked to remove the occupiers from the park," and later, the directives continued, "It was agreed that the goal is to remove the Stoney Pointers from the park as soon as possible; that public safety is paramount; and that the Crown Law Office — Civil will proceed expeditiously to obtain the injunction."

The notes from the meeting went on to state that any possible help from Kettle and Stony Point band Chief Tom Bressette wasn't necessarily desired: "if Chief Bressette offers help — wanted?" An aide from the Premier's Office rejected this, saying, "This government will not be seen as cooperating with the Indians."

A SECOND, MUCH SMALLER, and much more important government meeting took place in Toronto later that day. It was attended by Premier Mike Harris and thirty-three-year-old Minister of Natural Resources Chris Hodgson, from the Haliburton-Victoria-Brock riding. Like Harris, Hodgson had a small-business background, having worked in real estate, and, like Harris, he was from outside Toronto, beginning his career as reeve of Dysart Township.

Also at that meeting were OPP Superintendent Ron Fox (now working with the Ministry of the Solicitor General) and Larry Taman, deputy minister in the Attorney General's office. Taman, a former law professor, argued eloquently and forcefully that it would be wrong for the government to rush to get an *ex parte* injunction to bar the Natives from the park. An *ex parte* motion meant the Native protestors would be shut out of the court process and not given a chance to argue the merits of their case. Such an order was intended to be used only for the most extreme cases. What was the urgency here? Why not just let the police do their job? Hadn't that always worked in the past? Why change things now?

Taman's voice was not just that of another government lawyer. Once a clerk for Bora Laskin, chief justice of the Supreme Court of Canada, Taman had been associate dean of the Osgoode Hall Law School at York University before becoming deputy minister in the Ministry of the Attorney General. He was a particularly bright, highly educated man struggling to make a simple and basic point: Canada was not a police state and the police were not the tools of politicians. All citizens had the right to have access to the court process.

Taman carried the burden of being an NDP appointee and a bureaucrat, and he was trying to communicate to newly elected, hard-line Conservatives. His call for moderation seemed to be entirely lost on his listeners. A memo from the Solicitor General's office about the meeting made note of Taman's passionate plea for the government not to meddle with police operations at Ipperwash. The memo also indicated that the OPP commissioner, Thomas O'Grady himself, was now involved, as well as government lawyer J.T.S. "Tim" McCabe and Elaine Todres, the deputy minister in the Ministry of the Solicitor General and the Ministry of Corrections.

The following is an excerpt from the memo:

Sept. 6/95.

Ron Fox,

— Tim has asked for s.o. fr OPP to give *vive voce* evidence before J today in Sarnia

— now OPP commissioner is involved — decisions will be made at his level.

— he was called into Cabinet — Larry Taman was also there + was eloquent
— he — cautioned abt rushing in with *ex part* inj - + can't interfere w police discr.
— but Prem. + Hodgson came out strong
— Larry, Elaine Todres were at Cabinet.
Ron ws there for part of discussion. decision to go *ex part* appeared to have already been made.

The meeting was in the Premier's Office, and, according to the premier's itinerary, it was over by 1:00 p.m. It was clear that Queen's Park was asking the OPP to provide an officer to give verbal justification (*vive voce* evidence) for excluding the Native protestors from the court process (through an *ex parte* injunction). This would constitute an end run around the goals of the OPP's incident commander Acting Superintendent John Carson and his stated aim to resolve the conflict peacefully. According to the last line of the memo, the decision about the injunction appeared already to have been made.

THAT AFTERNOON, Kettle and Stony Point band Chief Tom Bressette received a disturbing phone call from someone who worked at Queen's Park. The caller was clearly agitated. Before going on, the person insisted that the message be treated in confidence. Bressette must never reveal the caller's identity. "Look, I'll lose my job if this gets out," the Queen's Park contact said. "I've got a family. I've got my life to worry about."

Reassured by Bressette that he wouldn't break the caller's confidence, the person at the other end of the line told the chief that there had been a meeting at Queen's Park that day and that now the caller feared there would be trouble at the park.

"I know you know a lot of First Nations people," the Queen's Park contact continued. "I don't like what may be going to happen, so you should let somebody know this."

Bressette didn't know what to do with the message. His relationship with the Stoney Pointers was already strained. If he went to the park with a threatening message, the whole thing might just blow up in his face. The protestors might just accuse him of trying to intimidate them. Quite likely, Bressette thought, they would have said, "Ah, fuck you." What was the point of me going down there?

The chief also knew that people in government often leaked messages to see how people would react. Why should he take this one seriously? "I thought it was a whole lot of crap," Bressette said after the events were over. "I wasn't convinced that anything like that would be accurate. I thought it was like a scare tactic. . . . There were so many rumours flying around. You hear things every day. You never know whether to take it seriously."

Still, there was something troubling in the caller's voice. The person clearly believed the threatening report — enough to risk their job. The Queen's Park contact was well placed and sounded rational. Bressette couldn't just dismiss the call. So the chief telephoned Lee Michaels, a reporter at Sarnia radio station CKOK, a station popular with Natives in the area. Michaels agreed to broadcast a warning to the Native protestors in the park, saying that, according to the chief, something bad might be happening there that night.

Later Bressette said he still wasn't sure this warning to the Stoney Pointers would amount to anything: "They'd made up their minds. They weren't leaving."

DESPITE THE MOUNTING PRESSURE from Queen's Park, Acting Superintendent John Carson still hadn't given up on negotiating. At 4:44 p.m., he advised Sergeant Margaret Eve to take her stripes off and go down to try to talk to the protestors. Perhaps they would see her more as a person than as a uniform. Not long afterwards, a report came back that the Stoney Pointers refused to talk with her, stripes or no stripes.

AS NIGHTFALL APPROACHED, the police were ready for action. As their notes state: "[Acting Detective Staff Sergeant] Mark Wright advise Sarnia jail has one full wing for natives, one prisoner van for 12 people at a time."

The police log entry for 6:42 p.m. reads:

John Carson states they are using women and children and it puts us in a tough position. John Carson advised [MPP] Marcel Beubien [sic] that he understands the residents [sic] concerns. John Carson reported to Marcel Beubien [sic] that we have 30 people on the ground at all times having the members talk to the residents to let them know our presence. Foot patrols are being completed around the residences — safety is important.

Marcel Beubien states that he doesn't mind taking controversy, if situation can't be handled by police services, something has to be done to handle the situation.

John Carson states that we want it resolved, but we don't want anyone to get hurt, wants everything that can be done to stress the point of no one getting hurt. John Carson also stated that we have a lot of good people, 2 teams on ground at a time. Officers doing a great job.

[OPP Inspector] Dale Linton advises Marcel Beubien that we appreciates [sic] everything he has done. Marcel Beubien talked to [Western Ontario Regional OPP] Chief Chris Coles . . .

John Carson brought up issue that if the park is cleared, what happens after that. Marcel Beubien is concerned about the residents. Stated that they had a meeting and 100 or more residents turned out, they are very frustrated. Instructed to contact me if something occurs and he would try to find out about things . . .

[Park superintendent] Les Kobayashi advises that there is great communication between the MNR and the OPP.

Marcel Beubien [sic] and Les Kobayashi depart at 19:05 hours.

THE STONE HIT the back of the blue Grand Am as it was driving away from the park area, leaving a nasty little scratch and a dent. At the wheel of the Grand Am was Gerald "Booper" George, the same man who'd called the Stoney Pointers "animals" in his recently published letter to the editor of the *Forest Standard*. On any other night, a fresh scratch on a car on a reserve wouldn't have attracted much police attention, but this wasn't just any night or just any reserve. That four-hundred-dollar scratch on the Grand Am would have repercussions that would be felt all the way up to OPP headquarters in Orillia and all the way down to the provincial legislature at Queen's Park.

Within a few minutes, Booper George had wheeled the Grand Am up to an OPP checkpoint outside the park. Police were easy to find this evening. He talked with Constable Sam Poole — an interview that would normally have been totally forgettable, even on a slow shift, but tonight it had different connotations.

Q. What if anything can you tell me about what just happened?

A. At about 7:51 p.m. on 06 September 1995, I went onto Army Camp Road from Ipperwash, are [sic] coming off the curve at the Ipperwash Provincial Park, when Stewart George, nickname "Worm" motioned for me to stop and I pulled onto the dirt. Stewart approached the car and he was angry over an article that I put in the *Forest Standard*. Stewart said that he, "was going to kick my ass." He was angry and drunk, so I proceeded to pull away and Stewart threw a rock at my sister's car and the rock impacted in the back left quarter panel [directly behind the driver's door] and I just drove away.

Q. How do you know Stewart George?

A. I worked with him for about the last three months building the new school at Kettle Point.

Q. Do you know how old he is?

A. 35–40, I guess.

Q. How do you know that he, Stewart George, was drunk?

A. I smelled him. It was strong with beer smell and his speech was slurred.

Q. Did Stewart have anything in his hands while he was talking to you?

A. He just had his fists resting on my door.

Q. Who else was standing with Stewart?

A. He came away from the other group. He was about 35 feet away from the group.

Q. Did you recognize who was in the other group?

A. No. I wasn't really looking at them. One of the young guys had a bat though.

Q. How far was Stewart when he threw the rock at the car?

A. About 12 feet.

Q. Did you see Stewart pick the rock up?

A. No, but as I was pulling away, I saw him wind up and throw the rock which hit the car.

Q. Who owns the vehicle?

A. My sister, Toni Jeannette George, age 26, owns the blue Pontiac, Grand Am with Ontario licence 439-KMZ.

Q. Do you wish to say anything else?

A. No.

Constable Poole recorded in his notebook that the interview with Booper George about the stone throwing ended at 8:21 p.m.

At 8:14 p.m., before Poole had even finished the paperwork on the incident, Acting Superintendent John Carson got a call at a private residence in Forest from Inspector Dale Linton that repeated a rumour that had begun to circulate. It greatly distorted the stone-throwing incident, saying that "a vehicle had been damaged by baseball bats and there was a crowd of Native people in that area at that time." The single stone had somehow morphed into multiple baseball bats and the impression was given that it was a mob attack and that Booper had been lucky to escape alive.

By 8:30 p.m. — nine minutes after Poole had completed his report — Staff Sergeant Kent Skinner of the elite, paramilitary Tactics and Rescue Unit (TRU) was called in. OPP Detective Sergeant Trevor Richardson would later tell investigators of the Special Investigations Unit (SIU), a civilian agency that looks into police violence, that he'd heard the car had been attacked with both bats and rocks. "It had escalated to a civilian motorist having his vehicle pelted with rocks and hit with baseball bats," said Richardson, who, along with the other riot squad members, was getting dressed in preparation for a standoff as Poole was finishing his notes. Richardson had completed his regular tour of duty at 4:30 that afternoon, but had been called back and told there'd been further escalation at Ipperwash Provincial Park.

A two-man OPP Sierra Scout Team — part of the Tactics and Rescue Unit — was sent out to the park to get a better look at the Native protestors. Even before they returned from the surveillance mission, Staff Sergeant Kent Skinner of the TRU told fellow officers that police had heard they had far more to be concerned about that night than Stewart George tossing a stone or Natives swinging baseball bats. As Skinner later told the civilian Special Investigations Unit (SIU), "This report stated there possibly were four AK-47 type assault rifles, some Ruger 14's and scoped hunting rifles in possession of those occupying the park."

How seriously did police take this latest report? Apparently not seriously enough to tell the riot squad members.

NOT FAR AWAY, ambulances were on standby, ready for those who might soon be wounded. St. John Ambulance personnel had been briefed by police, "to determine which hospital we would be taking casualties to," according to attendant Karen Bakker.

At 9:41 p.m. Inspector Dale Linton phoned his superior, Superintendent Anthony Parkin, from the mobile command post in the van that looked like a St. John Ambulance vehicle. The two men discussed problems created by the rumours that the Natives suddenly now had Russian assault weapons. Somehow the unsubstantiated information had bypassed any screening by police intelligence officers. Once the rumours hit the political level, they would take on a life of their own, much as how a single stone thrown at Booper George's car had somehow become an attack by a mob with baseball bats and stones. Now the police were fighting rumours more than Native protestors, and the rumours would be far harder to contain.

"Well, . . . it looks like we're in the thick of it," Linton said in a taped conversation. He noted that they were being pressured by local non-Native landowners to move against the protestors.

"There was a group of people," Linton said, "Bosanquet Township people. Met the citizens and they expressed their displeasure. Now this is the people that Fred Thomas was leading. He's the mayor of Bosanquet."

"Yes."

"Yeah."

"But right now I mean there's no way you could go in there and serve," Linton said.

"No, not to try and serve papers on a bunch of them," Parkin said. "They're probably all boozed up. They've probably been drinking."

There'd been no reports that the Natives were drinking, apart from Booper George's statement about Stewart George, who'd thrown the rock at his sister's Grand Am — just as there'd been no confirmed reports about assault rifles. Judas George had actually made it clear that he didn't want anyone drinking. There were enough problems without adding liquor to the situation.

"Yeah, yeah, they're setting fires," Linton said, then threw yet another unconfirmed rumour into the mix: ". . . there's some rumours they stole a thousand gallons of gas or whatever gas they could today from an MNR tank in there as well, and . . . the rumours of Molotov Cocktails . . ."

"Yeah."

"So it looks like tonight's the night they're . . . revved up for action. Their women and kids are leaving. It really surprised [me] . . . that they'd ah you know be this aggressive."

"Yeah," Parkin replied. "The women and kids are leaving. That's, that's a bit unusual too."

The fact that some of the Native protestors might be leaving because they had jobs and school to attend the next day wasn't considered. Parkin moved on to note the rumours about the Natives having military weapons, and how those stories had spread to the Ministry of Natural Resources at Queen's Park and to the office of the deputy solicitor general. "Well," said Parkin, "that injunction surprises me. . . . I guess John told you what happened today about the [rumour] going up the MNR [Ministry of Natural Resources] side about the possibility of automatic weapons."

"Yeah," Linton replied.

"And then that hit the fan down . . ."

"In Toronto," Linton said, completing Parkin's sentence.

"Well, that didn't come from us . . ."

"No, no, no, no. It went up through the MNR side. And then it got, the next thing it was sitting in the Deputy Solicitor General's office, so there was concern that you know, maybe we weren't doing the right thing."

Superintendent Anthony Parkin said the unconfirmed reports about the Native protestors passed on by people at the Ministry of Natural Resources circulated quickly at Queen's Park, where they took on a life of their own.

"[Lambton MPP] Marcel Beaubien was in tonight. He had talked to the Solicitor General," Linton said.

"Yeah," Parkin said, then went on to state that he wasn't comfortable with police entering the park that night to serve Natives with legal papers.

"And the Attorney General, they were comfortable," Linton said. "But he, he . . ."

"Well, that's right," Parkin said. "We called the Commissioner tonight. And he had been talking to [Solicitor General Robert] Runciman and that and they were more than pleased with what the OPP was doing, so there's no problem there. What happened though by that information about the automatic weapons going up the MNR side, they went from that regular type of injunction to the emergency type, which isn't really in our favour."

Parkin could see that going ahead with an *ex parte* injunction wasn't really in the favour of the police. Such an injunction would effectively shut the Natives out of the court process, as they would not be notified of, or invited to, any hearing before a judge. And yet the senior officer's hands seemed tied.

"Yeah."

"We want a little bit more time," Parkin continued.

"Yeap," Linton agreed.

"But, but they've gone for that and then that's why those papers must've come down tonight for us to serve. But I would suggest that it's not up to us to serve those initially."

"No," Linton replied.

"It's up to the MNR to serve those."

"Yeap."

"It's an MNR injunction."

"Yeap."

"And we would assist them in serving that."

"Yep."

"But this is typical . . . Ultimately the ball's gonna be in our lap anyway if they get this injunction tomorrow," Parkin said.

At 10:17 that night, Acting Superintendent John Carson phoned the command post and reached Linton. In addition to being the incident commander on the occupation of CFB Ipperwash since 1993, Carson had been the backup negotiator a couple of years before, when the TRU team in the area had shown up at the wrong house near Windsor. Bernard Bastien, a resident of that house, was sure they were armed criminals and grabbed a shotgun to protect himself. He was shot dead by TRU members. A member of that OPP operation, Wade Lacroix, was first-in-command of the Crowd Management Unit at Ipperwash. Carson had been ready to negotiate that night, but nobody ever called him. Clearly, Carson didn't want another tragic debacle like the Bastien case here at Ipperwash. This time, he had thirteen negotiators ready.

Carson: Okay, you were saying you were calling out TRU [the Tactics and Rescue Unit].

Linton: Yeah.

Carson: What are you gonna do with them?

Linton: Well TRU is probably gonna end up going in and doing an arrest.

Carson: Dale, don't do that.

Linton: No.

Carson: Don't do that. If you do that, we are in trouble, okay. Then are you asking my advice or are you just informing me, we better get this straight.

Linton: No, we, we need to discuss this . . .

Carson: What are you gonna achieve by using TRU that ERT [Emergency Response Team] can't do?

Linton: Well.

Carson: If somebody goes down, then what are you gonna do?

Linton: I think you've got a buildup inside, that's my concern . . .

Carson: Okay.

Linton: We were gonna do that with ERT once we got the statement.

My concern is that you have the schoolbus moving down there, you've got the dump truck moving down there, you've got people in the kiosk pulling the blinds all down and I think there's you know a threat here of maybe sniper fire, like they're doing something inside getting ready for us.

Carson: Okay, well, okay, well that's fine now. Let's evacuate those houses if you think.

Linton: Okay.

Carson: There's a threat of that nature, but don't go in there with TRU.

Linton: [inaudible]

Carson: If you go in with TRU and somebody gets hurt, we have nobody else to get them out.

Linton: No, what I'm doing is I'm getting TRU to come here.

Carson: Well, I wouldn't even do that.

Carson lost the argument and the paramilitary officers were called in. Years later, it would still not be clear how the command to bring in the Tactics and Rescue Unit made its way down the OPP chain of command. Whatever the case, Carson's plans for moderation were history.

WITHIN HALF AN HOUR, the riot squad was marched down onto the park, flanked by TRU team scouts and snipers. At 11:14 p.m., Carson's fears were realized. Another call came across on the police radio, saying, "We have possibly shot someone."

It was around this time that Ovide Mercredi, grand chief of the Assembly of First Nations, the umbrella group for Native people all across Canada, got a phone call in his Ottawa-area home from Chief Tom Bressette of the Kettle and Stony Point band. Bressette was clearly upset as he told Mercredi that one of his councillors, Cecil Bernard "Slippery" George, had just gone down to the occupied area. The chief didn't know that, as he spoke, Dudley George was dying of a gunshot wound and Slippery George was lying unconscious, with no detectable pulse. Tom Bressette just wanted to know if the grand chief could do anything to intervene. Mercredi agreed to do so.

Mercredi called the police command post at 11:32 p.m. and asked for whoever was in charge. He had hoped to speak with Chief Superintendent Chris Coles, who was responsible for Ontario's Southwestern Region but ended up instead on the line with Acting Detective Staff Sergeant Mark Wright.

Mercredi: I'm told that there's some thirty cruisers and some ambulances and some canine units on their way there.

Wright: Yes.

Mercredi: And I wanted to know if that's true.

Wright: Yes, that's true. We have a situation there.

Mercredi: And what is the intention there?

Wright: I'm not in the Command. I'm not the incident commander. He's kind of tied up with the situation here, but I can relay this stuff to you.

Mercredi: Maybe I should wait for him to talk to him then, because I want to know because I'm very concerned with what you're doing. I'm concerned about people's lives.

Wright: And so are we . . .

Mercredi: We have a common goal.

Wright: We certainly do. Okay, I'll tell you what, sir, if you can briefly tell me what you want and then I'll grab him and then, and then . . .

Mercredi: I want to know if it is your intention to move in [on] those people tonight?

Wright: To move into [sic] those people tonight. Okay, I'll pass that on to my commander.

Mercredi: [inaudible] I want to know that before, before I make any outstanding calls.

Wright didn't tell Mercredi that the police had already moved on the park that night, but said he would have to put the grand chief on hold. Instead, Mercredi passed on his phone number. Before he hung up,

Mercredi asked Wright why the police felt they had to move on the park at night. Wright couldn't answer the question.

> Mercredi: What's the rush? Why don't you wait until tomorrow after you've talked to them?
>
> Wright: I see.
>
> Mercredi: And why you're doing [inaudible] . . .
>
> Wright: I know exactly who you are, sir. I just want to know if you're their negotiator, you're their spokesman or what.
>
> Mercredi: No, I'm not.
>
> Wright: You're just . . .
>
> Mercredi: I'm concerned about Indian people. I represent them wherever they may be.
>
> Wright: Okay, and you're speaking on behalf of Tom Bressette or . . .
>
> Mercredi: No, I'm not.
>
> Wright: Or you're just speaking . . . You're the Grand Chief.
>
> Mercredi: I'm the Grand Chief. I'm speaking in that capacity.
>
> Wright: Okay, that's all I wanted to know, sir. Okay, I'm going. Do you want me to put you on hold or do we get back to you . . . ?
>
> Mercredi: Well you can get back to me. . . . I'll wait for the call.

Mercredi was uneasy after he hung up and phoned *Ottawa Citizen* reporter Jack Aubry, who had covered Native issues extensively, and told him, "I'm a little concerned somebody's going to get hurt." Mercredi also made a call to the news desk of the *Toronto Star*. As a result, night editor Paul Archer told the paper's roving "night stalker" reporter to head to Ipperwash.

Like the Kettle Point Natives, Mercredi felt that the police were less likely to do something violent if there were media eyes on them. Once his calls were made, he headed for Ipperwash himself. The return call from the police would never come.

AT 11:37 P.M. THAT NIGHT, as Pierre and Carolyn George frantically tried to get their dying brother to hospital, senior OPP officers Dale Linton and John Carson were on the phone again. Rather than seeing Mercredi as someone who could cool tensions, they saw him as one more potential headache.

Linton: ... Ovide Mercredi just called and wanted to know if we were going in the park. ... Nobody, nobody really said too much to him.
Carson: Okay, that's good. Where'd he call from?
Linton: Ah, don't know. It's a 6-1-3 number.

It was obvious that Carson's hopes of keeping everything quiet and away from the media were dying fast with Dudley George.

6

BLOODY AFTERMATH

"Minister has copy of burial ground record.
Shocked as well. Did not know it existed."
— OPP OFFICER'S NOTES

THURSDAY, SEPTEMBER 7, 1995

At forty-five minutes past midnight, Staff Sergeant Wade Lacroix gave Inspector Dale Linton a blunt message. "There is no doubt about it," Lacroix told Linton. "They tried to kill us."

The OPP log notes record Kettle and Stony Point Chief Tom Bressette angrily objecting to the use of force at night. According to the 1:28 a.m. entry for September 7, Bressette told police, "I told you I didn't support them, but I think this night-time business should have been done in the daylight. John Carson and Mark Wright agreed. . . . I've got a mob of people upset with me."

DOWN HIGHWAY 21 at Stoney Point, at the command post near the park, Acting Superintendent Carson was talking with military liaison officer

Captain Doug Smith about a plan to pump up the police presence so they could outnumber the Native protestors ten-to-one, should violence escalate. They already outnumbered them about two-to-one and had an overwhelming weapons and equipment advantage, with heavy equipment in the air, on the water, and on the ground — but that wasn't considered nearly enough now that Dudley George was dead. It was time for real military hardware. Unfortunately for the police, the Canadian Forces were already committed to an overseas peacekeeping mission in a real war, one that was publicly supported by elected officials. "There is a problem," the police notes said. "All the combat troops are in Petawawa, ready to go to Bosnia."

Marcel Beaubien had been at the police command post hours before the killing, and now, at 7:17 in the morning, the MPP was back again. This time, as he talked with the police, Beaubien called for peace.

"Beaubien stressed to Carson that he didn't want anyone hurt," the notes state. It was about six hours late for Dudley George. His bullet-torn body was being transported at that time to a morgue in London, Ontario.

At 8:23 a.m., as the people of Stoney Point and Kettle Point wept over the death of Dudley George and panicked over rumours that the OPP would be moving on the park again, Inspector Dale Linton reported that trauma councillors had arrived to counsel OPP officers shaken up by the bloodshed.

AT 9:26 A.M., an hour's drive away in Sarnia, something more than a little bizarre was occurring in Ontario Court, General Division (now the Superior Court of Justice), before Mr. Justice R.J. Daudlin. The police and government lawyers were still seeking an injunction requiring the Natives to leave the park.

The motion for the injunction was sought by both the attorney general for the Province of Ontario and the provincial minister of natural resources. No Native people were present at the hearing and no lawyers appeared on their behalf, which wasn't surprising, since they hadn't been notified of the hearing. Also notably absent and not invited was Ron "Spike" George, Dudley George's cousin, the reserve lawyer and former OPP inspector.

"We're here this morning, Your Honour, under the shadow of the grave and distressing events of last evening of which Your Honour may have heard media reports by this time," government lawyer J.T.S. "Tim" McCabe said in solemn tones.

"I have," the judge replied.

McCabe continued: "We are here partly in the expectation that the relief we are seeking will help to defuse this situation in and around Ipperwash Provincial Park before any more incidents like that of last night can occur. . . . [T]he decision to bring this motion this morning was made yesterday many hours before the trouble last night and, of course, before the tragic events of last night were foreseen. If Your Honour has had an opportunity to look at [the] material in this case, you will know that we are here to seek an *ex parte* injunction of ten days' duration restraining the occupation of Ipperwash Provincial Park . . . ."

"As Your Honour may appreciate . . . ," McCabe went on, "as the evidence unfolds here that, however, was overtaken by events last night, and there was no notice either formal or informal given to the persons in the occupation of the park."

The events that "overtook" the evidence the night before were not uncontrollable, unpredictable "acts of God"; they were a planned march by the riot squad and snipers on the park.

The judge asked why the police and the provincial government had taken so long to make their injunction request, since without it they could not argue with certainty that the Native protestors were in the park illegally.

McCabe answered that the law supported his request to bring the injunction motion *ex parte*, without the input of the Native people. He quoted Rule 37.07 sub Rule 2: "Where the nature of the motion or the circumstances render service of the Notice of Motion impracticable or unnecessary the court may make an order without notice."

Next, Acting Detective Staff Sergeant Wright found himself in front of the judge. He did not mention that the only charge laid against a Native before the riot police confronted the protestors at night was four hundred dollars' damage to Booper George's sister's car. Instead, Wright tried to impress the judge with the thoroughness of the police operation, noting, "We had a helicopter flying overhead on numerous occasions with a video taken and still photographer to that part of the camp — or the provincial park — that you cannot see from the outer barrier, as well as along the peripheral part of the part that I saw from the ground."

He did not present any actual findings of danger in the park by the police helicopter crew or the still and video photographers or by the police undercover officers or by the Native spy on the ground. The truth was that they hadn't seen any bona fide danger, and no police officers or equipment were hit with any bullets during the close-quarters confrontation the night before. There was no evidence that anyone but the OPP had opened fire the night before.

Despite the police helicopters flying low over Native protestors, the advance of the riot squad, and firing by snipers with submachineguns, Wright struggled to present the OPP as a culturally sensitive group that had tried for dialogue, even into the afternoon of September 6. "I arranged to bring an OPP Sergeant who's a policewoman," Wright told the judge. "In respect to their traditional values which are, if I may, Your Honour, native cultures — traditional native culture is that the females do the negotiating and the decision making."

This observation about traditional Native culture — that only Native women do negotiating and decision making — would have been news to the people of Kettle and Stony Point and any of the male chiefs who had negotiated with the Crown to set up the reserves back in 1827. And Wright's statement would have been a surprise for Mercredi, who was male and often acted as a mediator and who had hoped to help mediate the Ipperwash dispute. Wright continued to tell of damage Native protestors had done to picnic tables and police cars in an effort to show that the police were up against formidable opponents. While the Native protestors had done some damage to OPP and MNR property, their actions were far less provocative than those of other Native protestors at Oka and Gustafsen Lake.

"The damage was caused in all instances by rocks?" the judge asked.

"No," Wright replied. "The one [damaged cruiser] on the boat ramp area was a large — I believe it was a hockey stick through the rear window of the cruiser, and I believe the other two ones were rocks through the windows, and damage to the body of the cruiser."

Describing police intelligence, he said that police officers hadn't entered the park since the takeover on September 4, but they had flown over it. What they saw included Natives drag racing in the park, and they had flown low enough to read "OPP Who?" spray-painted on the side of one car, which had what appeared to be Ministry of Natural Resources lights and sirens on it, and homemade fins, like those popular in the 1950s. Its driver was racing, Wright said, "up and down and along the beach and . . . over the curbs and on the grass and all over the place."

He added that, on Monday night, a police officer saw the butt of a rifle in a car trunk by the boat launch, adding that at least eight of the Native protestors appeared to be itching for a fight. Asked how many police officers were currently in the area, Wright replied, "Well in excess of 100."

Despite the massive surveillance and spy operations, Wright could give the court no evidence that the Natives were armed. He could also give no proof that they had even planned to have firearms at the ready. The shooting had ended, he said, when the officers stopped firing. The clear conclusion was that there was no two-way gun battle. The judge was curious what, if any, effort had been made the previous night to let the Natives know they would be safe if they stayed inside the park. Did they know they wouldn't be pursued? Or did they feel they had to make a stand?

"I want to know," asked Mr. Justice R.J. Daudlin, "whether or not any effort was made when the CMU [Crowd Management Unit, or riot squad] did move the people back the first time and then the second time. Whether any effort was made by bull horn, or otherwise, to indicate to this crowd that if they remained behind and inside the park that there was no intent on the part of the officers to go any further."

Wright gave an answer that must have struck the judge as reasonable, although it did not match all other statements that would later be given by riot squad officers to the civilian Special Investigations Unit (SIU) or in later trials resulting from the confrontation. In later police statements, the SIU was told that the Native protestors were not told anything about the intentions of the riot squad that night. In fact, according to these statements, the officers were only doing "shield chatter" — that is, pounding on their shields with batons as they approached the park, making verbal communication impossible, according to riot squad officers interviewed by the SIU. However, that morning before the judge, Wright testified, "Yes, I think there was, just by the fact when they moved in yelling, 'Move back. Move back.'"

The judge didn't appear satisfied, and he pressed on, "My interest is in knowing whether or not there was any attempt to communicate to the eight to 20 people that were at that location at that time. Whether no attempt was going to [be] made to enter the park or pursue — that they were just to keep off the public access, keep off the public road, and remain in the park."

Wright appeared to relent a little, replying, "Well, to answer your question, sir, no there wasn't any direct made, but I think . . ."

"All right," the judge said. "You are saying that the inference was there that . . ."

"Certainly, that's what I'm saying," Wright replied, leaving it to the judge to determine exactly what inference a reasonable Native person in the park was to draw from the advance of a mass of baton-wielding, helmeted police officers.

"The basic point that I wish to make is this," said the judge, "— that this case is about the occupation of the park. It is about whether that occupation should be allowed to continue. It is about whether that occupation is *prima facie*, I suppose, lawful. The action and this motion are brought by the Attorney General in relation to a public nuisance."

Now, in the sealed world of the courtroom, the Native protestors were being discussed as trespassers and nuisances on what they considered to be their sacred land, and they could not reply, since neither they nor their lawyers could have been invited to attend to give their side of the story.

The government lawyers argued that an injunction was a much-needed legal buffer that would allow things to be sorted out. Out of respect for Dudley George, who had been shot to death by their forces, they agreed to amend proceedings to delete the name Anthony O'Brien "Dudley" George from the list of Native people mentioned as targets of the injunction. If nothing else, it showed how the world of paper can be much tidier than real life. Dudley was now safe from the injunction as his bullet-torn body grew cold in the morgue.

McCabe told the judge that the issue of the burial grounds had not been resolved. "There was only a suggestion," said the lawyer, "that there was a burial ground somewhere . . . within the boundary of the park." There had clearly been more than "only a suggestion that there was a burial ground" back in the late 1930s, when the provincial and federal levels of government reassured the Natives that the burial grounds would soon be fenced off, but the court heard no mention that these promises had been recorded and were filed away in federal and provincial government archives. Nor was mention made to the judge of the Native adolescent's skeleton found by the park superintendent's wife back in 1950 or of how the remains had been shipped to the University of Western Ontario. Nor was mention made of the decades of studies by archaeologists Wilfrid and Elsie Jury of the University of Western Ontario on Native burial grounds in the area. Certainly, no mention was made of the half-century of promises about the return of the adjoining military base and how this had concerned the current prime minister Jean Chrétien, back in 1972, when he was minister of Indian Affairs.

Mr. Justice R.J. Daudlin granted an interim *ex parte* injunction, but only for four days, until Monday, September 11, 1995. He also ruled that next time, the Native people were to be told what was going on. The judge indicated, furthermore, that this injunction order must be posted on the main gate or gate area no later than 4:00 p.m. on Friday, September 8 — the next day. He also required that fifty copies of the order be dropped by air on the park in areas where it was known to be occupied. "I trust that that can be effected without endangering the life of the crew that would be required to conduct that drop," the judge stated.

AROUND NOON ON September 7, about the time the court hearing was ending, some two hundred Native people from Kettle Point marched down the middle of Highway 21 into the built-up area of Camp Ipperwash as a show of support for the Stoney Pointers. Whatever tensions had existed between the two neighbouring Native groups were forgotten for the time being. Along the entire route of the one-hour march, Native youths dared police officers to try to stop them, but the police wisely stepped aside. Then many of the same youths who had taunted the police sobbed unashamedly when they reached the military base at Stoney Point. The death of Dudley George had pulled the Kettle and Stoney Pointers together, at least for the moment.

POLICE LOG NOTES from that Thursday indicate that the OPP were expecting two armoured personnel carriers to arrive soon, including the one from GM Diesel in London. "We will hide it in the arena," OPP notes for the day state. "It is just to be used for rescues only."

Another entry, for 9:40 a.m., states that the armoured vehicles were to arrive that day, "Moving from London. To bring under cover of darkness, and park with other. Suggest finding new place to store these vehicles. Some local people are aware of their being in the area."

There are easier things to do than hide an armoured personnel carrier in a small town, especially when one doesn't know how to drive it. Another log entry notes: "Relief drivers for Bisons on way to command post were involved in motor vehicle accident. Both persons injured and taken to hospital. Going to keep driver we have now in place. . . ." Only one officer involved in the riot at the park needed to be treated in hospital, but two were injured in their attempt to drive the personnel carrier.

That had to be a little embarrassing, especially for a police force that was ultrasensitive about how it was seen by the public. As one 3:00 p.m. police log entry states, "Be careful of our image. You are wearing the OPP uniform. Be professional. Be polite." The personnel carrier finally made it to town as another entry, from 7:59 p.m., noted: "[The] LAV [light armoured vehicle] bison is being stored at Lakeside Grain and Feed in the blue building." Ominously, the police log also noted, "Hollow point bullets approved by the military," referring to the extra-deadly type of bullets that tend to mushroom out upon contact with flesh — the type that had already killed Dudley George.

NORMALLY, ANTHROPOLOGICAL STUDIES don't send lightning bolts of shock down the corridors of the legislature, but something to that effect happened on September 7, the day after Dudley George became the only Native person in the twentieth century in Canada to be killed by police in a land claims dispute. Government notes from that day mentioned that a report was located in government files that suggested the Native protestors had been right all along in their claim that a burial ground existed inside the park. The revelation was contained in a Ministry of Natural Resources meeting note that also warned that if Native people were seen with guns, they could well be hunters, not criminals. "Deputy and minister weren't aware of commitment to de-escalate. Minister has copy of burial ground record. Shocked as well. Did not know it existed. Controlled deer hunt with shotguns starting Saturday morning. Officers may encounter hunters. Early goose hunt. No problems. Shot guns, archery and muzzle loaders. . . . Shock to minister will be relayed to proper authorities . . . ."

Those "proper authorities" apparently didn't include any Native people. There was no mention in the notes of any plans to apologize to the Natives. There was no plan even to admit that there had been a mistake. Instead, it was full steam ahead for the police and the government.

Government meeting minutes also note that two parallel groups from Queen's Park were dealing with the situation. One was the "Blockade Committee," made up of civil servants, whose role was to provide advice and prepare for what authorities feared would be a rash of copy-cat incidents at other reserves, including nearby Cape Croker and Akwesasne near Cornwall.

The other group was called the "Nerve Centre." Its point person for communications was Elaine Todres, deputy minister for the Ministry of the Solicitor General and the Ministry of Corrections. This core working group involved the ministers of Natural Resources and Corrections; the attorney general and the solicitor general; their executive assistants; a communications person from the Premier's Office; directors of the communications branches of the affected ministries; the commissioner of the OPP and/or a representative; public relations officers for the OPP; and others. Nerve Centre meetings were held daily in the Executive Boardroom, fourth floor, in government offices at 175 Bloor Street East.

A confidential internal government document revealed the Nerve

Centre's connection with Cabinet and the Premier's Office: "The core working group will . . . maintain contact with Cabinet Office and through the appropriate channels to the Premier's Office at all times and as events require on weekends." The intent was for the government to publicly present the mess as strictly a police matter, as confirmed by notes of the meeting which said, "Intent is to minimize public comment at the political level" and "This is a law and order issue, not a native issue." The notes also stated that the existence "of [the] committee should not be a matter of public record."

The alleged break-and-enter into park buildings was noted in the September 7 meeting, as it had been the previous day. Again, it was not mentioned that park staff had actually given the Natives a key to the main building in the park. It was again pointed out that this proof of Native wrongdoing would be useful for "damage control." It was also noted that there had been similar protests in the park in the past, which had run their course within a couple of weeks, without incident. And although the police were then maintaining that the Native protestors had fired upon them, curiously, minutes of the government meeting stated, "Armed? — no knowledge but no indication."

THE ESCALATION OF police power at Ipperwash continued, like some out-of-control machine stuck in high gear. Several media members who rushed in were angered to discover all the rooms at the better hotels in the Forest and Grand Bend area were taken, packed with out-of-town officers on overtime. Anyone wanting a meal at a local restaurant now had to wait for large numbers of police to be fed, at public expense. Fighting Indians, even ones who were only shooting deer and geese, was expensive work. To watch the OPP at Ipperwash, one would never have guessed that the police force was struggling mightily to cut some $17 million from its annual budget, in part by offering senior officers enhanced retirement benefits, closing smaller detachments, and giving pink slips to some three hundred clerical workers.

HOURS AFTER DUDLEY GEORGE was shot dead, the OPP sent its explanation of the killing to media outlets across the province. A more detailed memo was sent out by the military to military bases in Canada and abroad.

The memo, in English and French, was stamped "Confidential," and it read, "Subj; Security intelligence item . . . native militancy — shooting at Ipperwash Provincial Park." Among its comments were these:

1. . . . on Wednesday 6 September 1995 at 1955 hrs a disturbance occurred at Parkway Drive and Army Camp Road . . . A private citizen's vehicle [the blue Grand Am driven by Gerald "Booper" George] was damaged by a number of First Nations people armed with baseball bats. [According to Booper George, the Grand Am was actually hit by one stone, thrown by Stewart "Worm" George.] As a result of this, OPP crowd management team was deployed to disperse the crowd of natives which had gathered at the location . . .

2. (C) As the natives were dispersing into IPP (Ipperwash Provincial Park), OPP members were confronted by natives hurling rocks at them. [Exactly when the rock throwing began would depend on whom you believe.] When the crowd management unit was leaving the area a school bus, followed by a full size vehicle, drove through the provincial park fence striking a dumpster. The bus, pushing the dumpster, and the other vehicle then headed into the crowd management team. OPP stress that the occupants of the school bus and the vehicle, in addition to trying to run down OPP members of the crowd management team who were in the process of leaving the area, opened fire on the OPP officers with a rifle and a handgun. OPP returned fire. There were no OPP injured in the exchange of gunfire, however, there were three native casualties. Anthony O'Brien George, alias Dudley, (who had an extensive criminal record) was killed, Cecil George is in hospital with life threatening injuries, and 15 year old Nicholas Cottrell [sic] has injuries which are not considered life threatening. [This report implies that all of the injuries started to be inflicted after the schoolbus moved toward the police officers, not mentioning that the bus was driven out of the park only after the police officers began beating Slippery George. It also failed to mention the fact that Dudley George was not on the bus.]

3. . . . source described the mood of some local residents as quote paranoid

unquote. The entire area, around the IPP (Ipperwash Provincial Park) has been sealed off and the situation is being described as extremely tense.

. . .

6. (C) The chiefs of Walpole Island Reserve as well as the Kettle and Stoney Point Band (KSPB) are urging their people to remain calm. Although, as has always been the case, Chief Tom Bressette has no control or influence over members of the breakaway Stony Point group (SPG). [The Stoney Point natives were not a breakaway group. Stoney Pointers had been forced off their own reserve in the past and many had moved to Kettle Point.]

. . .

8. (C) The court injunction applied for by the Minister of Natural Resources was expected to be approved by 0900 hrs, 07 Sep 95. The OPP were originally intending to enforce it when it became valid, however given recent events, they will likely re-assess their options. On 06 Sep 95, prior to this incident, they also requested to borrow two military bisons [armoured personnel carriers], which were to be painted and decaled in OPP colours.

[Extensive portions deleted under the *Freedom of Information Act*.]

10. (C) . . . A native spokesperson is reporting through the media that four natives were shot. A . . . native may have sustained a minor gun shot wound which didn't require hospital attention. He also reported that the natives were quote medicine people unquote and therefore unarmed. [Some deleted]

11. (C) It is still too soon to judge how other native groups will react to the shooting death. [Some deleted under the *Freedom of Information Act*.]

The "extensive criminal record" of Dudley George had nothing worse on it than his teenaged arson at the lumberyard, when he was involved with a group of white youths who were not charged. The military had styled Dudley George as a long-time criminal, and since he was a dead man, he could not speak for himself.

Immediately after the violence, a Canadian Forces memo marked "SECRET" stirred the pot a little more, creating fears of a full-fledged Native rebellion. It also suggested more than a little panic in the police ranks. "OPERATING COMMAND POST, OPP MEMBERS WERE

UNSUCCESSFUL IN DESTROYING THEIR EQUIPMENT BEFORE IT WAS TAKEN." (The Natives had seized the mobile command post, which was painted as a St. John Ambulance van.)

ON SEPTEMBER 7, OPP Commissioner Thomas O'Grady issued a written statement of his own, which for months would be his only public comment on the matter. In it, he called the killing of Dudley George and the beatings an "isolated incident." He didn't say isolated from what. Commissioner O'Grady also didn't mention the massive nature of the operation.

In his written "clarification of events" immediately after the shooting, OPP Commissioner Thomas O'Grady said that police went to the park that night "to address a disturbance involving First Nations persons causing damage to private property in the area." He didn't say that it was a matter of four hundred dollars' damage to Booper George's sister's car caused by Stewart "Worm" George throwing one stone, and he did not mention that the police had not even arrested the thrower yet.

"OPP personnel did not enter the provincial park and were not there to remove those individuals occupying the grounds," O'Grady stated. "The officers were pelted with rocks and sticks. As OPP personnel were preparing to leave the area, two vehicles broke through the fence of the park and came at the officers. It was at this time that OPP personnel were fired upon from the vehicles. The officers felt their safety was endangered and returned fire, fatally injuring one man.

"This situation is an isolated incident. The OPP has a proven track record of many years of peacefully resolving issues with First Nations people. The events of last night are tragic, and we are committed to a course of action which will bring this situation to a peaceful conclusion as quickly as possible."

Commissioner O'Grady, who didn't enjoy the company of reporters in the best of times, never stepped forward to field any questions from the media. He simply directed his staff to send his comments to newsroom fax machines.

THE MORNING OF September 7, Mercredi decided to go with Tom Bressette, chief of the Kettle and Stony Point band, and Ontario Chief Gord Peters to see Premier Mike Harris. Ultimately, Mercredi reasoned, this was a political issue and that meant that Harris was the one who had to take responsibility. Within hours, after several telephone calls to Toronto, it was clear that Harris didn't want to meet with the chiefs. In an effort to flush him out, Mercredi urged Harris through the media "not just to say it's a police matter, because that leads to violence."

The tactic didn't work and neither Premier Harris nor Commissioner O'Grady would face the chiefs. The night of September 7, Mercredi, Tom Bressette, and half a dozen other Ontario chiefs met at the Kettle Point school with OPP Chief Superintendent Chris Coles, from A Division, which covered Ontario's Southwestern Region.

It was better than nothing but not nearly enough. Mercredi still stressed that Harris must ultimately be the one to meet with them, and the grand chief told reporters he was not going away. "Harris has no alternative but to meet with us," Mercredi said.

The premier was in Toronto that night at the gala opening of the Toronto Film Festival, and was still in no mood to meet with Mercredi, Bressette, or any of the other chiefs. He told the media that he wouldn't tell police how to handle the standoff, saying, "They receive no direction from politicians, nor should they." That was a rather unusual comment, given the later evidence of a meeting in the Premier's Office about the *ex parte* injunction and in light of the interministerial committee's statements about the need to "take steps to remove the occupiers ASAP."

Harris continued that he wouldn't negotiate until the Stoney Pointers stopped occupying the park. "There's an illegal occupation," Harris said. "They are trespassers on property that is owned by the Crown."

His comments were at odds with the OPP officers' notes from earlier that day, which state that senior government ministers were shocked to learn that the occupation might in fact be legal, since it appeared the Native people were right after all about the existence of burial grounds in the park.

Understandably, none of the reporters questioning the premier at the film festival knew about the notes, just as none of the reporters knew about how, just hours before the shooting, Larry Taman, deputy minister in the Attorney General's office, and OPP Superintendent Ron Fox of the Solicitor General's office had struggled to explain to Harris and others that it wasn't right for the government to interfere with police operations. So Harris escaped the questioning unscathed, and his night at the film festival gala wasn't ruined.

FRIDAY, SEPTEMBER 8, 1995

On Friday, September 8, 1995, two days after the killing, the incident was described in OPP press releases as the "attempted murder of OPP officers which occured [sic] at Ipperwash Provincial Park." If history is a story told by winners, then so are some press releases after police operations.

It was all a confusing jumble for the media, who like things in tidy packages. Premier Mike Harris did answer a few questions, but in the end also said very little. "If there are to be any discussions over what we all want to be a safe and peaceful conclusion to this illegal occupation, it should be with those in charge and that's the OPP," Harris told reporters at Queen's Park on Friday, September 8. In that short sentence, he dumped the problem squarely on the OPP. Meanwhile, the OPP and Commissioner O'Grady, except for O'Grady's one written statement, were saying nothing at all.

Confidential police and government documents show a much tighter relationship between the OPP and the government than the premier would have the public believe. The papers show the Ontario Provincial Police force was given the awkward job of making the Mike Harris government look credible during the Ipperwash crisis. While the politicians and police were publicly crowing about how it was inappropriate for government to meddle in specific police operations and vital for the police and politicians to be separate in a democracy, the secret documents show that before Ipperwash had become an issue, OPP Commissioner Thomas O'Grady was part of a government crisis team that met regularly, starting a month before Dudley George was shot dead. According to a confidential government document, one of the police-government team's goals was to enable "the ministry and representatives to emerge with the highest possible credibility," which sounded oddly like the role of a public relations specialist. Long before Ipperwash, the force had been nicknamed by critics, including some within the force, the "Ontario Political Police" — and that nickname seemed sadly appropriate now.

WHILE THE POLICE were tight-lipped, the media covering the shooting were far from home, uncomfortable, and confused. Worse yet, they had no good pictures. American author Susan Sontag once wrote that the mere act of photographing someone or something gives it a certain importance, and yet Dudley George, now the centre of media attention in death, had had few cameras pointed at him in life. Since no reporters or media camera people were present for the riot and shooting, the media had few compelling images to tell his story. This made it bad television, and by extension, somehow made the whole event seem less important.

Clearly something major had happened there. Still, the crisis lacked a defining image in the public mind. It was just so many words, and many of those were confusing. Were the Stoney Pointers a rebel band? Why were so many of them angry at Tom Bressette, who said he was their chief? How do you spell Stoney Point — with an "e" or without one? Exactly what had the Native people been promised in the past? Wasn't the incident somehow related to the shooting at Gustafsen Lake?

Almost all great conflicts have an unforgettable image, like the photo of the little Vietnamese girl Kim Phuc taken by Nick Ut of Associated Press, showing her screaming and running naked as napalm eats into her flesh during a Vietnam War bombing, or the Robert Capa shot of a soldier shot dead on a hill during the Spanish Civil War, or the flag being raised by American marines at Iwo Jima during World War II — taken by Joe Rosenthal of Associated Press. More recently, the defining photo of the Oka crisis was that of a Mohawk Warrior and a young Canadian soldier, standing nose-to-nose, neither blinking nor looking away — an image that was shot by several photographers. However, the shooting of Dudley George happened at night, and there were no media cameras aimed at him, only Acting Sergeant Ken Deane's submachinegun. If the OPP took

Polaroid photos and videos, as Project Maple had directed, they were never released.

Hours after the shooting, Sam George, Dudley's older brother, met with a *Toronto Star* reporter in the Kettle's On restaurant in Kettle Point, to try to find a photo of Dudley that would show that his brother was a real human being, not just a name on a police press release. The walls of the restaurant were lined with team shots of young Natives playing sports, but none of them showed Dudley. Sam George didn't have a lot of images of his brother to choose from, since Dudley never married and lived alone. Important moments in his life had passed without a photographic record. Now, in death, numerous photographs were being taken of Dudley George's body in the morgue, as his wounds were studied. The best photo Sam George could find that morning was one of Dudley the joker, mugging to a camera in a photo booth, pressing his face close to the lens and grinning his goofy Dudley grin.

As Sam George met with the reporter, he did have a strong picture of Dudley, but it was burned in his brain and not on film. It was of Dudley lying dead in the hospital, where Sam had seen him just hours before. That searing, awful image wouldn't go away. "I don't know what I feel right now," Sam said softly. "It's pretty hard when you go see your brother lying on a slab. . . . He's got a bullet hole in his chest."

Then a gentler image of Dudley came to Sam, of the final time they had talked. It was of Dudley's smile, which Sam knew now he would never see again. "I told him to be careful. He smiled. That's all he'd do was smile."

IN ADDITION TO lacking good photos and film, the story also lacked a quotable Native leader. No one was writing press releases from the perspective of Stoney Point. Ovide Mercredi and Kettle and Stony Point Chief Tom Bressette had titles and they were obviously Native, but they were both on the outside of the Stoney Point group. Among the Stoney Pointers, natural leaders like Judas George and Glenn George were not eager to step in front of cameras, partly because they had no elected position and partly because they feared becoming easily identifiable targets for the police.

Meanwhile, the government was doing its best to downplay the importance of what had happened. Thomas Walkom of the *Toronto Star* wrote a column for the September 12, 1995, edition of his paper which noted how "casually" the government was treating the killing.

> In 1990, the shooting of a police officer at a similar confrontation triggered what became known as the Oka crisis.
>
> Yet the shooting of an Indian by police last Wednesday night at Ipperwash northeast of Sarnia is treated as . . . an incident.
>
> Part of the reason is that we don't expect crises in Ontario.
>
> Part is that Ipperwash . . . has not been good television. At Oka, there were masked Indians with assault rifles. At Ipperwash, the protestors have no guns.
>
> In fact, one of the more intriguing characteristics of a public meeting last Thursday at the Ipperwash army base (now occupied by protestors) was the polite, working- and middle-class nature of the crowd. No fatigues; few angry young men — in short, virtually none of the images television has come . . . [to] associate with Indian protest.
>
> Nothing much to get excited about, it seems — and the province gets back to thinking about something else.
>
> Yet, in reality, Ipperwash will have consequences that are as far-reaching as Oka — maybe more so.
>
> For Ipperwash marks the first confrontation in decades in which an Indian has been killed.
>
> Don't underestimate this. The execution of Louis Riel, the 19th century Métis rebel, still resonates throughout Quebec as a symbol of English Canadian infamy. The 1990 shooting of a Quebec Sûreté officer at Oka shook Canada's non-native majority out of its romantic, Dancing with Wolves notion of Indian self-government.
>
> Similarly, last Wednesday's fatal shooting of Dudley George will not quickly be forgotten by Canada's Indian peoples. George may not have been a leader of the protest. This will not prevent his death from becoming to Indians a powerful symbol of native resistance.
>
> But the great question from Ipperwash is: Why? Why did the situation get so out of hand?

There was an obvious key difference between the crisis at Oka and the incident at Ipperwash. At Oka, it was a white police officer who was shot dead, while at Ipperwash, the victim was an Aboriginal protestor. While no one liked to pose the question, just how much did the public care about one dead Indian?

7

NASTY AFTERTASTE

"AUTH [authorization]TO SP [support] OPP HAS NOT BEEN RECEIVED"
— *CANADIAN FORCES SECRET MEMO*

The investigation into the fatal shooting of Dudley George wasn't a who-dunnit. On Friday, September 8, 1995, Acting Sergeant Kenneth Deane readily admitted to Detective Sergeant Trevor Richardson of the OPP and Wayne Allan, an investigator with the civilian Special Investigations Unit, that he had likely fired the fatal shot. Even without the statement, Deane would easily have been traced as the officer who killed Dudley George. The fatal bullet found in Dudley George's body could easily be matched to the submachinegun Deane fired that night. In what was officially known as his duty report, Acting Sergeant Deane didn't dispute touching the trigger to shoot the Native protestor. He wasn't admitting guilt, though. As Deane told the story, he was just doing his job.

Deane wasn't some nervous rookie. He was an experienced, senior member of the paramilitary Tactics and Rescue Unit (TRU) team. Only proven officers could even apply for the TRU team, and Deane was one of its

NASTY AFTERTASTE •

leaders and instructors, with experience that stretched back almost a decade. The night of the shooting, he was part of what was called the alpha team and was deployed strictly for support of the Crowd Management Unit, or, in Deane's words, "if the CMU members were faced with gunfire."

Deane told Richardson and Allan that he had reported for duty at 7:00 a.m. on the day of the killing. He'd gone first to the Pinery Park Meeting Centre where some of the officers were gathering and there he'd spoken with Staff Sergeant Kent Skinner. He was told that Native protestors had fired off some 100 to 150 rounds of automatic gunfire the night before. After the briefing, Deane and fellow members of the paramilitary unit prepared their equipment, readying themselves for action.

Deane's comments to Richardson and Allan were clinical and spare — all the drama and emotion of the evening flattened into bloodless police-speak. The near-fatal beating and arrest of Slippery George was condensed into one bland sentence: "One native was arrested and placed in the rear of the prisoner van."

Shortly after Slippery George's arrest, Deane continued, a schoolbus advanced toward the police. "As the bus got close to my position," he said, "I observed a distinctive muzzle flash come from the interior of the bus." Then "two distinct muzzle flashes originated from the bush area adjacent to the sand parking lot. I discharged approximately four rounds to that area."

A figure ran out from the bushes and out onto the road, shouldering a rifle, Deane told the investigators. "He was scanning our position with the rifle. I discharged approximately three rounds at the individual. He faltered, fell to the ground, got up, threw his weapon back to the ditch area."

And that was that. A listener might wonder why the Native man would leave a protected area for an open roadway where he would be an easy target. A listener might also wonder why a gunman, especially one under fire, would toss away his rifle. Someone who knew guns would question why Deane hit Dudley George only once. The strongest feature about Deane's lightweight submachinegun was its extremely high level of accuracy, and that night, it was equipped with a laser-guided night-vision scope to make his aim that much more true. And yet he had fired seven shots — four earlier and three at Dudley — and had hit a mark only once.

Richardson tried to draw him out on the gunshots which he claimed came from the bus, and Deane replied, "I heard two gunshots, as the vehicle was approaching . . . That's the only shots I heard."

Richardson then shifted back to the shooting of Dudley George, saying, "Okay and you see this individual, and then you see him get up and walk back towards the park?"

"No, the car [driven by Warren George] started to reverse, back towards the park. The individual gets up from this fence post area . . . And at that time he walked out onto the road shouldering what I took to be a long gun, a rifle . . . Okay? I watched him scan like across our position. At that time I discharged three rounds at his area, I think. I saw him falter, go to the ground, get up, threw what he had in his hand into the grass area where he had been hiding . . . He then got up and walked over to that area and hid down by the fence post at the corner."

"Do you know if you shot him two or three . . . times? . . . Do you know how many you think might have hit him?"

"If I hit him, I hit him with one round . . . I think I let three rounds go. I saw him falter just the once, and then going to the ground. Okay? So if I hit him I would have hit him with just one round."

"Okay, and then he go moves over to another spot . . ."

"Yeah."

"And then you see some people come out and get him?"

"Yeap."

He offered no description of Dudley George, and none of Dudley's supposed gun, other than that it appeared to be a rifle. Pressed about the lighting that night, Deane described a surreal scene, saying there were lights from several all-terrain vehicles driven by the Natives "going back and forth, and spot lights and headlights and moonlight shining all over the place."

He was adamant that he really did see muzzle flashes aimed at police. During the march to the park, the police mistakenly thought a man with a lit cigarette and walking stick was a gunman. "I've shot my weapon at night during training," Deane said. "I've also been shot at night so I can tell you that they were distinctive muzzle flashes."

"When you discharged your firearm at the flashes, could you see anybody?"

"No I could not."

"So you were firing into the bush where the flashes were coming from?"

"Yes."

An experienced officer might feel his stomach drop at hearing such a statement. Was Acting Sergeant Deane justified in firing into an area where he did not see a weapon? Could he be so sure they were in fact muzzle flashes? And could they not be muzzle flashes from other officers firing on the bus? Wasn't his fellow TRU member, Constable Mark Beauchesne, in that area? Hadn't he fired at about that time?

"When you discharged your firearm at the bush, why did you discharge your firearm?"

"Because of the two muzzle flashes coming towards our position."

"And you discharged your firearm at the individual with the rifle? The same question, why did you do that?"

"Because I thought he was going to shoot upon us."

Why didn't Acting Sergeant Deane also fire at the bus? Wasn't that a clear danger?

"Well, as it came forward . . . towards our position, there were CMU members in front of me, okay, and the bus gets closer and all of a sudden we have . . . certain [CMU] members diving over the fence so on and so forth. And it got close and close I see the muzzle flash and by that time the bus is past me."

He was asked if he commented to any other members about the man who he said was shouldering a rifle by the side of the road.

"No I didn't."

". . . Is there a reason why you didn't?"

"Timing I guess."

CONSTABLE MARK BEAUCHESNE, another member of Acting Sergeant Deane's four-man paramilitary unit, told the police and civilian investigators that he was stationed at the Pinery Provincial Park on Wednesday, September 6, when his pager went off, with a command to go immediately to the nearby Forest detachment.

Within three hours, Beauchesne was on a sandy patch of land outside Ipperwash Provincial Park, training his submachinegun on a car driven by Warren George that was coming out of the park toward some police officers. "I saw several members at the front of the car," Beauchesne said. "I thought there were guys underneath the car. The . . . tire spun and squealed and he backed out of the ditch and at that point I brought my weapon up and I thought if he takes another run at these guys, who were now sprawled all over the road, I'm going to have to shoot the driver. He backed about twenty metres down the road from me and stopped and at that instant I had my gun levelled as best I could at the door window where I felt the driver to be and I heard his tires start again, squealing the car, starting moving forward. I fired two rounds with my rifle. I heard other gunfire around me. At that time the car stopped."

"When is the first time you heard a firearm being discharged?" Ed Wilson asked.

"The first firearm being discharged was my own," Beauchesne replied.

Beauchesne's comments made one wonder if the flashes others reported as gunfire from the car were, in fact, sparks from his shots. "I saw sparks as I fired," he continued. "I believe that they could be my shots impacting."

Could those have been what Acting Sergeant Deane reported as gunshots coming from inside the car? Did other officers open fire because they mistook sparks from Beauchesne's bullets for shots directed at them? "Right after I fired, I heard several other rounds going off," Beauchesne continued. ". . . I believe I saw sparks from my rounds, but there were other officers firing at apparently the time."

WHEN CONSTABLE BRIAN SHARP was interviewed on Friday, September 8, by Detective Constable Mark Dew of the Lambton County Crime Unit, OPP, and Jim Kennedy of the Special Investigations Unit (SIU), he made no mention of the beating of Cecil Bernard "Slippery" George. Somehow, no one seemed to have seen much of it, except for the Natives, and Slippery George himself wasn't much good as a witness, since the police had been wearing visors and he had been unconscious for some of the beating.

Constable Sharp told the investigators that he had seen police hit by the car. When the motor revved up, he thought the driver was going to try to hit more police officers. That was when Sharp drew his pistol and squeezed off four or five rounds. "I formed the opinion that . . . he was going to try and run us over . . . I drew my pistol, and I fired at the car . . . I fired for the windshield area . . . When I stopped firing, I heard the sound of firing going on around me. It sounded like a pop pop pop pop pop. I had the helmet on and . . . I wasn't sure where it was coming from or who was firing."

". . . At anytime did you notice a person on foot?" Dew asked. ". . . a male native person on foot with a long gun, on the ground as opposed to being in the vehicle?"

"No."

"Did you at any time observe gun flashes from a gun being fired from either the bus or the car?"

"No."

Constable Bill Klym of the London TRU team told Dew and Kennedy that the snipers such as himself and Deane were supposed to act as "an advanced eye" for the Crowd Management Unit as they approached the park that night. Constable Klym said that the car that left the park appeared to have some officers trapped under it, and that's why he opened fire with his submachinegun, equipped with a silencer and set on semiautomatic. "I took aim and fired double [inaudible] at the centre box area of the driver and that time I observed sparkling on the car door and immediately upon completion of my double tap the car stopped its forward motion."

Now another officer besides Beauchesne had said that his bullets caused sparking on the car or the bus. Could other officers have mistaken this for gunshots from inside the vehicles? The most interesting aspect of Klym's statement lay in what he did not say. He said nothing of seeing any Native with a gun or of Deane warning others that Dudley was armed. Wouldn't Deane warn other officers about a gunman? Wasn't that his job?

IT TOOK STAFF SERGEANT Wade Lacroix, the Crowd Management Unit commander, almost an hour to complete his statement to Detective Sergeant Trevor Richardson of the OPP and Jim Kennedy of the SIU. He said that he'd completed his regular tour of duty on September 6 at 4:30 p.m., but that he'd been called back to the park. He didn't say who called him, but he did remember the reason. He'd been told that the occupation "had escalated to a civilian motorist having his vehicle pelted with rocks and hit with baseball bats." The incident Lacroix was referring to was the one stone thrown at Booper George's sister's blue Grand Am. No one had come near it with a baseball bat. Another Native protestor, standing well in the background, was holding a baseball bat, but he hadn't done anything with it.

"I had a feeling they'd know we were there by the full moon and sure enough, all of a sudden we were lighted up by portable floodlights onto us, glistened off the Plexiglas and that, and I knew we were kinda standing out in the open."

The Natives screamed abuse, like "White trash!" and "Get back on the *Mayflower*," but the riot squad didn't react verbally, Lacroix said. "Not one, not one individual in the Crowd Management Unit, or, or assisting teams, of TRU team spoke."

Lacroix's comments seemed to differ from the version of events given to investigators by Constable Chris Cossitt of the Crowd Management Unit. Cossitt said Lacroix shifted his visor to speak with the Natives before the fighting began. Lacroix indicated, however, that he was proud that no police officers had said anything to the Natives.

Lacroix also pointed out that the punch-out manoeuvre drove the Natives temporarily back into the park from the parking lot, but then police were hit with sticks and rocks and brilliant high-beam lighting. "They turned on the lights of cars, an ATV [all terrain vehicle] light and some portable flood lights trying to blind us from the projectiles I believe [were] coming in. And it was fairly effective. They had effectively blinded us."

Lacroix's comments were also at odds with Acting Detective Staff Sergeant Mark Wright's testimony before Mr. Justice R.J. Daudlin, when he'd told the judge that police officers had warned the Natives verbally as they marched toward the park.

Not all perceptions were the same. Not all versions could be accurate.

Lacroix was one of the very few officers who reported that he saw anything of the Slippery George beating. The staff sergeant didn't just say he saw the clubbing. He claimed credit for part of it, saying he was the man who'd dropped Slippery George after a man had broken his shield with a pole. Lacroix told investigators he caught Slippery George in the left clavicle, dropping him to the sand, where he lay in a fetal position. "I yelled out for arrest squads to come forward."

Then Lacroix spoke about the car driven by Warren George. "To my horror, I saw that the [CMU] members on the right ditch could go no further than the fence and the bus drove right down off the pavement, into the ditch, right along the fence. I could see the members there with their shields and sticks in their hands trying to get over the fence and I saw people diving. I saw members . . . trying to climb the fence, some diving over the fence and I was sure that they were going to be run over and was quite surprised later on to find out nobody was. So I drew my 30 inch sidearm . . . I knew there was no possible way of shooting a tire, and there was no possible way of shooting a radiator."

The car was nose down in a ditch now. "I ran . . . forward towards the driver, because I wanted to make sure that the bullets were slightly down and into the car because I was afraid it would riccochet [sic]."

Lacroix said that someone shouted, "We're receiving fire from the bus" and said he saw muzzle flashes from it, and so he opened fire with his .38 Smith and Wesson. In all, he fired four shots — two double taps of the trigger. "I fired around then, around that time, somebody yells out, 'There's a man on the road with a rifle.'"

No one else had reported hearing this. Yet Staff Sergeant Lacroix swore his statement was true.

"I yelled, 'Cease fire, cease fire.' Then all fire stops."

Did it strike him as odd that all firing stopped when he yelled, "Cease fire"? Why would Native people obey his command, if indeed they had guns? Weren't the police still vulnerable, easy shots? If this seemed strange to the staff sergeant, he made no mention of the fact. Instead, Lacroix ended his statement with a flourish of praise for the officers: "I guess I'd like to go on record also to say that I felt, under the circumstances, the ERT [Emergency Response Team] members and the TRU team members handled themselves very professionally . . . Thank God they had the training they had, and that they listened to commands. They split right, they split left, they took cover. TRU stepped in. I think we would have had a lot more injuries."

Lacroix did not mention, and may not have been aware, that only one police officer was injured, with a strained knee ligament and a twisted ankle.

CONSTABLE KEVIN YORK of the Emergency Response Team told the investigators that his workday on Wednesday, September 6, had begun at 6:18 a.m. with his arrival at the Forest detachment. Exactly when it ended wasn't clear, since when he put on crowd management gear that night, he lost track of time, as his heavy gear made it impossible for him to look at his watch.

He said he was told that the riot squad was going to the park that night for some sort of peacekeeping. "And basically I assumed our purpose was to . . . remove any persons from that area and arrest them for weapons dangerous."

He said that he shot at the car, but that he wasn't the first or second person to open fire. Shooting wasn't an easy thing to do, since he was trying to hold onto his shield and his baton with his left hand and shoot with his right.

"Did you see any gun fire from either vehicle?" Richardson asked.

"I did not."

Richardson pressed on, "Can you tell me how you felt during this whole thing?"

"I was scared to death . . . I really thought he was going to wipe somebody out . . . I wasn't so worried about me because I felt that personally I could get out of the way of that bus . . ."

OF THE FOUR MEMBERS of Deane's paramilitary team in the park that night, the one who could provide the most useful testimony, besides Deane himself, was his partner, Constable Kieran O'Halloran. If anyone could back up Deane's testimony, it would be his partner, since they were

A watercolour of Tecumseh, showing him with cap decorated with porcupine quills and a single eagle feather in his British uniform with war medals. Tecumseh was shot dead at about a 45-minute drive from where a fatal bullet hit Dudley George. — TORONTO REFERENCE LIBRARY (TPL), J. Ross Robertson Collection (MTL 2093)

The war chiefs at Sarnia. The shorter, older man is Chief Oshawanoo, or Shawanoe, Tecumseh's cousin, who lived in Kettle Point and who fought alongside Tecumseh with the British in the War of 1812. Three of Dudley's cousins would carry on the tradition of fighting for the Crown as members of the Canadian forces in World War II. — TORONTO REFERENCE LIBRARY (TPL), J. Ross Robertson Collection (MTL 2789)

Treaty totems from 1827, when land was freed for white settlers in the Ipperwash area. — SARAH EDWARDS

Clifford George, Dudley George's elderly cousin and neighbour, who returned from fighting in World War II to discover his family home at Stoney Point had been taken by the federal government to make way for a military base. — PETER EDWARDS, *Toronto Star*, March 5, 1996

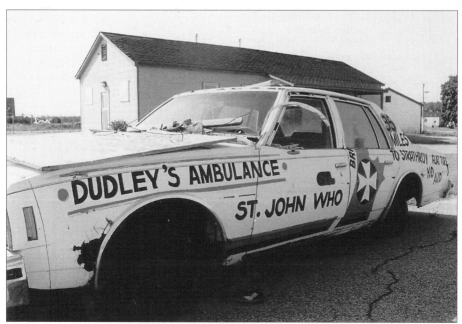

Dudley's ambulance, the car used to take Dudley George to the hospital the night he died. — PETER EDWARDS, *Toronto Star*

The roadblock set up near Stoney Point the day after the shooting. — PETER EDWARDS, *Toronto Star*, September 7, 1995

Dudley's Place, the trailer where Dudley George lived at Ipperwash in a former military base, was spray-painted with slogans denouncing the provincial government, the OPP, and Kettle Point band after George was shot dead. — PETER EDWARDS, *Toronto Star*, May 5, 1996

Dudley's sister Carolyn George, with members of ON F.I.R.E., a group of cottagers angry at the Natives. They are outside the first court appearance of Acting Sergeant Ken Deane, on trial for criminal negligence causing death, in Sarnia, Ontario, on August 13, 1996. — CANADIAN PRESS

Pam George, another of Dudley's sisters, is checked for weapons at Deane's trial. — PETER EDWARDS, *Toronto Star*, April 1997

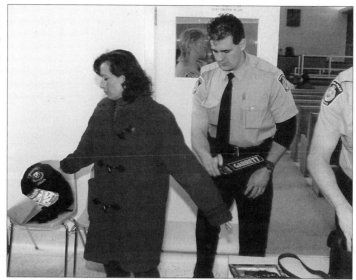

The "Team Ipperwash" logo, made up by some members of the OPP as a souvenir of the operation in which Dudley George was killed.

Team Ipperwash '95

A government memo from September 6, 1995, noting that Ontario Premier Mike Harris and cabinet minister Chris Hodgson attended the meeting about Ipperwash the day George was killed.

Sept 6/95.

Ron Fox,

Sam George (left), lawyer Delia Opekokew for the George family, Murray Klippenstein, and Veronica George in Ottawa appealing for a public inquiry into the death of Dudley George. — CANADIAN PRESS

The September 7, 1995, march by Kettle and Stoney Point Indians from Kettle Point to Ipperwash in defiance of the shooting the day before. — PETER EDWARDS, *Toronto Star*

Stacey (Burger) George (left). Burger was with Dudley George at the time of the shooting. — PETER EDWARDS, *Toronto Star*

Mr. Justice Hugh Fraser, the judge in the trial of Ken Deane, surveys the site of the shooting. Fraser found Deane guilty of criminal negligence causing death. In the background appears a wooden shrine marketing the spot where George was shot. — PETER EDWARDS, *Toronto Star*, April 27, 1997

Acting Sergeant Ken Deane (front, second from left) at his trial, surrounded by fellow members of the Tactics and Rescue squad. — PETER EDWARDS, *Toronto Star*, April 13, 1997

Dudley's brother Pierre George in Ottawa protesting for a public inquiry into his brother's death. — CANADIAN PRESS

In Toronto, Dudley's brother Sam, comforted by his wife, Veronica, crying as he calls for answers to the shooting. — PETER EDWARDS, *Toronto Star*, April 3, 1996

Nicholas Cottrelle, who was shot and injured at Ipperwash, and son Nicholas Leon Abraham Shipman "Little Nick" Cottrelle. — PETER EDWARDS, *Toronto Star*

Mike Harris's former aide Deb Hutton, who attended key meetings before the crisis, accompanies him to the Walkerton hearings.
— FRANK GUNN/CANADIAN PRESS

Liberal MPP Gerry Phillips, who has doggedly pressed Premier Mike Harris for an inquiry into the fatal shooting.

supposed to look out for each other that night. O'Halloran told Detective Constable Mark Dew of the OPP on September 11, 1995, that his job that night had been to look out for weapons, and that he and Acting Sergeant Deane were on the left, or lake, side of the Crowd Management Unit as they approached the park.

What was most interesting about O'Halloran's statement was what he didn't see or hear. As Deane's partner, he would have been standing close to Deane on the left flank of the Crowd Management officers, and he repeatedly scanned the Native people for guns or muzzle flashes. Yet he saw nothing. He also heard no report from Deane that night about seeing a Native person with a gun. O'Halloran wasn't involved in the hand-to-hand combat that night and he was trained to look out for trouble. Still, he saw no guns in the hands of any of the Native people, including Dudley George.

WHEN ACTING SUPERINTENDENT JOHN CARSON spoke with police and civilian investigators, he made it clear that he hadn't put too much stock in fears that the Native people were armed to the teeth and ready for bloodshed. "I didn't believe that the native people would use gunfire against us at that time. We . . . have policed Kettle Point for years and . . . I'm not aware of any incidents, in the recent past anyway, where our members were confronted with firearms, threatening their safety, if you would. Now there was no doubt that the overwhelming majority of them [Native people] have ready access to weapons and are . . . avid hunters . . . It's very normal to hear gunfire at night up there in that general area. There's no doubt there are weapons around all the time. At that point in time, were we expecting to come under fire? The answer would be no."

Carson continued that there were instructions to photograph and videotape everything, which instructions, he said, were carried out. That was news to the investigators. Why hadn't they received any police film of that evening? There should also have been a complete audio record, since there were recording centres both at the communications centre in Chatham and in the mobile command post. As soon as investigators got their hands on the audio and video tapes, there should be few questions remaining about what happened in the park the night Dudley George was shot dead and Slippery George was beaten nearly to death. The case should be easily solved if they could see the film.

AS THE POLICE dealt with angry Native people and curious investigators, government lawyers were planning to head back to the Sarnia courts. Their heads were still spinning over Mr. Justice R.J. Daudlin's instructions to hurl court papers from aircraft, so they headed back to court in an emergency hearing in London, Ontario, on Saturday, September 9. There, they pleaded with the court that it just didn't make sense to serve the Natives with the injunction notice as Judge Daudlin had ordered. No one had attacked the detachment in Forest, or any other nearby detachment, and police had not heard of any plots to attack them. Nevertheless, Acting Superintendent John Carson testified in this second hearing that security concerns were so great that police in the nearby detachment in Forest had covered their windows and required secretaries and janitors to wear soft body armour.

The court heard no mention of Project Maple, which Carson had prepared so meticulously, or why the police had inexplicably decided to abandon their plan to use thirteen negotiators. They did hear about dangerous Natives in general, but they were faraway Natives who had likely never visited Stoney Point and who had likely never been visited by Stoney Pointers. Carson testified that the OPP was in touch with the police at Gustafsen Lake in British Columbia. No one had been killed there, but the Natives at Gustafsen Lake had fired several times at police.

It would have been "irresponsible . . . and outright dangerous" to try to serve the Stoney Point protestors with papers ordering them out of the park, Carson testified. However, no proof was offered that they had weapons. No explanation was given as to why no police or police equipment were hit with gunfire in the close-quarters confrontation that killed Dudley George, even though the entire fight took place in an area smaller than a children's baseball diamond.

Carson asked the court to believe it would be dangerous for police to try to drop court papers out of an aircraft, as the previous judge had ordered.

"Surely, in an aircraft, you can be above gun fire?" Mr. Justice R.J. Flynn asked.

The judge didn't hear how, on the day Dudley was shot dead, the police helicopter buzzed the park from barely above the treetops, creating a wind so strong it knocked food off a picnic table.

"Well, the type of aircraft, sir, that — or the type of guns that we believe are available to these people, I would suggest would have a trajectory ability to be dangerous in excess of a . . . mile."

There is no mention in court records of the judge's reaction when Carson said that somehow the Natives could pick aircraft out of the sky from a mile away and yet could not hit literally dozens of police officers standing shoulder-to-shoulder in a tiny open area directly in front of them, just a few feet away, even if their lives depended on it, the night Dudley George was shot dead.

MEANWHILE, AS DAMAGE CONTROL specialists were downplaying what had happened, the OPP continued to quietly push the military for other support. The Canadian Forces weren't in the front lines, but they were there in the background, providing war equipment and feeding the OPP, for a price. An Operation Panda estimate was that it would cost about $7.52 daily for food for each of the three hundred or so OPP officers and staff at Ipperwash, meaning a daily ration cost of $2,256.00.

Once the cooks and other staff costs were factored in, even at the low Canadian Forces scale of $95 a day for corporals, and once fuel and garbage facilities, water and chemical toilets, and miscellaneous supplies like paper plates were added to the equation, the cost to the military was some $6,740.00 a day. The four-hundred-dollar damage to Booper George's car, which resulted in the only charge laid before the whole operation, seemed puny by comparison.

The OPP pressed for far more than low-cost food and chemical toilets from the military. On Saturday, September 9, a senior officer with the OPP sent a letter requesting that the Canadian Forces provide several pieces of military equipment, including fifty gas masks, material for the containment of chlorine spills, fifty pairs of night-vision goggles, equipment for intercepting cellular telephone calls, and one hundred bulletproof vests. "Additionally, should the tactical situation deteriorate, it is requested that two (2) Huey Helicopters be placed on Stand-By to assist with movement of Police Officers and possible extraction/rescue of Police or civilians.

"As manning levels now exceed 250, it is suggested that a military style Field Kitchen be deployed to accomodate [sic] the feeding of large number in a short time at odd hours."

Another Canadian Forces memo, also dated September 9, shows the military was now less keen to go along too far with the police. There was now considerable reluctance to give the OPP everything they wanted: "Has legal auth [authority] been obtained for cell phone intercept?" the military memo asked. "All pers [persons] dealing with the OPP," it went on to say, "must clearly understand that auth to sup [support] OPP has not been received and consequently no assurance of sp [support] can be provided."

Also that Saturday, another military memo suggests the Canadian Forces in London, Ontario, were turning over the Bison armoured personnel carriers in case a rescue operation to take nearby cottagers to safety was required — even though none had been attacked and many still felt secure enough to remain in their homes: ". . . Many cottagers have voluntarily left the area and voiced concern for their physical protection. Aboriginals threatened them. Roads leading to the cottages are narrow and open to ambush. OPP have been planning rescue mission."

A memo sent out of the London detachment on Sunday, September 10, noted that about fifty gas masks were needed "to conduct rescue ops [operations] in smk [smoke] fm [from] bonfires, burning cars/houses — needed for crowd control if cs [tear gas] used."

There had still been no attacks on whites, three days after the shooting. There still was no confirmation that the Native protestors had guns in the park. Still, the memo ominously continued that "Up to 400 lbs of chlorine aval [available] in the pumphous [sic]. As the SPG [Stoney Point group] now controls the prov pk [provincial park] and pumphouse chlorine could be used in some way."

Among other things, the memo stated that "two addition Bison armoured personnel carriers are needed, and a devise [sic] for intercepting cellular telephone calls. The memo also suggested that "two Huey helicopters, like what American forces used in Vietnam, be put on standbye [sic] as OPP hel [helicopters] have no capability to carry more than 4 pers at a time, pilot incl [included] . . . — would be used in rescue ops [operations] or for emergency evac [evacuation] to a hospital."

THE MILITARY CLEARLY wasn't comfortable with the pressure from the OPP, since they still had not obtained proper authorization. The situation was reviewed at the lofty level of the Judge Advocate General, which provides legal advice to the defence minister, and suddenly a halt was ordered to the flow of equipment to the OPP.

DUDLEY GEORGE WAS to be buried on Monday, September 11, a week after he and the other Stoney Pointers had begun their occupation of the park. The OPP issued a solemn news release: "The Ontario Provincial Police wish to recognize the dignity of the Funeral ceremony . . . The First Nations desire for privacy during this solemn period will be honoured."

Not everyone in the OPP was as earnest as the writer of the press release. It was about the time of the funeral that Dudley George's sister Pam went into a shop on Forest's main street and saw some coffee mugs with curious crests. She took a closer look and read, "Team Ipperwash 95." The cups also sported OPP crests and an arrow, and there were crests with a feather lying down under the OPP symbol. Pam was horrified to realize that these were souvenir mugs for the police operation that had killed her brother, and that commemorative T-shirts and sweatshirts were also on sale as a reminder of the bloody operation. They had been ordered by on-duty police officers in uniform and the store owner later insisted that they were sold only to police. The owner said they stopped selling the novelty items altogether when George family members said they found them deeply offensive, but not before officers had bought mementoes of their role in the operation that had killed Dudley George.

The upbeat mood among some of the police officers might be explained somewhat by the sense of bonding that comes from such an operation. But it may have been aided by their hefty overtime pay rates. When the overtime for Ipperwash was finally tallied, it was discovered that some $1.27 million in overtime had been paid out for a twenty-seven-day period that September, which translates into an average of $4,980.00 for each of the 255 officers involved — in less than a month.

THE MORNING OF the funeral, it was decided that Dudley would be buried deep in the military base, among the oak, pine, and birch trees and far from the eyes of gawkers. The spot near the parking lot where he was shot dead was marked with a simple shrine, shaded by a frame structure of saplings and tree boughs.

As the Native people prepared to bury Dudley George, the OPP and the military braced for more trouble. A military memo from the funeral date states, "This afternoon . . . Dudly [sic] George was buried in the camp graveyard. An attempt was made by a faction to bury Dudley George in the parking lot of the provincial park. Fol the intervention of the family it was agreed that he be buried in the graveyard.

". . . After the burial most natives left the park. OPP estimate 100 natives remaining in the park. They are under the supervision of the native spiritual leaders. It has been stated that there will be no drinking and the native spiritual leaders will keep control on young men."

THE DAY AFTER Dudley George was buried, the chiefs still had not met with Premier Mike Harris. It was painfully obvious that they were not going to get anywhere as long as they were in Kettle Point and the premier was in Toronto, so they decided to make the three-hour drive to the big city uninvited.

As they drove to Toronto, Tom Bressette, who had slept little over the past few days, worried that he would lose his temper and start swearing at the premier. The prospect of the mammoth chief shouting at Harris was unsettling for Mercredi, who said, politely but firmly, "Look, let me do the talking."

When they got to Toronto, no one did any talking with the premier immediately, as they were told curtly by an aide to the premier, "He's not going to see you."

Mercredi replied that they were going to stay outside his office until the premier did deign to talk to them. There was a media buzz now, as the standoff in the hallway gave the killing a political flavouring. There wasn't much to report from Ipperwash, though the standoff continued, with Native flags at the occupied military base flying at half-mast and a Canadian flag flying with the maple leaf cut out.

After about ninety minutes in the hallway, an aide to the premier appeared outside Harris's office and said that the premier would finally meet with them. It was now late in the afternoon of Tuesday, September 12, and the premier was clearly unapologetic about the wait of almost a week — or about anything else.

Bressette said in an interview that Harris gave them a blunt, forceful message: "I want to make it clear," the premier said, according to Bressette's recollection, "I didn't kill anybody. I never gave orders to kill anybody."

Harris demanded that they listen to him. The gist of Harris's comments was that the Ipperwash crisis was strictly an OPP affair, and that Harris had no blood on his hands. "He denied knowing anything about anything," Bressette recalled. "If Harris was to be believed, the police had done it all."

Also at the meeting was Charles Harnick, who held the joint title of attorney general and minister responsible for Native affairs. Harnick, unlike Hodgson, was not at the meeting held in the Premier's Office on Wednesday, September 6, hours before Dudley George was shot dead. However, Hodgson was shielded from having to attend the unpleasant post-shooting meeting with the angry Native chiefs, while Harnick was placed front and centre. Bressette was struck by the shell-shocked look on Harnick's face. It looked as if he was wiped right out.

The premier emerged grim-faced from the meeting to face the press outside his door, insisting the government had passed on the message to the chiefs that Ipperwash was "a police matter."

"I believe First Nations leaders should be treated with courtesy and respect," Harris read from a press release distributed to assembled journalists. "Therefore, I personally delivered the government's message that we will not discuss the illegal occupation of Ipperwash Provincial Park." He continued by saying that the Ipperwash occupation was being handled by the OPP and that the civilian Special Investigations Unit would probe the shooting death of Dudley George. "Our government is committed to restoring hope, economic opportunity and jobs for the First Nations people of Ontario," he said. Once his statement was read, Harris refused to answer reporters' questions and was whisked back inside to his office.

When it was his turn to speak, Mercredi said federal and provincial politicians must be willing to sit down with Native leaders and discuss problems if future standoffs are to be prevented. He told reporters that both sides agreed to keep the lines of communication open, which was a polite way of saying they hadn't really agreed on anything except that they shared a big, complicated problem.

Mercredi continued that there was "a common understanding" that the legal status of the provincial park must be addressed. "The only difficulty that stands in the way of progress is the position that the Premier takes that it [the government] will not negotiate with anyone so long as the park is being occupied," Mercredi said. "So in a sense, I guess you can say that while we've opened up understanding about the fundamental issues to be resolved, we have not really settled anything."

As Bressette drove back to Kettle Point, he felt a profound wave of dissatisfaction. It was almost a week since the march on the park, and still nobody was stepping forward to take any responsibility for the death of Dudley George.

THE SPOT WHERE Dudley was hit by the fatal OPP bullet was still marked with a simple shrine of pine boughs, on which Native friends had placed boughs and a pouch of sacred tobacco. Within a few days, someone had painted "Dudley is a Dud" on a stone nearby and thrown beer bottles and garbage on the shrine. Natives painted over the graffiti, picked up the debris, and once again, the spot in the sand had a simple dignity.

THE IDEA CAME to Sam George, Dudley's brother, six months after the killing. They had no answers to the questions surrounding Dudley's death and there was no prospect of any coming. So Sam decided that the family would file a lawsuit against Premier Mike Harris, OPP Commissioner

Thomas O'Grady, and all the government workers and police officers who they believed knew something about what had happened that night. The government clearly did not want to call an inquiry, so they would have an inquiry of their own. It would come in the form of their lawsuit. They could get all the answers they sought in the examination for discovery, when people being sued are requested to answer questions. They would still get their answers.

It wasn't going to be an easy task. Sam George's lawyers, Murray Klippenstein, Andrew Orkin, and Delia Opekokew knew they would literally have to make history to succeed. To date, no premier of Ontario had ever been compelled to testify in a lawsuit as a defendant while holding office.

A lawsuit threatened to be an expensive, draining, and joyless exercise for the George family, but also a necessary one. And if the government committed itself to calling an inquiry, the suit could be quickly dropped. Either way, they felt they had to launch the suit in order to get real answers from the premier.

Sam George didn't feel he had a choice. What he really wanted was to spend more time with his family, but he also felt he could not really get on with his life until there were full answers about the death of his brother. So he filed the suit, accusing Harris, Harnick, and former Solicitor General Bob Runciman, by then minister of consumer and commercial relations, of personally directing the OPP to get tough with the Natives in the park. Something had to be learned from the death, he would later say. "My tradition is we learn by our mistakes and if you're honest with yourself, it only helps you to be a better person."

Government lawyers acting for Harris, Runciman, and Harnick argued that there was no legal basis for naming these politicians in the case. The OPP officers weren't fair game either, they argued. The police officers were simply exercising their best professional judgement. And without the politicians and the police, there was no one to sue or no one who could explain what happened. Clearly, no one in power wanted to take responsibility. It was clear also that, if they were going to get answers, it would take considerable time and a massive fight.

IN THE ABSENCE of an inquiry, the press began digging for answers of their own. On March 31, 1996, the *Toronto Star* quoted the OPP's Southwestern Region Chief Superintendent Chris Coles as saying that a decision had been made to confront the Natives at Ipperwash on September 5, a day before the fatal shooting. This contradicted Commissioner O'Grady's explanation that the violence was merely an "isolated incident."

Another *Toronto Star* front-page story, published May 29, 1996, broke the news that Debbie Hutton, a key aide to Premier Mike Harris, had been part of a secret emergency meeting about Ipperwash the day of the police operation that killed Dudley George. This challenged Harris's position that the shooting was strictly a police matter, free of any political interference.

MEANWHILE, ATTORNEY GENERAL and Minister Responsible for Native Affairs Charles Harnick stuck to the government line that it wasn't time to call an inquiry — yet. In June 1996, he urged a gathering of some four hundred provincial Native leaders to be patient until the Special Investigations Unit had completed its long-awaited probe. Perhaps then it would be time to call the inquiry they so badly wanted.

"I don't want to do anything to jeopardize the SIU's investigation," Harnick told the chiefs. "I have to be very careful."

8

CHARGES
LAID

". . . the investigation is frustrated by the fact that
no one can identify the officers involved."
— THE CIVILIAN AGENCY INVESTIGATING THE BEATING OF
SLIPPERY GEORGE COMPLAINS OF A LACK OF COOPERATION FROM POLICE

There were plenty of chuckles and raised eyebrows in June 1996 when James MacLean Stewart was appointed for a term of only one month as the head of the province's police watchdog body, the Special Investigations Unit. "Why so long?" joked Toronto lawyer Mark Wainberg to *Toronto Star* reporter Harold Levy. "Why didn't they just rent him by the hour?"

No one grew old as the director of the SIU. They just felt that way. There were constant rumours that the SIU, a creation of the former New Democrat government, was on short-term life support with the new Tory government anyway, and that the plug could be pulled any day now. Meanwhile, the name plates kept changing on the office of the SIU director. In June 1996, Stewart became the fourth director in eighteen months, replacing Graham Reynolds, a federal prosecutor, who'd lasted seven months into a one-year term before taking a job as provincial assistant deputy attorney general for criminal law. Reynolds had replaced Dana Venner, who'd also weathered seven months on the job.

All SIU investigations are supposed to be completed within ninety days, which was three times the length of time of acting director Stewart's appointment in June 1996. However, at that point, the delivery date was so long overdue, at nine months and counting, that any quibbling over time periods seemed meaningless. In the absence of a report on Ipperwash, there were plenty of questions and rumours. Had some of the police unwittingly fired at each other that night? Had they mistaken sparks from their own bullets hitting the bus and car for shots coming from the vehicles? Hadn't the Natives said that Dudley George wasn't even on the bus or in the car, and didn't police say that the firing had originally come from those vehicles? Shouldn't officers know what they are shooting at? And the shield chatter as they approached the protestors was also profoundly disturbing. Isn't that what Zulu warriors used to do to instill terror in their enemies? Was that any way for a paid peacekeeper to act?

It was no rumour that there were also deep tensions between the civilian investigators and the police, who never welcomed what they considered to be the SIU's intrusions. That tension was now palpable. Many SIU investigators were former police officers, but they were no longer treated as members of the brotherhood. At the time Stewart was appointed, the SIU was battling in the courts to win access to I.D. photos of police officers at Ipperwash to show to potential witnesses. The OPP Association (which defends the interests of OPP officers) was arguing that to release these photos of individual officers would be an unjustified intrusion into their personal privacy.

When Stewart took the job, he must have realized that intense political overtones would accompany any Ipperwash decision. Liberal MPP Gerry Phillips (Scarborough-Agincourt) was now continually hammering at Premier Mike Harris in the legislature, drawing attention to Harris's failure to call an inquiry into Ipperwash. "I share the frustration with a lot of people about the length of time that the SIU investigation has taken place," Harris replied in the legislature, not even addressing the question of when or if he might call a public inquiry.

As the politicians argued on, police critics like Toronto lawyer Mark Wainberg also expressed a loss of confidence in the agency, which they considered to be too soft on the police. In 1995, 176 incidents of alleged police misuse of force were reported to the SIU — including two firearms deaths, 18 firearms injuries, 20 custody deaths, 68 custody injuries, and 10 sexual assaults — yet not a single charge had been laid against any officer in the province.

There was talk suggesting that the SIU was a lame duck that should be put out of its misery. "I don't think it matters who they appoint," Wainberg said. "Since the Harris government doesn't support the SIU and won't fund it properly, it cannot possibly be effective regardless of who the director is."

The SIU investigation was actually completed when Stewart began his term, but the final report had yet to be drafted, and that was the tricky part. Stewart was to be director from June 17, 1996, until July 14, 1996 — about a third the length of the average student summer job — and he was to study investigators' findings and make recommendations to Queen's Park concerning possible charges before he, too, vacated the director's office.

After all the missed deadlines and director shuffles, the SIU issued a press release on July 23, 1996, that threw Ipperwash back onto the front pages. The decision from Stewart's office was a week overdue, past its latest deadline, and when it finally came, it hit the police community like a bombshell. Acting Sergeant Kenneth Deane of the Ontario Provincial Police Tactics and Rescue Unit was charged with criminal negligence causing death.

The SIU's choice of charge prompted some head scratching and a new rash of conspiracy theories. One might argue that the charge of criminal negligence causing death was extremely severe, since it, like murder, carried a maximum penalty of life imprisonment. It might even be seen as tougher than a murder charge, since if Deane was charged with murder, he would automatically have a jury trial. Canadian juries have proven to be extremely reluctant to convict police officers, and it would be easy for even a modestly skilled defence lawyer to telegraph to a jury that a murder conviction would mean serious jail time, making a conviction that much more unlikely.

However, the criminal negligence causing death charge could also be seen as ridiculously light. It carried no minimum penalty, meaning a convicted killer could be found guilty and still walk free from the courthouse without serving a day in jail. If the Ipperwash shooting had happened just a couple of months later, Deane would have faced a minimum four-year sentence if found guilty, in accordance with tough new legislation passed by the federal government. Ironically, that legislation came after successful lobbying by police, among other groups, to crack down on crimes committed with weapons.

Everyone in the legal community agreed that criminal negligence causing death was extremely difficult to prove. All it would take for Deane to escape the charge was to successfully argue that he had had a mistaken but honest *belief* that Dudley George was armed and dangerous. He didn't have to be right. He just had to convincingly argue that he had honestly *believed* it. The nature of the charge meant the trial would be a trip inside the mind of the man who killed Dudley George.

When the charge against Deane was laid, Dudley's family renewed calls for a full public inquiry, saying they were worried that Deane might be made a scapegoat, to shield others from public censure. They wanted to know why Deane was in the park at night with his submachinegun in the first place. They were interested in bigger fish, ones that swam at Queen's Park. "This [Deane's trial] is a starting point," said Dudley's sister Carolyn George.

However, Paul Rhodes, senior media advisor to Harris, said the government remained firm in its position that it was inappropriate to call a public inquiry as long as there were cases before the courts. Now, ironically, the Deane case was one of those before the courts which the Harris team said was blocking any talk of an inquiry. The fact that a police officer was charged lent a certain amount of support to the Natives' claim that something unjust had happened that night. However, it also prevented them from getting a full look at why something had gone horribly wrong. "As long as there is outstanding court action we will not even discuss an inquiry," said Rhodes.

Meanwhile, Ontario Provincial Police Association president Brian Adkin was unapologetic. He wasn't going to argue that officers he represented were used as dupes by politicians. Instead, he simply said his organization was "disgusted" by the charge. "The members of the Ontario Provincial Police are constantly faced with dangerous and violent situations in the line of duty," said Adkin. "These situations require our officers to take the most appropriate steps available given all of the difficult circumstances they face." Whether or not that situation had been created by Queen's Park was an issue he wasn't about to address.

The July 26 statement by the SIU did more than announce the charges laid against Deane. Even though the trial had not yet begun, it went on to vindicate Dudley George to a degree. The press release made no mention of any gunfire from any of the Native protestors and made a point of stating that Dudley George was not in the bus when he was shot dead. Immediately after the shooting, the OPP said that they had been fired upon from the bus. As the police originally explained things, Dudley George had been shot dead when police returned fire coming from the bus, in order to defend themselves. Now, obviously, the SIU investigation did not back up the original police story. Even Deane didn't agree with this, saying that Dudley had been standing on the roadside holding a gun when he was shot.

As for the beating suffered by Slippery George that night, the SIU said its investigators could not determine which OPP members had beaten Slippery George, but not for lack of effort. Some 250 witnesses had been interviewed before they'd finally thrown in the towel. "The director concluded that Cecil George's injuries were the result of a violent confrontation between 'Slippery' George and officers of the OPP," the SIU press release said. "However, the investigation is frustrated by the fact that no one can identify the officers involved."

Only thirty-two officers had been in the Crowd Management Unit at the park that night, and Native witnesses said eight to ten of them were beating Slippery George. That made the officers' inability to remember the details of the event all the more baffling, or aggravating, depending on one's point of view. Since the OPP Association had blocked the release of officers' I.D. photos, the SIU could also not properly investigate the Native allegation that an OPP officer had threatened Dudley George on the last afternoon of his life. Unlike the officers who'd beaten Slippery George, this officer's face had been visible, and he'd allegedly made his comments in broad daylight. Still, somehow, he could not be found. "This is extraordinary that a police force has simply clammed up," said Andrew Orkin, one of the lawyers for the George family. "If they had cooperated with the SIU, then the SIU would have been in a position to lay charges."

THE NEXT DAY, July 24, 1996, OPP Commissioner Thomas O'Grady broke months of silence to comment, reading a public statement at OPP head-quarters in London, Ontario, less than an hour's drive from where Deane had killed Dudley George. O'Grady stated that he had declined to comment throughout the SIU investigation out of respect for the legal process.

At the press conference, O'Grady said twice that he did not take "operational" direction from the government and once that he did not take "tactical" direction. These were irrelevant points, since no one, not even O'Grady's harshest critics, was saying that Queen's Park officials had told the OPP exactly what to do that night. The problem was that the provincial government had pressured the police force to replace an effective and often-used approach of negotiation with confrontation. That wasn't "tactical" direction, but the provincial government had opted to make sure the Natives were physically removed from the park before the team of thirteen Project Maple negotiators had been given an opportunity to do their work. That physical confrontation had deadly consequences.

The September 6, 1995, meeting of the Emergency Planning for Aboriginal Issues Interministerial Committee came to the following conclusion according to a meeting report: "Police have been asked to remove the occupiers from the park." The statement makes no allowance for the implementation of Project Maple or any other negotiation. Instead, it focuses only on getting the Native occupiers out of the park. Further handwritten notes by Hutton's name suggest that the provincial government wanted the Aboriginals out of the park and "nothing else": "Premier last night — OPP only Maybe MNR — out of Park only — nothing else" and "want to be seen as actioning."

In his lengthy statement, O'Grady did not mention that the Project Maple peace plan had been abandoned at the last moment and the negotiators were never called, even though thirteen had been listed for the job. In his statement, O'Grady also talked of rifle fire at a Canadian Forces helicopter in August 1993 (the shot to the wing of the aircraft manned by the squadron just returned from Somalia). He spoke as well of a bus smashing into a drill hall and a jeep at the military base in July 1995, saying, "These incidents provided every indication that violence would escalate." These were acts of violence perpetrated by the Natives, but the two incidents occurred almost two years apart, and no person was hurt or killed in either case. It was never proven that the shot to the helicopter wing had come from a Native person's gun, and the drill hall smashing was an act of exasperation after approximately half a century of waiting for the federal government to make good on its promise to let the Stoney Pointers return to their reserve lands after World War II was over. In his statement, the commissioner also praised himself for sending an officer to monitor the dispute at Gustafsen Lake in British Columbia but said nothing of any links between the two incidents, likely because there were no direct connections.

O'Grady also justified the OPP's baton-drumming march on the park as a means of allaying the fears of local non-Native residents: "The OPP took into consideration the highly populated area and the possibility that friction could have erupted between the large numbers of non-natives and the occupiers. The OPP continued to respond to calls from area residents who feared for the safety of themselves and their homes."

What evidence was there that those fears were at all well founded? Didn't the confidential memo sent out by the Canadian military after the shooting describe the mood of "some local residents" as "paranoid"? And O'Grady did not elaborate on the fact that the only charge laid before the march on the park resulted from the throwing of a single stone at a car, in which both the stone thrower and the car's driver were Native. No one was injured, and a high estimate of the damage was four hundred dollars.

O'Grady went on to tell the news conference that heavy military equipment had been brought in for purely defensive reasons, "to evacuate our members or members of the public should the need arise. . . . Fortunately it was not needed and never used." O'Grady also claimed that the snipers and riot squad members had marched on the park without warning late at night, "to keep the peace, ensure public safety, and to uphold the laws." Ironically, the peace was broken only after the CMU officers began marching forward, beating their shields with their batons. No mention was made that the provincial government had been the first to break a promise by failing to fence off the burial ground inside the park. However, it was acknowledged that the confrontation had occurred over a land claims dispute — unlike Premier Mike Harris who repeatedly stated that it was not a land claims dispute.

When O'Grady spoke of how the OPP were working to keep open lines of communication with First Nations people, he failed to note that his officers had not followed up on Ovide Mercredi's offer the night of the shooting, when the grand chief of the Assembly of First Nations had pleaded over the telephone line for an opportunity to mediate, before things got out of hand. Furthermore, O'Grady gave no explanation for why the OPP suddenly dropped their Project Maple plan, which called for thirteen negotiators. And if dialogue with Native people was so important to the OPP, why did they not ensure that Natives or their lawyers were allowed to defend their position at the injunction hearing the next day? Why was Slippery George clubbed unconscious when he approached police, offering to act as a mediator on the night of September 6, 1995, just before the shooting?

And why, even before Acting Sergeant Deane's case had gone to court, did Commissioner O'Grady say: "[O]n the information I have, I am confident our officer acted in good faith in the performance of his duty?"

Not surprisingly, the media-shy commissioner did not field questions after his remarks. Instead, he turned on his heels and marched quickly out of the room, trailed by junior officers.

THE MOOD WAS ugly at the Sarnia courthouse on August 27, 1996, when Acting Sergeant Kenneth Deane was to make his first court appearance. It was just a routine scheduling matter, involving no arguments or testimony. Deane wasn't expected to even open his mouth. Nonetheless, it was the first time he would appear in court in relation to the shooting. Finally, almost a year after the event, people would get to see the man who pulled the trigger on the gun that had killed Dudley George. Outside the courthouse were about eighty members of a group of people who lived in the area or owned summer homes there. They called themselves ONFIRE (Ontario Federation for Individual Rights and Equality) and they chanted, "We support the OPP!"

There were also about thirty Natives and their supporters outside the courthouse, and one of them shouted at the ONFIRE crowd, "You only support the OPP because they kill Natives!"

About thirty off-duty OPP officers briefly watched the ugliness outside, then went into the courtroom. There were so many officers and the courtroom was so small that when the George family and the media arrived, two uniformed OPP officers told them that there was no room and they would have to leave.

As Dudley George's family stepped back outside, they could hear Richard Schultz of ONFIRE opining into a megaphone that there was "no law and order" in the area around the park. Schultz wasn't complaining about the police and their late-night shooting and beating. He wasn't talking about how the Native people were paid too little for their land in 1927 and how the federal government had reneged on its 1942 promise to let the Stoney Point people return to their reserve after World War II was over. Schultz said nothing about how the OPP had no injunction to remove the Native protestors when they'd marched on the park on the night of September 6, 1995. He said nothing about how the Ontario and Canadian governments had broken promises made to the people of Stoney Point. Instead, he complained that he and other members of his group had experienced property damage or had seen their land values plummet as a result of the controversy.

Schultz said his position wasn't racist and that ONFIRE was prepared to work with Native people at nearby reserves to allow the parkland to be returned to the bands, but then offered no details as to how this might be done.

When a reporter asked Dudley George's sister Carolyn how she felt watching this, she replied that she had known many of the opposing group for years, and suggested sadly that they were "definitely in need of a history lesson."

IN THE VICINITY of London, Ontario, Norman Peel was the lawyer police called on when they had serious problems. It didn't hurt his reputation that newspaper reports often noted he'd been counsel to General Jean Boyle at the time of the inquiry into wrongdoing by the Canadian military in Somalia. Peel would look reporters in the eye and seem genuinely interested, no matter how stupid the question, which often proved to be a daunting challenge. He was the type of folksy, easy-to-like person who could somehow appear rumpled, even when wearing neatly pressed, expensive clothes. If Norman Peel appeared to be fumbling, it only worked to his advantage as it had for TV detective Columbo. Peel might look like an absent-minded professor, but one got the impression that, under the rumpled surface, Norman Peel was as smart as a fox.

Peel was the lawyer Deane's paramilitary unit had called upon during one of its darkest moments — in 1989, after a series of blunders led to the shooting of Bernard Bastien, a thirty-four-year-old Windsor autoworker. TRU team members had shown up early in the morning of August 14, 1988, at a house outside Windsor, ready to deal with an armed and suicidal teenager who, they had heard, was bent on goading police into a shootout. The police were ready for battle, but they were also at the wrong address. The Bastien family beagle, Buster, was understandably startled by the strangers in commando gear who arrived in the dark. An officer silenced Buster, who was tethered on a chain outside the house, with three shots from a .223 carbine, killing the pet.

The noise awakened Bastien's elderly mother, who in turn woke up her son, Bernard. He emerged from the house with a shotgun, looking for prowlers. The strangers in camouflage gear said they were police, but Bastien couldn't believe police would act this way and ignored their warnings to drop his weapon. What happened next is unclear. Police maintained they were fired upon first, before Bastien was hit with thirteen bullets, including at least three nine-millimetre softhead copper jacket bullets from an MP-5 submachinegun, the same type of high-tech weapon that killed Dudley George. Dr. Pat Allevato, the pathologist who performed the autopsy, determined Bastien had twenty-five exit and entry wounds, making it the worst case of gunshot wounds he had seen in emergency departments in Windsor or Detroit.

Similarities with the Ipperwash shootings didn't stop with the fatal use of MP-5 submachineguns and the odd coincidence that both cases included police attacks on dogs. They also both occurred in the dark and also both involved Staff Sergeant Wade Lacroix. Lacroix's movements that night weren't just troubling to the Bastiens. Windsor Police Staff Sergeant Brian Greenham told public hearings into the fiasco that Lacroix, then the TRU team leader, did not advise the police incident commander that they were moving into Anderton Township. If the dispatcher for Anderton Township had known about the move, Windsor police could have informed Bastien's wife, Debbie, when she called to report that her husband was outside the family home confronting prowlers.

In the Bastien hearings, Peel tried to deflect at least some of the blame to the police officers' portable radios, which he said were either in short supply or malfunctioning, creating a "nightmare" for police. "One officer isn't hearing another," Peel said. "There's a breakdown of safety."

The police backup negotiator that night was a Sergeant John Carson, the same John Carson who was incident commander the night Dudley George was shot dead. He was not called to negotiate the night Bastien was fatally wounded, just as negotiators were not called the night Dudley George was killed.

In the public hearing on the Bastien death, Bastien family lawyer Leon Paroian warned that Lacroix's TRU team needed to be placed under much tougher scrutiny. "This is an extraordinarily deadly unit," Paroian said. "And if it's not managed properly, if it's not equipped properly, if it's not trained properly, it shouldn't be out there."

Paroian noted that it was easy for officers to get confused at night and falsely assume that they were being fired upon. He theorized that when an officer sprayed the beagle with three bullets, fellow officers mistook this for a shotgun blast, and fired at Bastien.

The inquest into the Bastien death also heard about "Tackay psyche." At least two police officers were experiencing this little-known phenomenon that describes the almost hallucinatory effect stress can place on a person who is in a life-threatening situation. Police officers in gunfights commonly experience auditory and visual distortions, including tunnel vision, or a feeling that events are moving in slow motion. It is possible for people in high-stress situations to hear shots that aren't fired, to "see" bullets fly through the air, or to fail to see things that would normally be obvious.

Regarding the shooting of the Bastiens' pet beagle, Buster, Paroian asked, "What possible, possible reason could there be for that kind of lack of restraint? The evidence is absolutely clear in a minute the dog wasn't armed." At another point, Paroian warned that the TRU team, which was formed to combat possible terrorist infiltration at the 1976 Montreal Olympics, had perhaps outlived its usefulness. "You might recommend keeping this team as an anti-terrorist unit but don't let them out on the domestic scene . . . That [TRU] team is a military organization . . . trained in the military sense."

Norman Peel, on the other hand, painted the officers outside the Bastien house that night as victims and pleaded with the jurors not to "get rid of the little guys . . . We'll never know what happened. The TRU team went out into the night in a dangerous situation and there was a tragic result. I don't try to hide that for one minute." The "little guys," in Peel's words, were the armed police officers who killed the beagle and then its owner. "It sounds as though [Paroian] is laying boots . . . laying boots to the little people," said Peel.

Peel had it down to a simple formula: blame the radios, blame the pressure, blame the fates; blame the night and even blame the beagle for barking. Blame pretty well everyone and everything, until the cloud of blame is so thick that everyone forgets who pulled the trigger.

Paroian was clearly frustrated that, amidst all the talk of blame, no one really seemed to be taking responsibility for what should have been an avoidable tragedy. "Who do you blame?" Paroian rhetorically asked reporters. "Do you blame Bernard Bastien? Do you blame the night? Do you blame the dog?"

In April 1989 the inquest ruled that a series of human errors and misadventures had led the OPP tactical squad to mistake Bastien for the suicidal teenager. In reaching this conclusion, the jury also ruled that there was "no conclusive evidence" that Bastien had fired the first shot and concluded that he was "legitimately protecting his family and home."

The case did differ from that of Dudley George in at least one significant respect: there was an inquest into Bastien's death within a year of the killing.

IT WAS TOUGH to figure out what Norman Peel had up his sleeve as he prepared for the Deane trial, but he was too intelligent a man and too experienced a lawyer to wander in casually with no plan. He elected trial by judge, which seemed a bit unusual. Trial by judge meant there was no preliminary hearing, and that seemed a bit risky. A preliminary hearing would have given him the opportunity to see his witnesses in action and to fine tune his case. He could always change his mind after the preliminary and switch over to trial by judge. The OPP was paying the bill, so money wasn't as much of a problem as if Deane had been paying his legal fees himself. Norman Peel must have something big planned, but it was difficult to determine just what that might be.

One thing was clear, however. Peel wasn't going to allow this to be a trial about the historical treatment of Native people by whites. He immediately defused things on that front, telling reporters that Native people have had a sad time of things. His case, however, was not about the history of Canada. It involved one man, Acting Sergeant Kenneth Deane, and a very short period of time on the night of September 6, 1995: the night Dudley George was shot dead. No one at Queen's Park had to worry about Peel pointing fingers in their direction.

Peel was well acquainted with his courtroom adversary, Ian Scott. Scott was no relation of the former attorney general of Ontario by the same name, who had also been minister responsible for Native affairs — but he had made quite a name of his own prosecuting cases of police and Crown malpractice. The Ian Scott of the Ipperwash case was a graduate of the University of Western Ontario's law school, where one of his professors had been none other than Norman Peel. Easygoing and chatty outside the courtroom, Scott was totally focused when arguing a case, with the type of single-minded intensity associated with champion prize fighters or highly bred hunting dogs.

Scott didn't have to be told that he faced an almost impossible task. Peel wasn't going to deny that Deane had fired the fatal shot. The officer had readily admitted that. Peel didn't have to prove that Dudley George was armed either. He just had to prove that Deane had a reasonable and honest *belief* for a split second that George was armed and dangerous. Peel didn't have to prove this to a certainty either — just enough to establish reasonable doubt. All Deane needed to do to walk free was to look credible and say, "I think he had a gun. I still think so. I pray I was right. I had to act quickly to protect my men."

THE TRIAL WOULD be heard by Mr. Justice Hugh Fraser from Ottawa. Not too much was known about him outside the Ottawa area. His reputation there was that of a judge who believed in the system and wanted to play a role in making it work well. He was also black, and neither the police nor the Natives knew what, if anything, to make of that.

Some of the police were happy to hear that the judge was black. If Deane was acquitted, liberals couldn't bleat about racist justice, since the judge himself was a member of a visible minority. Liberals, however, hoped that the judge's racial background would make him sympathetic to the treatment of a member of a minority group.

Fraser would probably have been far better known if Canada had not boycotted the 1980 Moscow Olympics. He had been a member of the Canadian relay team that reached the finals of the 4 x 100–yard relay in the 1976 Montreal Olympics, despite nursing an injured hamstring at the time. By 1980, he was in his physical prime and a legitimate medal hopeful. However, Canada supported the boycott of the Olympics over the Soviet invasion of Afghanistan and Fraser retired as an athlete, never knowing how well he might have done.

Those who asked around heard that Fraser was a serious, thoughtful, hard-working man. The son of a Justice Department lawyer, he had trained for the Olympics while carrying a full law-school course load at his father's *alma mater*, Queen's. "When I wasn't training, I was studying," he told Bruce Ward of the *Ottawa Citizen* in 1993. "When I wasn't doing one, I was doing the other — with a minimum amount of sleep in between."

There was no master plan to have a non-white judge handle this racially explosive case. The story was that it obviously had to be an out-of-town judge to handle such a volatile situation, and that when the call went out for volunteers, Fraser was the first and only candidate to volunteer.

9

THE TRIAL
OF KEN DEANE

"They covered the whole road ... They were
marching down the road just like the Gestapo."
— ISAAC "BUCK" DOXTATOR TESTIFIES DURING THE
TRIAL OF ACTING SERGEANT KENNETH "TEX" DEANE

Security wouldn't have been much tighter in the Sarnia courtroom if it had been the Pope and not Acting Sergeant Ken Deane who was arriving. He came in a convoy of sport utility vehicles, and bomb-sniffing dogs checked out the building and parking lot before he stepped out, barely visible in the midst of a phalanx of a dozen members of his fellow TRU team members in plainclothes. Even those who did manage a view of him found it tough to gauge how he felt, since his eyes were shielded by wrap-around sunglasses.

For his trial, there would be no unseemly rushing for seats as there had been in his first, pretrial day in court when off-duty OPP officers filled the courtroom, leaving no place for the George family or the press. The actual trial was being held in a far bigger venue. There were some two dozen on-duty police officers visible, including eight in the courtroom and five in a hallway outside. The officers in the courtroom wore bullet-proof vests and looked grim as they whispered messages into their portable radios. Everyone entering and leaving was frisked for weapons and required to pass through a metal detector. Much of the security was handled by Deane's own TRU team.

It was now a year and a half since the night Dudley George had been killed, and finally the world would hear the story from the mouth of Acting Sergeant Kenneth Deane. People in the packed courtroom leaned forward a bit to hear his voice as he was asked how he pleaded to the charge of criminal negligence causing death. In a flat, firm tone, he replied, "Not guilty," staring straight ahead. Like Dudley, he was a smallish, stocky man, and like Dudley, he had been largely anonymous until the night of September 6, 1995. Now, both men were forever tied together by a few minutes of late-night violence, both seen as symbols now more than as actual humans.

There was no denying that Deane had fired seven shots that night, including the one that tore into Dudley George's chest and killed him. The Crown's task was to prove that Deane had been wrong in firing at Dudley George, and that he hadn't simply been doing his duty.

In a criminal trial, the Crown introduces its case first, allowing the defence to determine if the charges are even worth answering. The first witness called by senior Crown Attorney Ian Scott was Kevin Stanley Thompson of the Special Investigations Unit, who carried with him a brown paper bag. From it he produced a T-shirt, caked in what appeared to be dried blood, with a hole in the shoulder. As the bloodied, bullet-torn shirt was held up, a fifteen-year-old cousin of Dudley started sobbing. The T-shirt was such an ordinary, common thing, and yet now it also sent a message that was unspeakably powerful and tragic to the young girl.

Then Thompson pulled out the cheap grey pants with a rope belt that Dudley used to wear and rolled up the leg to show two ragged tears in the legs, where another bullet had hit him. More sobbing was heard from the back of the courtroom. Thompson reached into the bag again and held up some cheap running shoes, with what appeared to be caked blood on the instep and treads. Next, Thompson produced the state-of-the-art, finely engineered submachinegun that had produced the blood and the torn shirt and pants, with its sure-fire night light and ultra-accurate laser lighting device. Thompson noted that the laser sights had already been given back to the police, as it was a "specialized piece of equipment and vital to their operation which was ongoing at the Ipperwash scene."

Finally, Thompson showed the court two tiny pieces of metal, in a vial about the size of a pill bottle. One, he said, was the copper jacket of a bullet and one was the lead core material of a bullet. That bullet had been positively matched to Deane's submachinegun and had been cut from Dudley George's lifeless body, providing an indisputable link between the shooter and his now–dead-and-buried target.

LAWYERS ARE OFTEN accused of conducting major makeovers with witnesses to make them appear nonthreatening and even angelic in court. Bikers routinely cover tattoos with suit jackets, hookers dress in formless dark clothing, and free spirits crop their hair to look like corporate bankers. Only the truly innocent or the hopelessly criminal actually look guilty in court. But no one could have accused Scott of attempting such a stunt with Isaac "Buck" Doxtator, an Oneida from the nearby Muncie Reserve, and it was doubtful that Buck Doxtator would have played along with it anyway. He appeared for court in head-to-toe camouflage hunting gear, offset with a fatigue-coloured headband, sunglasses, two drop earrings, and an American Indian Movement T-shirt. It was a complete head-to-foot, militant-Indian look, and one that was wholly authentic.

Doxtator, a large, imposing man, had a conviction for assaulting police from 1971, a suspended break-and-enter conviction from 1975, and a 1988 break-and-enter. He didn't flinch when his criminal record was read into court and made it clear from the opening moments of his testimony that he wasn't going to try to cozy up to anyone in the legal system. He said he'd arrived at Ipperwash "the day before the murder." That day was purely social, he said. "We went fishing, swimming, whatever. Visiting."

Doxtator recalled that he could feel heavy tension between the police and Natives on September 5, 1995, the day before the shooting. He and another man were sitting on a picnic table outside the park when a police cruiser pulled up and an officer called to them, "Welcome to Canada" and yelled racial slurs.

The night of the bloodshed, Doxtator said he used portable spotlights powered by car cigarette lighters to light up the police as they marched on the park. The police were clearly trying to intimidate them, he recalled. "They covered the whole road . . . They were marching down the road just like the Gestapo."

Doxtator said that things turned ugly fast, after the riot squad marched on the park and a black dog belonging to a protestor ran out at police, barking loudly. Several officers kicked at it, according to Doxtator. "The dog was barking. It made a yelping sound. And I never heard it no more."

Native supporters must have been holding their breath as the blunt-talking witness began speaking about the protestor's dog. There must have been a collective sigh of relief on the Native side of the courtroom a few minutes later, when Scott's questioning moved on past the dog incident. There was only one black person in the courtroom, and he was the only person whose opinion truly mattered — the judge. The Native people thought it was just as well that Judge Fraser hadn't heard the black dog's name — "Nigger."

After the dog was kicked, Native protestors rushed out of the park and "the fight was on," Doxtator said in a flat voice. He said they were not armed, but used clubs and sticks to fight police, who wore full riot gear and shields and batons.

Slippery George dropped suddenly when he was hit by a police officer. "They had a bunch of police around him. Kicking him and hitting him with clubs." Doxtator said he charged at the police, trying to free Slippery, and he could clearly see a circle of officers around Slippery, as officers kicked and beat him. "I grabbed a club and went to try to get Slippery back. We were outnumbered . . . I probably hit one of them pigs who were beating on him."

"We're going to call them police officers today," Scott corrected.

A couple of Native members of the audience smirked, while some police officers' faces tensed up. It was another reminder that whatever hatreds had exploded that night in September 1995 had not been extinguished. Doxtator pressed on, and his voice became even more earnest as he spoke of the gunfire. "I heard the first three shots, then a fully-automatic, one hundred or more rounds fired. The shots were hitting the sand. I could see them hitting the ground in front of me. I just froze."

He said police grabbed Slippery George and took him somewhere, then a schoolbus came out of the park gate, and police scrambled out of the way. He could hear someone say, "I'm hit," and he saw a man, who, he later realized, was Dudley George, holding his chest and walking backwards. The man collapsed on the sand and protestors put him into a car.

DEFENCE ATTORNEY NORMAN PEEL seemed delighted at the opportunity to cross-examine Doxtator, who looked like someone central casting would send in answer to a call for a dangerous-looking Indian. The cross-examination began in almost friendly tones. Peel asked Doxtator about his "camis" — camouflage clothing — and Doxtator was happy to reply, noting that he had several outfits of camouflage wear, in different colour combinations. "Were you wearing camis that night at all?" Peel asked.

"No," Doxtator replied, declining to elaborate.

"Why didn't you just go home, with all of them pigs around there?"

The lawyer was mocking him now, but Doxtator wasn't fazed, remaining stone-faced and continuing to speak in a flat monotone. "That would have been easier said than done," he replied. "How are you going to get out of there?" Things then turned testy as Doxtator said he'd originally considered the police ridiculous, not scary. "They came stomping down here, trying to scare us."

"Anybody swinging anything?"

"Just the police."

Until the dog ran out, it was all a big joke for the Indians, he said, still not mentioning the dog's unfortunate name. "We sat there laughing because we thought they looked like fools."

Peel tried to egg Doxtator on, and Doxtator was more than happy to take the bait and run with it. Obviously Peel didn't know Nigger's name. If he had, he would have been able to score major points there.

"Did you stand your ground pretty well?"

"I must have. I'm still here."

Peel pushed a little more on this, and Doxtator replied, "I guess the police got their ass kicked because they ran back."

The cross-examination hit a low when Doxtator told Peel he thought the police smelled of alcohol. "I smelled booze. They were half drunk or something."

NEXT TO TESTIFY was Stacey "Burger" George, an artist and the twenty-five-year-old younger brother of Cecil Bernard "Slippery" George. He said Slippery was only trying to make peace when he walked out alone toward the police riot squad that night. "He was telling the police that these were unarmed occupants and things like that. . . . They dragged my brother down the road by his hair, and they were still beating on him."

Stacey George said he heard three distinct shots, and then "a whole bunch" of police fired rapidly. At first, he said he thought the shooting was just another police scare tactic and that they were either using rubber bullets or firing into the air. Then he heard bullets whiz past and the sound of glass shattering. He covered his head with his hands, as if this might offer protection, and ran back into the park.

In a sad, soft voice, he recalled seeing his friend Dudley George lying on the ground, curled up in a ball, and hearing Dudley say that he'd been shot. "I froze," Stacey said. "I was standing beside him, looking at him, and I took a couple of steps back and sat down in the sand."

Another Native witness, Elwood George, described the same sense of disbelief as he heard about a dozen bangs. It was only after he'd heard that Dudley George had been shot that he realized those banging noises really were gunshots. His brother Stewart told the court that he'd asked for a stick as a weapon against police when he saw Slippery George beaten. "That's when all of us went out there because he was just one man and there were thirty to forty of them."

Kevin Simon was one of several Native witnesses who gripped an eagle feather for strength as he talked of how he thought he too might have died that night. "I thought everybody was getting shot," Simon said in a quiet voice, with no hint of bravado.

Officers weren't just shooting at the bus, but also at a group of Natives walking behind it, Simon said. "They [police snipers] weren't pointing at the bus. They were pointing at that group of people."

"I was kind of surprised he [Dudley George] was the only one [hit]. I thought I was going to get shot myself."

Simon had a faraway look in his eyes as he described seeing Dudley George, lying in the sand and clutching his chest. "He didn't look so good. His eyes weren't focusing. I shook his hand. I said he did a good job."

Simon told the court that he'd sometimes stayed at Dudley George's trailer on the military base, and that Dudley had never owned a gun and didn't have one with him that night either. None of the Natives had guns that night, Simon said.

Simon testified that as Dudley George lay on the sand, his grip was weak. Dudley tried to say something, but could manage no words.

Scott asked if he'd seen anything in Dudley George's hands.

"They were just bloody," Simon replied.

THERE ARE PLENTY of courtroom experts-for-hire who make thousands of dollars a day, saying pretty much whatever the lawyer paying the tab wants to hear, but Dr. Michael Shkrum of London, Ontario, a staff physician at Victoria Hospital and expert in pathology who had lectured at the Ontario Police College, was clearly not a medical mercenary. It was the Crown's contention that none of the Natives, including Dudley George, were armed that night, and Ian Scott called on Dr. Shkrum to give his exhaustive findings from the autopsy of Dudley George.

Dr. Shkrum was rigid, cautious, and professional, staying within the bounds of what he knew to be true, as he told the court that no gunshot residue was found on Dudley's hands, obviously suggesting that he had not fired a weapon. As he spoke, he thumbed through colour photographs of Dudley George's body, lying in a white body bag.

"The bullet would have come from above," Shkrum said. He held the bullet, now in two fragments, in its small vial, and George's family members and Deane stared at it as well, as if the pieces of damaged metal might explain something. The bullet had been recovered from a back muscle behind a rib on the left side. "It resulted in considerable blood loss, which would have caused shock. Basically, the heart would not have had enough blood to pump." That led to organs failing, the brain failing, and, soon afterwards, Dudley's death.

From the angle of the bullet, the deceased was bent over at about a forty-five-degree angle and twisted to his right when he was shot, the doctor concluded. "I have no idea what he was doing with his hands." There was also a curious scraping of his mid-right leg, which could have been from a grazing bullet wound. Before Dudley George collapsed from shock, he would have been able to walk for several minutes.

Dudley George's family members looked particularly sombre as the doctor conceded to Peel that his bent position could have been consistent with his holding a gun. Peel suggested that handling some guns does not leave a powder residue, but the doctor demurred, saying, "I think I'm getting out of my area of expertise."

And that was it for the Crown case. There had been some deeply moving testimony. Obviously, something had gone horribly wrong. It seemed a miracle that more Native people hadn't been killed by police gunfire that night. But did the five days of testimony by prosecution witnesses prove beyond a reasonable doubt that Acting Sergeant Kenneth Deane had knowingly shot an unarmed man that night? Was the testimony enough to convict a police officer? Was it enough to send him to prison for the rest of his life? Ian Scott and Crown witnesses had all presented a strong case, but it still seemed that, once the defence wound up its case, Deane would be walking free.

DEFENCE LAWYER NORMAN PEEL wanted to send the message that his client was a straight-ahead, no-nonsense guy who wanted to get on with things, and so he made Acting Sergeant Ken Deane his first witness. Deane wasn't required to testify at all, since all Canadians are presumed innocent until proven otherwise beyond a reasonable doubt. However, by standing before the court, Deane showed he was not afraid to face the charge before him.

He wore a navy blue suit, white shirt, and steel blue tie, making him look businesslike, if a little cold. Deane's voice betrayed no emotion as Peel began walking him through childhood memories. It was quickly clear that Deane liked cop-talk, and Peel seemed happy too, as they talked about "sierra observation units" and "alpha squads" and the CMU and the TRU and the need to make "discerning observations about . . . objects." They drew diagrams of where Deane was at various phases of the operation. It sounded more like engineering than the dissection of a fatal shooting, and the sound of the cop-talk made Deane seem more comfortable and it had the effect of making him appear cool that night in September.

"Did you hear any racial slurs being called by any Crowd Management Unit people?" Peel asked.

"No, I did not."

Deane said he saw flashes of light from the barrel of a fired weapon coming from the bus that was being driven at the OPP officers. "It was an attempt to shoot a police officer," he told the court. However, he didn't open fire upon it because he didn't want to hit the officers who were in the way. "I saw a distinct muzzle flash originate from the interior of the bus."

Deane said he looked back toward the park and saw two "threatening" muzzle flashes aimed at police from a sandy area outside the park. "As soon as I saw the muzzle flashes, I discharged approximately four rounds from my carbine."

He didn't say anything about taking a good aim, and it seemed hard to believe he could have, since his German-engineered submachinegun was deadly accurate and yet he apparently hadn't hit anyone or anything with his first four shots. The lights he'd fired at could only have been shots from a gun and not camera flashes or lights or cigarettes or anything else, he said, noting that he has taken night training classes. Deane confidently told the court that he knew what it was like to be fired upon and he knew what a muzzle flash looked like. "I know they were muzzle flashes. . . . The two flashes from this area were threatening fire."

Shortly after his first volley of gunshots, Deane said that a car came out of the park and hit three or four riot squad members. At the same time, someone left the area where he'd first seen the flashes and moved across the road. That person then came into the middle of the intersection near the retreating police officers and pointed a gun at them, Deane told the court.

"I observed him shoulder a rifle and in a half-crouched position, scanned [the rifle] over our position," Deane said, matter-of-factly. He said he fired three shots "as quick as I could."

"He immediately went down on one knee and immediately got back up," said Deane. Then the man on the road looked to his right and left and got up again, walked a few steps. It was at this time, Deane swore under oath, that the man did something quite odd for someone who was mortally wounded, with a broken collar bone, cracked ribs, and a punctured lung: the man threw his rifle into a grass-covered field, far away from Deane, leaving himself both unarmed and totally exposed to police fire.

There was no hint of wonder when Deane said this to court. His eyes did not shift. He just carried on with his testimony, explaining that electronic communication equipment allowed members of his paramilitary unit to talk with each other while maintaining separate positions. Superiors at a command post about half a kilometre away could also join in.

Under cross-examination, Deane told Crown Attorney Ian Scott that he didn't know the name of the person he had shot when he pulled the trigger. He said he didn't know his bullet had killed Dudley George until about two days later.

Deane said that all of his TRU team had gathered at the Bluewater Hotel in Grand Bend hours after the shooting, but that he'd been alone when he wrote his notes about the incident and he hadn't discussed them with fellow members. "The only person I spoke with from my unit about this incident would be my commander, Staff Sergeant Skinner."

The night of the shooting, there was a microphone directly in front of his mouth from his headset, but he didn't have time to use it, he told Scott.

"Is it possible you didn't get on your headset because there were not muzzle flashes?" Scott asked.

"No, it's not . . . I did not have time . . . The whole sequence took place in twenty–thirty–thirty-five seconds."

"You didn't think that was important?"

"I did think that was important. At the time, I did not have time to get on the com system."

Scott wasn't about to let the point rest. "Did you say, 'There's a rifle in the ditch which may be a threat to us, if a Native got a hold of it'?"

"No, I do not believe I said that."

"Wasn't it important to say that a man with a rifle was dropped by gunfire?"

"Yes, that is important," Deane replied. "I do not believe I said that. I cannot recall that."

Scott noted that there was no mention in Deane's notes of the shooting or muzzle flashes. "These notes make no mention of muzzle flashes. The notes make no mention that you shot a man."

Deane said he was too exhausted immediately after the fighting to write his notes.

"There wasn't a meeting of any kind before you wrote them?"

"No, there was not."

The question hung in the air for a few seconds, then Scott asked Deane if he truly believed the Natives were armed. Deane replied that the TRU team members had been briefed that night that the Native protestors were armed with AK-47s, hunting rifles with scopes, and Molotov cocktails.

Scott pressed Deane on how he could have taken that seriously, since the riot squad still marched on the park in plain view of the Natives in the park. Everyone who knew anything about weapons knew the AK-47 was a particularly fearsome weapon. It had been the standard rifle of the Soviet army for decades and was capable of blasting out 600 bullets per minute, each of which has a killing range of 1,500 metres or a metric mile. That meant there was enough firepower for one gunman to pump at least fifteen bullets into each police officer in the riot squad in just one minute. Clearly, that wasn't something anyone should take lightly, yet Deane made it sound as if they believed there was more than one AK-47 in the hands of the Native protestors. No one in his right mind would consider marching directly into such firepower.

Scott asked Deane again if he truly believed the Natives had such weapons.

"We had totally credible information," Deane replied, adding that the TRU team's assignment included backing up the Crowd Management officers if they were fired upon.

Clearly, Inspector Dale Linton and Superintendent Anthony Parkin hadn't considered these reports "totally credible" when they'd spoken on the phone early in the evening of the shooting. Back then, they'd complained about how such unsubstantiated rumours about AK-47s had somehow caught the ear of some powerful politicians at Queen's Park. Now Deane was describing those same reports as "totally credible."

Scott pressed on. "So if you got a line-up of officers with shields, batons and the [Natives have their] lights on, and someone in the dark is hiding with an AK-47, for all intents and purposes you're sending those CMU officers to their deaths?"

"No," Deane replied bluntly, declining to elaborate.

Scott did not let the point rest. Surely, the officers at the scene "did not take this information [about weapons] seriously, or they would never have permitted the Crowd Management Unit to walk into . . . the Canadian equivalent of the Charge of the Light Brigade. They would have been sitting ducks."

Then Scott shifted his focus and returned to the rifle Dudley had allegedly carried. Why hadn't Deane tried to recover the rifle allegedly thrown away by Dudley George? "Did you not have any concern that another aggressive Native might pick up that rifle and do what Dudley George did?"

"At the time I felt it prudent to make sure all our officers were accounted for," Deane replied.

Scott then had Deane mark on a map where he was that night. Deane showed where Dudley George had been at various points that evening, freezing in time key moments of the fateful night. When he stepped down from the witness stand, Deane was still showing no emotion whatsoever.

SERGEANT GEORGE HEBBLETHWAITE gave the impression of being honest and straightforward and definitely not someone you'd want to get on the wrong side of. He looked like the type of guy who drove a pickup truck with standard gearshift and who, if he drank, took his whisky straight up. Big and powerfully built, he looked like a cop's cop as he marched up to the front of the courtroom. Hebblethwaite was second-in-command for the Crowd Management Unit, behind Staff Sergeant Wade Lacroix, and he'd been front and centre with the unit as they'd marched on the park that night. He'd been right in the middle of the fighting.

The sergeant made no bones about the fact that he was one of the officers who'd kicked the black dog that had run out from among the Native people. It was a threat to the continuity of the unit, and he told the court unapologetically that he'd booted it in the rear, sending it yelping back toward the park. It didn't seem nice, but it made sense, as Hebblethwaite told it. He wasn't trying to present himself as a lovable guy, just someone who was going to tell the truth.

Aside from Deane, Hebblethwaite was the only testifying officer who could recall having seen Dudley George that night. "I saw this person holding an object which I perceived to be a pole or a stick and I saw this person turning or spinning in a clockwise fashion back toward the park, turning as he stood," Hebblethwaite said. "My first thought was this person has been shot. He went down hard on his right knee but he was up almost as quickly as he went down."

There were shocked looks in the courtroom now. Hadn't the blunt-talking sergeant just said that Dudley George was carrying a stick, not a gun? Hadn't Deane earlier described, in great detail, Dudley George's alleged gun? Clearly, both Deane and Hebblethwaite could not both be telling the truth.

On cross-examination, Sergeant Hebblethwaite testified that he had not seen any muzzle flashes apart from his own. Again, the defence witness who looked like the cop's cop had contradicted his fellow-officer Deane, who'd told the court that the police were under fire from gunshots from within the park and from the schoolbus that had left the park. Hebblethwaite had no choice here. If Dudley truly was armed and threatening police, Hebblethwaite would have been obliged to shoot him too. Hebblethwaite's gun was drawn but when he looked at Dudley George's hands, he didn't see a gun. He saw what appeared to be a stick.

IF HEBBLETHWAITE'S TESTIMONY did not entirely shore up the case of the defence, neither did that of Constable Chris Cossitt, one of the junior officers in the riot squad. Cossitt was the only police officer other than Ken Deane who'd said he'd actually seen a gun on the bus. Now, as Deane's trial began, Cossitt could now also recall having seen a Molotov cocktail fly past him and land on the sand nearby. Oddly, not one other police officer or any Native person could recall this, even though the Natives and the police were all packed together in a very small area. Cossitt went on to say that he'd been able to see the gasoline bomb very clearly in the night, in the heat of battle, and he'd even noticed that it contained a quarter to an inch of liquid and had a wick at one end. "It landed in the sand, sir," he told Scott.

Scott pounced on the testimony. He was clearly feasting on the witnesses served up to him by the defence. First it was Deane, saying that Dudley had somehow thrown his gun far away when he was shot, then Hebblethwaite, testifying that he hadn't seen Dudley George with a gun. Now a previously unidentified Molotov cocktail had appeared. In a tone that sounded alternately disgusted and mocking, Scott noted that there was nothing in Cossitt's original notes about any Molotov cocktail. "That's correct," Cossitt agreed. "I have an independent recollection of that, sir."

Scott noted that Cossitt also had not mentioned the Molotov cocktail almost hitting him when he later gave an interview on December 7, 1995, to Ed Wilson of the SIU. He also had not recalled this when testifying at the trial of Cecil Bernard "Slippery" George in July 1996.

"I'm going to suggest to you that there's no mention because you never saw anything like a Molotov cocktail being thrown at you," Scott said.

"I did, sir."

Scott bore down on him now, asking once more why he had never mentioned the bomb before.

"It's just an oversight on my part," Cossitt offered.

"It's a curious oversight, wouldn't you agree?"

"I guess so."

"Do you have a tendency to exaggerate?" Scott continued.

"No sir."

Scott moved on to test other parts of Cossitt's memory, and in particular, what he'd seen of the near-fatal beating of Slippery George.

Cossitt could recall swinging his steel baton, but he said he could not remember whether he'd hit anyone or anything. "I'm not certain if I did make contact," he said.

"Did you see other officers strike out and hit him?"

"No sir."

"Can you help us at all [to explain] why he was hospitalized after that incident?"

"I have no information on that."

Scott was now using the beating of Slippery George as a way to test an officer's credibility. Slippery George was pummelled in the middle of a cleared area where there were dozens of police officers, and yet virtually none of them said they could recall having hit him or having seen other officers hit him.

When Constable Kevin York took the stand, Scott also asked him what he recalled of the near-fatal beating.

"I did not see any of that," Constable York said.

"You can't help us at all, on how he got multiple injuries?"

"I have no idea."

CONSTABLE MARK BEAUCHESNE was the type of man people liked to believe. He had a B.A. in psychology from Carleton University, with a concentration in criminology. He was athletic as well, appearing to be someone expected to move high in police ranks. He had more than six years' experience with the TRU team, and painted a picture of Deane as a competent, professional, well-trained officer.

Beauchesne went back a long way with Ken Deane. They had been together in 1991, when they and others had earned commissioner's citations for their work at the tiny Grassy Narrows Reserve in northwestern Ontario near Kenora. At Grassy Narrows, OPP Sergeant Tom Cooper had been killed with a blast in the face from a .22 rifle and Constable Kevin Orchard had been shot in the shoulder. In the investigation that followed, four other officers collecting evidence had been fired upon, and yet another, Constable Bill Olinyk, had been shot in the hip. After a three-day search through thick bush and swamp, Constable Beauchesne's team had found the suspect — hungry and barefoot — under a clump of bushes. It was, by any standard, an impressive piece of police work. Deane's defence attorney, Norman Peel, made sure that Mr. Justice Hugh Fraser heard clearly that the suspect — who wasn't harmed even though he was suspected in the murder and wounding of police officers — was Aboriginal.

The night Dudley George was shot dead, Beauchesne was part of Deane's four-man sniper team. He was carrying a microphone and headset, as well as night-vision equipment. His mission was to provide an advance eye and cover for the CMU unit against any potential threat from firearms or incendiary devices. Beauchesne told Peel that each of the paramilitary officers, like himself, had a microphone and headset exclusive to himself, so that all the officers could talk freely to each other. Staff Sergeant Kent Skinner at the command post in the St. John Ambulance van up the road was able to listen in on their conversations. The conversations of the TRU team were also supposed to be recorded.

Beauchesne told the court that he scanned with his night-vision goggles and saw two men, one of whom appeared to have a gun. The two men squatted and kept looking in his direction. The marching police of the Crowd Management Unit split and took sides of the road, while Beauchesne moved twenty to thirty metres down the road. There, he could see the object in the man's hands was not a firearm, and the CMU marched past without a shot being fired.

As the riot squad rounded a bend in the road and entered the parking lot in front of the park, Beauchesne moved to a grassy dune, which made a good observation point. While Natives and police fought toe-to-toe below him, Beauchesne kept looking for Native people with guns. He was looking carefully at what the protestors were carrying, assessing them person by person.

He thought of shooting at the bus driver as officers scrambled for safety, then decided it was too late to stop it anyway. Then came the car, which hit several CMU officers. He fired at it twice, then heard other shots. When the car and bus no longer appeared to be threats, Beauchesne started looking around again for any Natives with guns.

He hopped the fence and asked Acting Sergeant Deane if anyone needed help on that side of the road. At this point, he said Deane asked him, "Did you see the guy with the gun?"

It wasn't an appropriate time to call in a description of what had just happened, he said. "We were still in the middle of it. . . . It wasn't the time to get on the radio and start debriefing."

On cross-examination, Ian Scott asked Constable Beauchesne what he would have done if the object in the person's hands had turned out to be a gun.

"I would have assessed what he . . . [was] doing as to whether he could actually see us," Beauchesne replied. "This is in the dark. I have night vision. We are deployed invisibly. He can't, he shouldn't really be able to see us."

". . . All right, so if you were, let me get this straight then, if you continue to be invisible, to use your word, and if the CMU was out of the line of fire, then what would you have done if you saw this person scanning [with] what you thought was a rifle?"

"I would be assessing as to whether he could actually see us. We have been in circumstances before where people have fired shots at random. If you can determine that they are not being directed at an individual, therefore they're not, you feel comfortable enough that they're not an immediate threat to yourself or another officer or another person, I would not be shooting."

"So . . . shooting, even at an individual who is posing a fairly imminent threat, is the option of last resort, is that fair?" Scott continued.

"Yes, any time you would shoot somebody would be an option of last resort."

"So when you pull that trigger it's not an attempt to disarm," Scott said. "It's an attempt to disable the individual and if he is mortally wounded in the process that is just a consequence of that action at that time, correct?"

"Yeah," Beauchesne said. "Regrettably you want to stop him as soon as possible."

Beauchesne continued that he never saw a firearm in the hand of any Native that evening. Unlike Cossitt, he also didn't claim to have seen any Molotov cocktails, despite his fine vantage point.

Now Scott wanted to know about his conversation with Deane after the bus and car had retreated back into the park: ". . . tell us exactly what he said to you?"

"We exchanged some information and one of the things he said was, 'Did you see the guy with the gun?'"

"What did he say next?"

"I don't recall in terms of — that was one of the parts of the conversation," Beauchesne said. "We were trying to form the team up, confirm that the Sierra teams were there. That was exchanged. Do we have our people? Was there anybody hurt?"

"Let me get this straight. He says to you, 'Did you see the guy with the gun?' Then you say, 'No,' and then you moved on to do a head count. Is that right?"

". . . That may have been the first information shared or . . . the last information shared or in the middle. I really couldn't tell you."

"Well, all right," Scott said. "Let's go back. I want to hear everything he said to you about the guy with the gun. Have you told us everything that he said to you at that point about the guy with the gun?"

"As far as I can remember that's basically what he said to me about the guy with the gun. That's it."

Scott's head snapped back a little, as if he couldn't quite believe what he had just heard.

"Let me get this straight, sir. Your job was to look for people with guns, right?"

"Yes, sir."

"Sergeant Deane, from your perspective, is a reliable source, correct?"

"Yes."

"He says to you, 'Did you see the guy with the gun?' You're telling that today under oath, right?"

"Yes."

"You say 'No' cause you never saw a guy with a gun, right?"

"That's right."

"In your head, in your mind when he said to you, 'Did you see the guy with the gun?' did you think that he saw a guy with a gun?"

"Yes."

"Well, tell this court why you didn't follow up on this?"

"We were in the process of getting everybody together, organizing the team and covering withdrawal. He put it to me in the past tense. It wasn't an immediate threat at that time. It was him sharing information with me."

"Well, how did you know it wasn't an immediate threat?"

"Because . . . his behaviour would have been much different, I imagine, if it was an immediate threat. He was speaking in the past tense. There was no point to say, 'There's a guy with a gun.' This was, 'Did you see a guy with the gun?'"

"Did you ask him, 'Is the guy you saw with the gun out on the roadway?'"

"No."

"Did you ask him, 'Did the guy with the gun, might he shoot me?' Did you ask him that?"

"No."

Scott reminded Beauchesne that he was under oath, but Beauchesne didn't appear at all rattled. Scott regrouped, then pressed ahead with the same line of questioning, saying, "So let me get this straight. In your view, Natives with guns were armed aggressors, correct?"

Beauchesne agreed.

"A Native with a gun would be considered a high threat, yes? . . . To you personally, correct?" Scott continued.

"To anybody out there. To certainly all the police officers out there."

"And you made absolutely and utterly no follow-up inquiries with respect to that question asked of you by Sergeant Deane. Is that correct?"

"That is correct."

The frustration rose even higher in Scott's voice. "All right," Scott continued. ". . . Did you ask Sergeant Deane, 'Well did the guy with the gun shoot anybody?'"

"No, sir, I didn't ask that."

"Did you ask Sergeant Deane if he shot the guy with the gun?"

"No sir."

"Why didn't you ask him that?"

"Because we weren't debriefing the occurrence at that time."

". . . You're in the middle of this operation still. Isn't that right?"

"That's right."

"Wouldn't it have been of interest to you to find out whether or not this armed aggressor had been shot by Sergeant Deane?"

"It would be nice to know. I'm making assumptions during this exchange that the way he put the statement to me, it was in the past tense. I did not take his actions as indicative of an immediate threat and since we were in the process of withdrawing, I also made the assumption that the man with the gun would have been down towards the park, so my area of threat or concern would obviously be in that direction."

If this had been a boxing match, Scott would have been throwing hard leather with both hands now, doing serious damage but still not quite able to connect with Beauchesne's chin. If he was going to win, it would have to be on points, not by a knockout.

"But you don't know any of this, sir," Scott continued. "You never asked Sergeant Deane where this man with the gun went, right?"

"No, I didn't."

"And for all you know he was just around the corner, or just behind a tree, with a gun trained out on the roadway, right?"

"The way it was said to me led me to believe that it wasn't an immediate threat. If there was any indication that he was in our midst or off to the side, then, yes, I would have had a concern."

"Well, one [way] you could have found out whether or not it was an immediate threat was to ask Sergeant Deane if he shot the guy with the gun, isn't that right?"

"That's right."

"But you didn't do that, did you?"

"No, I didn't."

Scott took a deep breath, then bore down yet again. He noted that the TRU officers had been together when they'd turned in their weapons less than three hours after the shooting. Three of the officers in the Tactics and Rescue Unit led by Staff Sergeant Kent Skinner — Deane, Constable Bill Klym, and Beauchesne — had arrived in the same car at their hotel in Grand Bend after the shooting. They'd waited there, in the same room, before going, one by one, to see their lawyer, Norman Peel. When this was done, they went in the same car back to the Pinery Provincial Park. Clearly, they'd had plenty of time together to talk. Obviously, they must all have been thinking about the shooting.

"You wrote your notes after the meeting with Peel and after spending a significant time with other TRU officers?"

"Yes, sir."

Scott wanted to know why he'd waited so long before committing anything to paper.

"I was waiting until I was well rested. We were up all day and all night before . . . And then I made up my notes at the earliest convenience after that."

Scott wasn't about to let the point rest. He asked Beauchesne if there had been discussion among the three officers about "bits and pieces" of what had just happened in the command post when they turned in their guns and in the hotel and the car.

"Perhaps," Beauchesne replied.

Scott wanted him to explain just how he perceived the threat to the Crowd Management Unit. Couldn't they have been mowed down if there were Natives waiting for them with heavy carbines? It wouldn't have been a battle. It would have been mass slaughter.

"That would be a major concern," Beauchesne replied.

Wouldn't the officers have been killed if the Natives truly had guns? Scott asked.

"That would be a major concern," Beauchesne repeated.

So why, then, did he permit the march to go on? Why didn't he at least say something?

"The way we were briefed, I thought we were taking the necessary measures."

Later, Beauchesne added that he'd had trouble with his microphone that night. He then told of watching the Natives, looking for guns. "I used the flashlight a few times. I don't think I used the night vision at all." They were intermittent flashes from his light, he said. "Sometimes to illuminate them — to make them feel they were monitored . . ."

Scott asked Beauchesne if he saw no guns in the park that night.

"Yes."

"Your job is to look for guns?"

"Yes . . ."

"You're trained to look for guns?"

"I'm trained in observation, yes."

"You never saw a firearm in the hands of Natives?"

"Yes."

Scott repeated that Beauchesne was on an elevated area, looking out for weapons.

"On the point of Molotov cocktails, did you ever see any?"

"No."

Like the others, he also swore he hadn't seen the beating of Slippery George.

"Did you see him kicked on the ground?"

"No."

"Did you see him hit with batons on the ground?"

"No."

Asked why, Beauchesne replied, "I'm looking for the threats — the firearms."

"Do you recall any communication over the headset about a rifle being thrown . . . ?"

"No."

A little later, he was asked yet again about whether he'd observed any Natives with guns.

"The first weapon I heard fired was my own."

Scott again pressed him about why he hadn't pursued Deane's alleged comment about seeing a man with a gun.

"Did you think that he saw a guy with a gun?"

"Yes."

"Tell the court why you didn't follow up on this."

". . . He put it to me in the past tense. It wasn't an immediate threat."

Scott clung to the point like a hungry dog with a bone.

"Did you ask him, 'When did you see a guy with the gun?'"

"No."

"Sir, you're under oath right now. I'm going to suggest that you're lying."

The gloves were off. Any pretence of politeness was long gone. Beauchesne stayed cool, but Defence Attorney Peel was immediately on his feet to protect his witness.

Scott wasn't fazed, asking if, anywhere in Beauchesne's notes, there was any mention of Deane's alleged comment, "Did you see the guy with the gun?"

"No."

Moments later Scott asked, "Did you put in your notes anywhere that Sergeant Deane might have seen somebody with a gun?"

"No."

"Well, sir, your whole *raison d'être* for being there is to look for somebody with a gun, is that right?"

"Yes, sir."

"You receive reliable information that somebody is out there with a gun, right?"

"Yes."

"And you don't do anything with it?"

". . . The information was already out there that there was a concern about firearms. Obviously Sergeant Deane was confirming that he had seen somebody with a firearm."

"Right," Scott said.

"It did not change the way we were going to be behaving or responding from that point. We were in the process of withdrawing."

"Okay, you're standing in the roadway with Sergeant Deane at the time he tells you this, right?"

"Yes."

"And there's what, thirty, forty CMU members behind you?"

"Yes."

"And if there was someone with a gun, and did you even ask him, do you think it was a submachinegun or just a single shot rifle? Did you ask him that?"

"No, sir."

"Okay, so you didn't ask him where this person was who you say had the gun, right? So you didn't know where he was, correct?"

"No."

"You didn't ask him when he saw the person with the gun, so it might have been less than five seconds before he made the statement, correct?"

"His demeanour," Beauchesne said. "This was an exchange of information. I trust that in this exchange that if it was a threat, or an immediate threat then his demeanour would have been different and his way of relating information would have been different."

Scott was all over Beauchesne again now. He said he simply couldn't believe that Beauchesne asked no follow-up questions, if Deane in fact did tell him that he saw a man with a gun.

"Sir, I'm going to suggest to you that you're not telling the truth right now under oath."

The attack was withering but Beauchesne didn't flinch. Now Scott was suggesting collusion. "Have you ever talked to Sergeant Deane about the evidence you're going to say today?"

"No sir."

Scott repeated that there was no statement in Beauchesne's notes about Deane saying anything about seeing a man with a gun. What sense did it make to leave this out?

Beauchesne said that they had discussed the incident, but that they had not discussed his evidence. "Nor am I lying under oath," he added, still keeping his cool.

In his re-examination, Peel tried to salve the wounds a little. It was a time for wounded dignity, although Peel seemed more upset than Beauchesne.

"Sir, have you ever had the insult in advocacy of ever being called a liar before?"

"No sir."

With that, Beauchesne stepped down from the witness stand, still looking cool.

Fraser intently followed the drama, as the mood in his courtroom was now decidedly ugly. The only expression on the judge's face was one of concern.

THE NEXT DEFENCE WITNESS was Staff Sergeant Kent Skinner, who had been the leader of the paramilitary TRU team that night. With an elaborately waxed and curled moustache, the lanky officer looked a bit like a television cowboy.

The night of the shooting, Skinner was in the mobile command post down the road from the shooting. He made it sound as though police weren't too worried about the report that the Native protestors had hunting rifles, AK-47 Russian assault rifles, and Molotov cocktails. His team could handle the risk, he said with a shrug.

Deane was Skinner's second-in-command that night, and would have been beside him in the mobile command post, operating a tape recorder, if not for a strange twist of fate: another officer had injured his back, so Deane was called upon to replace him and walk into the darkness shouldering a rifle, instead of recording the night's operations.

The officer with the bad back who was supposed to have been managing the tape recording had also had a bad time that night, the court heard. Skinner said there should have been a complete audio recording of everything that all the officers — including Deane — had said that night.

"I believed it to be recording at this time," Skinner said.

Skinner's comments about the tape recorder recalled the Bastien case, when faulty radios were blamed in part for the fatal police shooting of the autoworker. That time, the radio faults were cited as a factor in the actual killing; this time, the audio equipment malfunction was offered as the reason why the court would never hear Deane's exact recorded words the night he shot Dudley George dead. The court would have to accept the word of the testifying witnesses.

Skinner's answers were short. He told the court that, when Deane had returned to the command post shortly after the shooting, "he told me that he had discharged his weapon at an armed individual and that he had seen that person fall down." Then Skinner added, "His first reaction was that he wanted to go forward to assist but he couldn't because of the situation."

Norman Peel then posed this question: "During the time . . . the unit [was] assembling and looking for injured people . . . would you expect him [Deane] to go on the channel and start to advise you of the history of what happened?"

"No sir."

"Why?"

"He has other duties at that time, sir, to ensure the security of his fellow officers and the CMU members."

On cross-examination, Scott once again zeroed in on officers' notes. Skinner testified that he had completed his on September 7, less than a day after the shooting. Some of the notes had been written as he was waiting for Peel at the Bluewater Hotel in Grand Bend.

The night of the shooting, Skinner said that he was in the cube van that was used as the mobile command post, monitoring the CMU and TRU radios, while Constable Rick Zupancic was in the back, making notes about radio communications. Up front on the passenger side was Acting Superintendent John Carson.

Skinner said that Carson wasn't present when Deane had told him about the shooting, and that Skinner had independently relayed this to Carson.

"What did you tell Inspector Carson?"

"I may or may not have told him that Ken Deane had hit an individual."

Scott pressed Skinner. Did he tell Carson that Deane had shot an *armed* individual?

Skinner said he couldn't be sure.

"Isn't that pretty important?"

"Yes sir."

"But you didn't do it?"

"I'm telling you that I don't recall."

Before the march on the park began, Skinner went on to testify, he'd briefed the TRU team and told them that the Natives might have heavy-duty military machineguns, but for some reason, the message hadn't been passed on to the Crowd Management Unit. As Skinner told it, this wasn't a particularly big deal.

"None of that caused you sufficient concern that you suggested the mission be aborted?"

"That's correct."

Scott's question hung in the air, begging for a fuller answer.

Scott returned to the fact that there was no record of Deane telling Beauchesne that he'd seen a man with a gun.

"I was relying on the tape recorder," Skinner said.

Scott pushed for details, and Skinner continued, "The recorder was not in the record position. . . . [There were] two buttons, play and record . . . He [Zupancic] clicked one and not both."

That was clearly human error, as Skinner told it. However, Scott noted that in June 1996, Skinner had told another officer that there had been electrical problems with the tape recorder.

"Was it a mechanical problem or a human problem?" Scott asked.

Actually, Skinner replied, it was a combination of both. He seemed almost to welcome the question, saying that the engine had failed in the truck and that this had affected the taping system.

"It's just not on tape?"

"Correct."

Why didn't Skinner put these recording problems in his notes? Scott wondered.

"I recalled the tape not working without needing my notes, sir," he replied, hitting the word "sir" particularly hard.

Regarding his face-to-face conversation with Deane, which would not have been tape recorded, Skinner said, "He told me that he shot an armed person."

"But you didn't put it in your notes."

"No sir."

Scott wasn't as blunt as he'd been with Beauchesne, but he drove home the same argument. "Sir, I'm going to suggest to you if he had told you he had shot an armed Native, this would have been the talk of the town. . . . That you would have run to Inspector Carson and told him that we had a huge problem here."

Now Skinner added another twist. He said that Deane had said that he'd shot *at* an armed person, but that the person might not actually have been hit. "I don't think I said 'struck,' sir. I'm saying that he shot *at* an armed man. . . . Ken said he went down and got up . . ." Scott saw a huge opening here. The answer sounded absurd.

"Staff-Sergeant Skinner," said Scott, "there's obviously a relationship between firing and falling. . . . Are you suggesting that Sergeant Deane fired and Dudley George had a heart attack?"

"He didn't know for sure if he hit him," Skinner replied, not directly answering the question.

Scott now shifted his focus slightly, asking Skinner if he'd asked Deane whether the gun Dudley George had supposedly carried was still in the field.

"I didn't ask him that."

"You don't recall him saying to you, 'He threw the rifle in the ditch?'"

"No."

A few moments later, Scott asked, "You never told Inspector Carson anything about Deane shooting an armed Native?"

"My recollection is I did, sir."

Scott noted that this was not mentioned in Skinner's notes or in a duty report Skinner had filed on the incident, and that Carson had also indicated that he had not been told. There should have been plenty of records of this and yet, somehow, there was not a mention before now of such a critical comment.

Mr. Justice Hugh Fraser interrupted with a few questions of his own. The judge wanted to know about Constable Rick Zupancic and note-taking. Skinner said that he believed Zupancic had been making a written record of conversations that night.

Then Scott was again the one asking the questions, this time about Staff Sergeant Skinner's meeting with Deane at the mobile command post, after the shooting had stopped.

"What do you recall him telling you?"

"Sergeant Deane told me . . . he had discharged his weapon at an armed individual. That he saw that person fall down. His first reaction, he told me, was to want to go forward to assist but realized he could not because of the situation. He told me that person was then carried back in the park."

Pressed further by Scott, Skinner testified that he had no recollection of Deane saying anything over the communication system about seeing muzzle flashes. He also made no notes of any reference to muzzle flashes. Again, Skinner testified that he recalled being told by Deane that he had shot an armed person. Again, he agreed that he had not included that point in his notes.

"Tell me, Sergeant," Scott said. "Tell me when Sergeant Deane told you about shooting this armed individual. Did you ask him about the rifle of the armed individual?"

"No."

"Did you ask Sergeant Deane if the rifle was still out in the . . . theatre of operation, is that the correct term?"

"It serves its purpose but, no, I didn't ask him that."

"Okay, well, did that cause you any concern that . . . [it] could be out there in the hands of Natives who could use it?"

"I was already aware that there were weapons in the hands of Natives because there had been an exchange of gunfire."

"Did Sergeant Deane tell you what the Native that he shot at did with the rifle?"

"Not that I recall, no."

"You don't recall him saying to you he threw the rifle in the ditch?"

"No, I don't."

And that was it for Staff Sergeant Skinner, as the defence case sunk yet another notch.

AT THIS POINT, the judge announced that he was going to take a break from the courtroom and take a silent walk-through of the site where the shooting had occurred.

Defence Attorney Norman Peel didn't seem overjoyed by the judge's decision, but all he could do was comment: "The defence has the utmost respect and trust the court will be cognizant of the differences. We go by day. They went by night." He also noted that there would have been leaves on the trees then, but not now, and that the road line was slightly different. But, Peel allowed, "The fundamental landmarks haven't changed."

Throughout the testimony, Judge Fraser had carefully charted where Deane and Beauchesne and Hebblethwaite and others had said they'd been at key times that night. As he walked alone around the sandy parking lot at Ipperwash Provincial Park, the judge occasionally glanced at the maps.

The breeze was gentle and the large trees swayed quietly. The peace of that beautiful sunny spring day was so much at odds with the violence that Judge Fraser was trying to mentally reconstruct.

Now a pine bough shrine had been built to Dudley, but it seemed more restful than sad, blending in with the trees. The whole area where the violent confrontations had taken place appeared tiny and restful, small enough that a child could throw a stone across it.

The Stoney Pointers seemed happy with the judge's visit. "I think it's good," said Leyton Elijah, who was in charge of security for the Stoney Pointers. "The people here like it because he's going to . . . see how close Deane was to Dudley."

Glen Bannon, police chief of the Anishinabek Police Service, also said he was pleased, saying, "Our traditional teachings teach us the truth never changes."

10

JUDGEMENT DAY

"My father told him that this was our land."
— SAM GEORGE SPEAKS OF HIS BROTHER DUDLEY'S TIE TO STONEY POINT

When the trial returned to the courtroom, it was time to hear from Dr. Werner Spitz, a seventy-one-year-old professor from Wayne State University in Michigan. He had assisted with the 1970s House of Representatives investigations into the assassinations of President John F. Kennedy and civil rights leader Martin Luther King, Jr., and more recently, he had appeared as an expert witness in the Goldman family lawsuit against O.J. Simpson.

This was a man who knew death. He had performed between fifty-five thousand and sixty thousand autopsies, which perhaps explained his extremely confident manner and his flat, lifeless voice. In a grumbling, Germanic accent, Spitz told the court in tedious detail that it was very remotely possible for a person to have no gunpowder on their hands after firing a long rifle. The absence of gunpowder residue did not necessarily lead to the conclusion that a person had not handled a rifle.

"He could have handled it and he could not have handled it," Spitz said, somehow making something so dramatic as a gunfight sound deadly dull.

Peel took a wooden pointer, held it like a gun, and contorted himself into an odd firing position. Then he asked the doctor if Dudley George could have been standing in a position like that when he was hit.

"Absolutely," the doctor said.

The mark on Dudley's leg could have been a grazing wound from a bullet, the death expert added, noting that bullet wounds aren't always painful, even when they're fatal. "The bullet goes through the skin so fast that the so-called pain is so short that before you realize it, it's terminated, because only the skin has pain receptors."

That offered a temporary relief to Dudley George's family — the thought that somehow Dudley hadn't been in extreme physical pain when he died. Then the doctor pressed on, noting that the bullet that killed Dudley George had also shattered his collar bone, which can be extremely painful. This didn't make it physically impossible for Dudley to move his arm, however, since "the muscles moving the shoulder have not been disrupted." He was also mobile, the doctor said. Someone shot like this could possibly move one hundred feet after being shot.

Things livened up considerably during the cross-examination. Expert witnesses such as the doctor are paid thousands of dollars to appear in court, and Scott wanted to make it clear who was footing the bill for this appearance — the Ken Deane defence team.

Scott asked Dr. Spitz if he considered his gunshot residue conclusions completely neutral.

"I was asked a number of questions and I gave a number of answers," the doctor replied flatly. "Why don't you ask me a question and I'll give you an answer?"

Scott obliged, asking, "If he did not have a firearm in his hands, he would not have gunpowder residue on his hands? Is that fair?"

"Yes."

Scott asked the doctor about a report he'd made on the shooting, after seeing the post mortem and X-rays.

The doctor admitted that, when he'd prepared the report, he had not seen the colour photos of Dudley George's wounds. "I think I did not. That's correct."

Scott pressed the doctor about the scenario that suggested Dudley had been shot in the back of the leg first, then twisted around and put his hand on the wound before being struck by the fatal shot.

"It might and it might not" have happened that way, the doctor replied. "You might want to bend over to see why you are being irritated, yes. You might and you might not."

Scott asked him how Dudley was standing the instant he was shot dead, in the doctor's opinion.

The doctor adopted an ungainly and obviously uncomfortable twisting squat. "You'll have to hurry up," the doctor said. "I can't hold this position."

For one of the few times in the trial, the judge smiled briefly as the doctor contorted himself. Then, in an act of mercy, Scott enlisted Susan Peel, the wife of Norman Peel and Peel's courtroom helper, to take over from Spitz in demonstrating the position Dudley might have been in, the instant he was shot.

The testimony wound up as the doctor said there was no way to forensically determine whether or not Dudley George had been holding a firearm. "I really couldn't tell . . . No, I cannot tell you what he was doing with his hands."

The judge asked the doctor if Dudley George could have fired a gun.

"Yes, he could. Not for a tremendous length of time, but he certainly could for some time."

With that, the doctor was free of the witness stand. It had been an odd spectacle, with entertaining moments, but exactly what he'd said was up for debate. It seemed that he had just testified that either the scenario suggested by the prosecution or the one put forward by the defence was possible. That was his expert opinion.

CONSTABLE RICK ZUPANCIC had had a chiropractor's appointment for his aching back on September 6, 1995, the day Dudley was shot dead. Instead of getting medical treatment, however, he was recalled to his team and given the job of monitoring radios for the Ipperwash operation.

Interestingly, he was rushed back to rejoin the TRU squad *before* the stone-throwing incident which police had used as a reason for the march down onto the park.

Zupancic told Peel that idling problems with the command post cube van meant that the recording device had to be restarted every time the van was started up again. "I believed it was being recorded," he said. However, he said, he later learned that this was not so. "I failed to activate the record portion of it. . . . It appeared to be working properly. The tape was going around. The counter was countering. I believed that it was working."

Scott was curious. "Does it have a light on when it's recording?" Scott asked.

"Yes, it does."

"Did it go on and deceive you?"

The officer said that a green light went on. "There is nothing on the tape of the incident."

After the operation, that tape from the cube van went into his locker at the TRU team headquarters in London, Ontario, he said.

Scott asked if that locker was locked and the officer said that it wasn't.

"So it has been in an unlocked locker for about a year and a half?"

"Yes."

Constable Zupancic's notes weren't much help, providing only what the officer called a "general overview." That overview said simply, "Report of police being fired upon and returning fire."

"Did you ever hear Sergeant Deane say anything about seeing muzzle flashes?"

"I don't recall."

"Did you hear Sergeant Deane say anything about seeing a Native with a longarm?"

"No . . ."

"Did you hear him say anything about shooting a Native?"

"No."

ACTING SUPERINTENDENT JOHN CARSON told Scott that he also didn't recall Deane saying anything about muzzle flashes. Although he had a steno pad beside him that night, he said there was also no record in it of Deane referring to muzzle flashes.

He said his notes for 23:09 the night of September 6, 1995, were, "Native shot. Ran into park." He said he thought he heard something about muzzle flashes, but he wasn't sure whose voice it was. "There was so much going on. . . . Those words could have been said and I may not have heard them."

"You don't recall and you don't have a note?" Scott continued.

"That's right."

Moments later, the defence team rested its case.

SEVERAL NOTEWORTHY THINGS *did not* happen in the defence case. Peel didn't call upon Deane's partner that night, Constable Kieran O'Halloran. If anyone could back up Deane's testimony, wouldn't it be his partner, who was standing close to him? However, there was no report anywhere in the statement O'Halloran made to investigators immediately after the shooting about seeing Natives with guns or about gunfire from the Native ranks that night. O'Halloran also did not report that Deane said anything about seeing a Native with a gun. Wasn't that something you'd tell a partner?

Defence Attorney Peel also did not call upon Constable Bill Klym, the fourth man in the TRU "four-man immediate action plan team." In his September 8, 1995, interview with the OPP and the civilian Special Investigations Unit, Klym said nothing of having seen any Natives with guns. Like O'Halloran, he also made no mention of Deane having said anything that night about seeing a Native with a gun.

All that was left now was for Mr. Justice Hugh Fraser to deliver his verdict. He told the court that this would come in ten days. Then he quickly gathered together his papers and returned to his life in Ottawa.

THE DAY THE DECISION was to be given, on April 28, 1997, the George family's lawyers held a press conference in a hotel across the road from the courthouse. There they told reporters that no one should be surprised to hear the words "Not guilty" from the judge's lips. It wasn't enough for the judge to determine that Dudley George had been unarmed. The judge had to conclude that, beyond a reasonable doubt, he was confident that Deane had *knowingly* shot an unarmed man. All it would take for Deane to walk free was for the judge to conclude that Deane had a mistaken but honest split-second *belief* that Dudley George had been armed. It was a gloomy message for the George family legal team of Murray Klippenstein, Andrew Orkin, and Delia Opekokew to deliver, but the last thing they wanted was Deane's acquittal — if that was the verdict — to be taken as an overall vindication of the police operation that night. So they prepared for defeat, and then hoped, against hope, for victory.

There are judges who clearly like to entertain and who clearly relish the cut-and-thrust of the courtroom and the attention they receive in a high-stakes legal battle. From their raised bench, they literally sit above the debate, interrupting whenever they feel the urge, and then they have the final say. People hang on their every word and chuckle at their every quip, even the not-so-witty ones. Mr. Justice Hugh Fraser was not one of those judges. He had the deadly serious air of a man doing a dirty but necessary task when he ordered the courtroom locked shut, so that he could pronounce his verdict.

"Let me just say at the outset that it is going to take me a few minutes to give the reasons for my decision and I want to make it clear that should there be any unnecessary disturbance or disruption while I am doing this, I will ask that the individuals be removed as soon as possible," Judge Fraser said. His voice was still soft but he clearly meant business. One sensed that he was not a man who shouted when he was angry.

Things were far more polite now than during Deane's first court appearance, eight months earlier, when police scrambled in and took all the seats, leaving the George family and the press standing outside the courthouse, listening to pro-police demonstrators shout into megaphones. Now, in the bigger courtroom, special accommodation had been made for both Thomas O'Grady, OPP commissioner, and Ovide Mercredi, grand chief of the Assembly of First Nations. The prime spot in the courtroom was front and centre in the middle aisle, and that is where both leaders had been placed, so neither would be offended. They shared the front middle spot, sitting shoulder-to-shoulder in icy silence.

Verdict day was clearly a police get-together as officers from across the province renewed acquaintance. Smiles and nods were exchanged, and there was a visible sense of camaraderie, and the feeling that a great burden would soon be lifted. All that was needed was for the judge to say two words — "not guilty" — and the celebration could begin.

The judge took a deep breath and then began reading, "The defence evidence just summarized requires the Court to accept the following points. First, that Dudley George left an area of safety to go to an open area on the roadway. Secondly, that the accused either was unable to or chose not to use his sure light flashlight device or laser-light features before or after Dudley George was shot. That immediately after seeing Dudley George assisted back into the park, he turned to his right and spoke to Sergeant Hebblethwaite with regard to the head count. Further that Sergeant Deane walked twenty metres but did not have time to get the message over the communication system re: the muzzle flashes or danger from the sand berm. Further that Sergeant Deane watched Dudley George move from the position where he was shot to a location in closer proximity to the CMU, still carrying the rifle in his hand and still, according to Dr. Spitz's evidence, with the ability to fire a rifle. And not knowing how seriously he had injured Dudley George did not fire his weapon again to keep Dudley George from posing any further threat. Further that Dudley George having just sustained a bullet wound to his chest, which fractured his collar bone completely, punctured his left lung, partially fractured his left eighth rib, completely fractured his left ninth rib, tore a number of blood vessels, that he established as his next priority, the disposal of the weapon he was allegedly carrying."

The police weren't smiling anymore. Often judges scare the accused before giving a positive verdict, but this was going a little far for their liking.

The judge continued: "Furthermore that having made this decision Dudley George moved towards the police officers to dispose of the rifle, rather than heading immediately towards the park where his friends and relatives were. Further that Dudley George having sustained the injuries described above was able to throw [this underlined in actual written decision] the rifle into the field or ditch. Further that Dudley George threw the rifle into an area where Constable Klym and Constable Beauchesne happened to be. Also that after the threat was over he sent a message over the communication system but that message did not include any reference to shooting a man with a rifle, or the rifle having been thrown in the ditch. Also that someone with the responsibility to insure the security of his fellow officers and the CMU members would not warn them about the rifle. The Court would also have to accept that Constable Beauchesne having been involved in the Grassy Narrows incident which resulted in the death of one OPP officer and the wounding of two other officers, having been involved in tracking a suspect through the woods until he was arrested; having received a commissioner's citation for his efforts, was nevertheless not the least bit concerned when Sergeant Deane asked him if he had seen the guy with the gun. Also that Constable Beauchesne who gave the impression to the Court of being an intelligent, highly competent member of this elite team, suddenly became disinterested in the subject of a native with a gun because of some telepathic message given to him by Sergeant Deane."

The Natives and the police looked equally stunned at this point. Clearly, the judge was mocking Beauchesne's testimony by using the word "telepathic." But judges are notorious for appearing to lean one way in a ruling, then doing an about-face at the end, veering suddenly in the opposite direction with the single word, "however."

The judge pressed on, pausing only briefly for a sip of water: "Further that Sergeant Deane chose not to say anything to Sergeant Hebblethwaite no more than 15 seconds after he saw Dudley George being helped into the park. Further that Sergeant Deane decided to save this question for his meeting a short time later with Constable Beauchesne.

"Counsel agreed that this case was fact driven and that there was no need for a lengthy discourse on the law as it relates to criminal negligence causing death.

"I am therefore going to make reference only to one case which is often cited in matters where credibility may be an issue. In the decision of *R. v. (D) (W), (1991), 63 C.C.C. (3rd) 397*, a decision of the Supreme Court of Canada. The Court confirmed that even in cases where the credibility of the witnesses plays a determining part in the judge's verdict, the issue is, as always, whether the Crown's case had been proved beyond a reasonable doubt."

Here we go, courtroom observers thought. Now the judge was going to let Deane off the hook by arguing somehow that the case against him had not been proven beyond a reasonable doubt.

"If the accused is to be believed, I must acquit him," Judge Fraser continued. "If I do not believe that accused, I may still be left with a reasonable doubt as a result of the accused's testimony. Even if the accused's testimony does not raise a reasonable doubt I must decide whether I am left without a reasonable doubt on the basis of the evidence that I do accept."

He sounded like the George family lawyers, when they'd explained to reporters that morning just how difficult it was to get a conviction of criminal negligence causing death in this case, which had begun before the new, stronger legislation had been introduced.

"These are findings that the Court is prepared to make at this time. I found Sergeant Hebblethwaite to be a helpful witness, a credible witness before the Court."

Hebblethwaite seemed to tense up when the judge mentioned his name. This was praise he apparently didn't welcome.

The judge pressed on, referring now to maps of where Hebblethwaite and Deane had been standing the instant Dudley George was shot: "I will not make a lot of reference to the exhibits except to say that . . . what we find is that Sergeant Hebblethwaite is no more than a few metres behind Sergeant Deane when Dudley George is shot."

Now, it became clear what the judge had been doing when he'd surveyed the area where Dudley George had been shot. He'd been getting a mental picture of where Deane and Hebblethwaite had been standing the instant the fatal shot was fired. Obviously, he'd noted that they were very close together, with Hebblethwaite standing behind Deane. Hebblethwaite was the taller man, so Deane would not be blocking his view. If Deane had seen a gun in Dudley George's hands, why had Hebblethwaite seen a stick?

The judge continued: "It follows from that that Sergeant Hebblethwaite was further away from Dudley George than was Sergeant Deane yet he had no difficulty distinguishing what he recognized to be a pole or stick. I also find that Dudley George was in Sergeant Hebblethwaite's line of vision. I accept Sergeant Hebblethwaite's testimony in this regard and that this fact would have been unknown to Sergeant Deane at the time of the shooting. I find that Sergeant Hebblethwaite did not see any muzzle flashes other than his own. And that Sergeant Hebblethwaite did not see any firearms in the hands of any native protestors that evening."

Hebblethwaite looked horror-struck now as the judge continued: "There were no Crown witnesses or defence witnesses that saw any weapons in the hands of the First Nations people except for Sergeant Deane and except for Constable Chris Cossitt. The Crown called his testimony amusing, which is one word. I might choose others." The judge continued: "Rather than scrutinize Constable Cossitt's testimony for any grains of truth that might fall out, I have dismissed it entirely as being clearly fabricated and implausible."

Some of the Native people in the audience were smiling just a little now. At least the judge was making the police sweat.

"I accept Sergeant Hebblethwaite's evidence that he saw a man turned in the direction of the park after he got up from his one knee, that he was bent at the waist and facing the park, before Sergeant Hebblethwaite turned his attention elsewhere," the judge continued.

Hebblethwaite appeared distraught as he dropped his head into his hands. Sam George could feel himself going a little numb. He had expected an acquittal, even though he was sure his brother had been unarmed. He hadn't really come to the courtroom that day expecting justice, but he also couldn't stay away.

"In the Court's view this is not a situation of honest but mistaken belief," the judge continued. "The accused has maintained throughout that Dudley George was armed. And the accused was able to even describe some of the features of the rifle that he saw Dudley George holding."

The judge appeared to be nearing the homestretch now. What the Natives and their supporters had thought to be impossible seemed about to happen. "I find that Anthony O'Brien (Dudley) George did not have any firearms on his person when he was shot. I find that the accused Kenneth

Deane knew that Anthony O'Brien Dudley George did not have any firearms on his person when he shot him. That the story of the rifle and the muzzle flash was concocted *ex post facto* in an ill-fated attempt to disguise the fact that an unarmed man had been shot."

The only sound in the courtroom was the judge's voice. "The accused testified that the Court heard essentially the same version of events that was given to the Ontario Provincial Police and the Special Investigations Unit in September 1995.

"I find, sir, that you were not honest in presenting this version of events to the Ontario Provincial Police investigators. You were not honest in presenting this version of events to the Special Investigations Unit of the Province of Ontario. You were not honest in maintaining this ruse before this court. I have considered all of the evidence presented in this case, and on the basis of the evidence that I have accepted, I find you, Kenneth Deane, guilty as charged."

Deane stared straight ahead, still showing no expression. He must have felt something when he heard "guilty as charged," but no emotion registered on his face. For a few seconds, there was nothing but silence. Then, from across the courtroom, on the Native side, Pam Matthews, an actress who worked in the office of the George family's lawyers, shrieked with as much volume as her lungs would allow. It was raw and loud and seemed to unleash something, because suddenly the courtroom was filled with sounds of Natives sobbing for joy as the police quietly walked out, looking dazed and deflated.

THE FRESH RUMOURS BEGAN within days of the guilty verdict and kept surfacing throughout the three weeks between the verdict and the sentencing phase of the trial, set to begin May 27, 1997. Word was that a former high-ranking OPP officer, who was now a private detective, was trolling the Ipperwash area for fresh evidence. The story — invariably from police sources — was that he was digging into Dudley George's past and coming up with some interesting things. It could tear the prosecution's case apart, the story went.

The day sentencing hearings began, a middle-aged woman sat in the back of the courtroom holding a Bible. She said the case touched great biblical themes, like the perils of pride and the strength and dignity of the humblest people in society. She seemed to be on the side of the Native people, although she did say, "Judge not lest ye be judged," shortly before Mr. Justice Hugh Fraser entered the courtroom, then leaned forward intently to watch the next scene of the drama.

A look of righteous indignation can be valuable to a courtroom lawyer, especially when he's badly losing an argument. That indignant look was on Defence Attorney Norman Peel's face as court began, and he stood up and bluntly asked for the trial to be called a mistrial. Being accused of a mistrial is something of an insult to a judge, meaning that he or she allowed things to be so severely botched that the verdict became worthless. However, Peel carefully tried to channel his display of outrage toward Scott, not the judge. Peel said that he and his client had been victimized and that the Crown had agreed in pretrial meetings not to allege that shooting at muzzle flashes was negligent.

However, Peel claimed, this agreement had not been upheld, since throughout Scott's cross-examination, Scott had asked witnesses about what was *not said* to the accused. The defence had objected, repeatedly and forcefully, only to be overruled each time, Peel sadly continued. "The Crown then questioned the accused about what he had *not* said to his superiors about the ground-level muzzle flashes."

In keeping with the deal that Peel claimed had been made before the trial, the defence had not bothered to call witnesses who could have testified about dangers in the park, so that Deane would not have appeared negligent when he opened fire. Shooting at muzzle flashes or not shooting at muzzle flashes hadn't seemed particularly crucial during the trial, but now Peel was depicting the muzzle flash issue as if it was at the core of everything and at the very foundation of the Crown's successful case.

Peel appeared more agitated the more he talked. Because of his trusting nature, he said, he had allowed himself and, more importantly, his client to be sadly duped. "That position left the accused defenceless. It was an assault on his credibility that he could not answer."

Peel sadly said that he'd been left with the clear impression, when he'd walked out of the pretrial conference, that he and the Crown had made a deal about not mentioning muzzle flashes. Such conferences are vital for effective justice, since without them, lawyers could end up calling 170 witnesses, instead of 10. "As a defence advocate, I say to you that I was fundamentally misled."

Peel was picking up steam, working himself into even more of a funk. If credibility was indeed an issue, new lawyers who were untainted by the original trial would be needed, he volunteered. He and Scott would have to become witnesses themselves. "Credibility is the issue," Peel said, "and I'm not going to be libelled like Deane."

Ian Scott was now up on his feet, looking bewildered and calling Peel's allegations presumptuous. He continued by saying that he would not be treated like a witness.

Judge Fraser sounded like a frustrated parent as he asked Peel: "Why isn't it possible for him [Scott] to say that he's seeing it differently? It's not possible that it's a matter of different interpretations?"

And then the court recessed.

WHEN EVERYONE RETURNED to the courtroom, less than an hour later, Scott brought with him memos and a voice-mail transcript and challenged Peel to come up with anything in writing or on tape regarding the pretrial sessions that showed an agreement about not mentioning muzzle flashes. "My friend, in my respectful submission, knew precisely what the agreed statement of facts were and in no way was misled," Scott said. Peel's arguments were, he argued, "simply fallacious," and he continued: "I don't know why he's doing this today. . . . What matters is the record. The record speaks very clearly as to where we were going as a result of that pretrial conference."

Scott ridiculed the suggestion that his former professor was somehow a "babe in the woods," who had been misled. "He's been at this bar a lot longer than I have." Then he noted that Peel had actually lectured Scott's class some twenty years before and added that Peel's long career had included time in the Crown Attorney's office. The Crown's position, that none of the Natives had guns that night, was immediately and clearly stated as the trial began, Scott said. Then he argued it was time to get off this tangent altogether. "It's a long and winding and ultimately fruitless road that will ultimately take us nowhere."

It was again Peel's turn to speak. He harkened back to his teaching days, saying, oddly, "One of the things I did teach when I was in the law school was there was a distance between the position of counsel and the facts."

The bickering wound on for almost an hour, when Dudley George's sister Pam got up and left in disgust. Other Natives followed her out, some grumbling about legal mumbo-jumbo that sounded like games played by well-paid white folks.

As they left the courtroom, Peel returned to his argument about how pretrial meetings were needed to pare down witnesses. "This trial could start at 1492 and carry on to the Estey Commission and then some," he said, referring first to the date Christopher Columbus sailed across the Atlantic Ocean and then to the investigation conducted by retired Supreme Court of Canada justice Willard Estey into violence between the OPP riot squad and striking Ontario Public Service Employees Union workers outside the provincial legislature in March 1996.

Peel said he thought the pretrial meeting was "the clearest meeting of the minds . . . Whether I was . . . Elmer the fool to have believed that, that was what I relied upon . . . That was the bedrock of my defense."

One sensed that Peel would gladly have spoken forever, if given the chance. Scott refrained from calling Peel "Elmer the fool," arguing instead: "He continues to suggest that he's a babe in the woods who has been mis-led by some sinister Crown."

With this, the court recessed, leaving the judge with the unenviable task of restoring order. When he returned, Fraser ruled that the factum filed jointly by the lawyers at the onset of the trial was a result of correspondence between Peel and Scott and that the Crown had clearly stated its position that none of the Natives in the occupation had guns in their possession on the night of September 6, 1995. The Crown had maintained this position throughout the trial. "The court is of the view that it must deal with the record before it."

With those words, the sentencing hearing was back on track, but the courtliness with which the trial had begun was but a distant memory. Scott was testy and waved off a Peel attempt at familiarity. "I'd like it on the record. I can't speak to Mr. Peel off the record anymore."

It was the painful job of Dudley's brother Maynard "Sam" George to explain what Dudley's death had meant to his family. A youth worker at Kettle Point, Sam George wore a ponytail and gold-coloured wire-rimmed glasses, and he held an eagle feather for strength as he pulled out a prepared statement. He was a likeable, humble man, with no hint of theatricality about him. It was impossible not to wonder how much Dudley was like him.

"Dudley was the lively one of our brothers and sisters. He always had a smile on his face, or something to laugh and joke about. Even when we were adults, Dudley would come by and make sure that there was something to laugh about. He was a person with spirit. He was full of the spirit of life.

"Since that night of September 6, 1995, my brothers and sisters and I have been trying to make sense of what happened. This has been terrible for us. For many months, it seemed like we are alone against the world."

Sam took a deep breath, blinked his moist eyes, and tried to explain how deeply it mattered that Dudley's name was cleared. "The day after Dudley was killed, the police announced that the demonstrators at Ipperwash Park had fired on the police. Our brother and the other men, women, and children in the park were being set up as killers who the police had to shoot because they were a threat to the police officers' lives."

The official police story, that the Natives, including Dudley, were armed and shooting at police, was devastating, Sam continued. "This was what the police told the public. We always knew that this was a lie. Dudley's memory was being destroyed because of these lies. But we did not know what to do about it."

The support of First Nations communities and others, including church groups, meant a huge amount, Sam continued. He then explained something about his family. He told of how his parents had done their best to provide for their ten children and how their family, and seventeen others, were removed from their land at Stoney Point in 1942, ten years before Sam was born. "All of the children at Stoney Point always knew that it broke our parents' hearts when they were taken off their land."

Things seemed to spiral downhill after that removal from the land, Sam continued. There was substance addiction, suicide, and abuse. The new George family home burned to the ground twice and Sam considered it a miracle that no one had been killed in those fires.

Through all the upheaval, Sam continued, Dudley still seemed happy-go-lucky and full of jokes. Sam always thought that Dudley was particularly sensitive and that humour was his way of coping with the world. The jokes were his shield.

Sam said he wanted the truth to be told about Dudley, and this included the fact that he wasn't a saint. He told of how, after the death of their mother, when Dudley was fourteen, he seemed to badly need to escape, although he wasn't sure where to go. He started hanging around with non-Native kids in the neighbouring community of Forest and was convicted for arson for burning down a warehouse in a lumberyard in a stupid teenaged stunt with a group of other young people — all of them white. After his jail term, Sam said, Dudley did odd jobs with their father and listened intently as he was told how the federal government had moved his family off the land when Dudley's father was just sixteen. "Our father told us that it was his dream to return there," Sam said.

"It was our father that planted the seed of returning to the family's land in Dudley's heart," Sam said. ". . . My father told him that this was our land. He also told him that the government had promised to return it, but 50 years had gone by and they never had. Dudley put up a big sign on his trailer at the base that said, 'Dudley's Place.' We were glad for him. He had come home. Dudley told me he was living at the base for our Dad.

"Dudley asked me to join the occupiers. I did not, because I had three children and five grandchildren, a house, and my job as a youth counsellor at Kettle Point to think about.

"I am glad that my parents were not alive to know that Dudley was killed while he was trying to get back our family's land. Our parents would have been proud of him, the same as we are. But Dudley's death would have broken their hearts one more time."

Some of the Natives in the courtroom were crying now, and it was clear that Sam wanted to weep with them, but instead he continued softly: "The death of my younger brother has changed our life and my family's life completely. When a loved one dies of natural causes, it is hard to deal with. But when a loved one died from a gun shot, and did not have to die, you not only deal with death, but there are also many questions that need to be answered. The pain does not go away."

Sam tried to explain that more than Dudley died on the night of September 6, 1995. It wasn't just a George family problem. It went far beyond that. "When my grandsons ask me why Uncle Dudley died, it's very hard to explain to a six-year-old what happened. It breaks my heart not to be able to answer all those questions. But my grandchildren, and all the other children at Kettle and Stoney Point, know that Dudley was killed by a police officer."

The only sound in the packed courtroom now was that of sniffles, as Sam pressed on, his voice still soft and determined. "I am a parent, and a grand-parent, and a youth worker. I must speak about the impact of Dudley's killing on our children. We have tried to raise the next generation of native children to believe that things were slowly getting better in Canada.

"We have tried to teach them that if they get an education that they would get ahead. We have tried to give the next generation of native children more faith in the government and the police than our parents had.

"The bullet that Sergeant Deane used to kill Dudley also killed some of our hopes. Our young children now fear the police. We see them thinking of the police as soldiers who killed the uncle they loved. Killed him like an enemy.

"All across this country, history changed for native kids on September 6, 1995. First Nations kids learned on that day that they have started shooting Indians again in Canada." Sam noted that Dudley and the other demonstrators had been unarmed, and that they'd waited for the park to close for the tourist season and for the last campers to leave before they occupied it. "They wanted the police and government to know what their plans were. And they spoke to the park superintendent before going in."

Sam was sure that the demonstrators were rowdy when they went into the park.

"I am sure that Dudley and his friends shouted some things to the police that would not be said in church. But Dudley and his friends did not intend any violence. This was always Dudley's way.

"Hundreds of First Nations from across Canada have serious complaints against the government. Many First Nations lands have also been taken away from them. There are many places that are similar to Ipperwash.

"The bullet that was shot into Dudley's chest was a terrible lesson for young natives across this country. The way they see it, Dudley and his friends were not armed, but they were shot anyway."

His words were frightening now, although he did not raise his voice. "From the testimony in the trial, it seems that the police advanced on the demonstrators. The police would never have advanced on the demonstrators if they had believed for one second that my brother and the others were armed.

"So the lesson from Sergeant Deane's bullet for young people in Canada is that you might be better off if you are armed. You might be better off at a land claim demonstration if the police know you are armed. Dudley and the others got shot even though they had no guns. So why not have guns?"

Sam then returned to the terrible personal effects the death had on his family. "It has taken more than eighteen months for the facts about what happened that night that Dudley was killed to start to come out. Last March, my brothers and sisters and I launched a court case against the government and the OPP about Dudley's death. We only want to find out the truth about how our brother died.

"But because of all of the lies, all of the facts have been kept secret. We were only able to see the autopsy report on Dudley when this trial began. We only found out how he died on the day this trial began, more than a year after he was killed.

"The amount of work that is involved in this has caused a lot of stress on myself. It started to effect [sic] me so bad that now I have developed diabetes, which my doctor said is caused by the stress. I was disabled from my work last year for three months. I have been to see my family doctor, traditional healers and one of the top psychiatrists in Ontario seeking help from the stress.

"I could not do my job as a youth counsellor for fear of making a mistake. This only added to the stress until I had to take time off work to try and get healthy.

"I never have time for my own children or to play with my grandsons because I am always tired or gone someplace working on this issue. I am lucky to have my wife. I sometimes feel bad for her because I can't give her the kind of life we used to have. Now it is all work and more work.

"All I want is for someone to tell me the truth. I watch as it tears at my brothers and sisters and when they get mad I have to take the anger they feel. I sometimes wonder why I am the one who has to take all of the anger.

"Someone is also trying to take my peace. This has cost me so much, how can I ever replace my brother? I can't. I hope I can make up the time I missed from my job, and what about the young clients I used to work with? Everyone is not as understanding as my children.

"I said that all I want is for someone to tell me the truth. I believe in the Creator and in telling the truth. When Sergeant Deane put a bullet into Dudley's chest, it was also the truth that died.

"Will I ever be able to say, 'Now my brother can rest in peace?' Will my wife and I ever get our life back? I know one thing for sure. I will never be able to sit down and talk to my brother. I will never be able to give him a hug."

It was clear that Sam was fighting hard to keep the tears away now, but he still didn't break down. "I can only go to the cemetery to talk to him, but I will never again hear the sound of his voice, or a joke from Dudley ever again. It was an honour having Dudley for a brother. On the day this court ruled that Dudley did not have a gun, my brothers and sisters and I began to feel a little less like victims.

"We thank you for this chance to speak to the court."

Sam finally sat down. The judge had leaned forward to take in every word.

DUDLEY'S SISTER CAROLYN always had more trouble controlling her emotions, and this day was no exception as she told the court: "After our parents died, the kids were a lot closer to each other. Especially after Dad died." Carolyn later married, and when that marriage ended in divorce, Dudley became a father figure for her family, though he was younger than Carolyn by seven years. Carolyn had four children, and she noted proudly that they had all finished high school, and one had earned a B.A. in sociology. "I don't know if I would have been able to get my kids through all of that without the help of Dudley," she said.

Her children loved to visit their Uncle Dudley at Stoney Point, she continued. "That was where they should have grown up. My kids felt at home there. They went there mainly because Dudley was there. I went to Dudley when I had problems. I don't have anyone to go to now. . . . You don't just go and build trust with anyone . . . I had so much taken away from me . . . After that [killing] happened, I had no sense of security."

Dudley was a joker, but sometimes that was a good and necessary thing, she noted. When Dudley died, so did his laughter. "He'd always give you a laugh . . . I believe that's why my kids went to him. He would make them feel happy too . . . Now, it's like I've lost everything except my home — the former army camp."

Nowadays, she said, she suffered near-panic attacks whenever she heard the sound of helicopters. One of her daughters who used to love to go to Stoney Point didn't like going there anymore, saying she had been harassed by police too many times. That daughter had earned a university degree, yet she was still regarded with suspicion by police in her own homeland. "It was a slap in the face with her to be treated that way.

"I believe there has been a great void created in our lives," she continued. "It's going to take many years for my children to get a sense of security . . . for myself to get a sense of security."

Carolyn wiped tears from her eyes and sat down.

WHEN THE CHARACTER WITNESSES for Acting Sergeant Ken Deane spoke, he was also portrayed as a victim. Long-time TRU team member Staff Sergeant Brian Deevy said that he had been to more than one hundred high-risk occurrences with Deane, and that he had been able to judge his character under pressure. "Ken Deane is a very honest person. He's a very direct, straight-forward person."

Deevy talked of a hostage-taking call with Deane in June 1996 in the northern Ontario town of Dryden, when a man with a rifle was threatening two women. That call lasted for several days and was contained and negotiated. When the team finally entered the house, it was Deane who was first through the door. "It's a very dangerous thing to do." No shots were fired. In fact, Deevy said, there was "no use of force whatsoever . . . He does not react emotionally . . . I have never seen him lose control."

He said that the TRU team is a full-time job, with no room for people who are not team players. "If you are a loose cannon, if you're a rogue, if you're a person who looks for confrontation or enjoys that, and we see that, you don't get on." Deevy called Deane stable, disciplined, patient, brave, sensitive, humble, and professional.

Scott stood up at the end of Peel's examination to ask if Deevy had ever heard Deane express any remorse over his killing of Dudley George.

"He felt he did what he had to do," Deevy replied.

Insurance broker Kim Black said he had been a neighbour of Deane for years. Black described him as a man with strong Christian values, who went to the United Church. He was also a respected competitive slo-pitch player. "Ken seemed quite dedicated to his team. With the younger players, he seemed to have a very stabilizing influence."

Detective Constable Patrick Morrissey of the OPP said he had worked shoulder-to-shoulder with Deane at the Oka reserve standoff in Quebec and at Grassy Narrows in northern Ontario, when a fellow officer was shot dead. In his work with Native people, as with everyone else, Deane showed compassion and professionalism and chose talk over bullets, the court heard. "His integrity was always top-notch."

London Police Chief Julian Fantino spoke Deane's praises loudly and clearly. He recounted an incident in September 1994, when three desperate individuals had come to town, wanted for "murders, attempted murders, many robberies, weapons offenses and on and on it goes." Deane acted in an exemplary way in that arrest, paying careful and meticulous attention to the safety of everyone, "including the suspects," Fantino noted pointedly.

Detective Jerome Branagan of the Windsor Police Services, a member of his force's tactical unit and a trained negotiator, said Deane impressed him

when executing warrants on the Lobos motorcycle gang for narcotics traf-
ficking and firearms offences. "I find him a very competent tactical officer."
The defence testimonies were derailed temporarily when, in the midst of
the glowing officer testimony, Ovide Mercredi, grand chief of the Assembly
of First Nations, was called to the stand by Scott as part of the victim
impact statements. A scheduling problem had meant that Mercredi was
available only on a day when all other witnesses were for the defence.

It worked better for Scott this way anyway, as Mercredi reminded the
court that there was more involved in the judge's sentencing than the future
of Acting Sergeant Kenneth Deane.

Mercredi began by stating that on September 6, 1995, he'd received a
"frantic call" from Chief Tom Bressette of the Kettle and Stony Point band.
Bressette badly wanted Mercredi to intervene, saying that councillor Cecil
Bernard "Slippery" George had just gone to the park. Bressette urged
Mercredi to call the police "to see if I could prevent them from moving in
on the people in the park."

Mercredi said he made the call, asking the OPP why they were moving
on the park at night. If they felt they had to move, why not do it in the
daytime, when it would be safer for everybody? "Too often the white
politicians send the police to do their work for them . . . The general
feeling is that our people have been reminded once again about who the
police work for."

He spoke of the psychology of Native people, reminding the court that
those with power over their lives are often from different cultures. "The
authority figures are the priests or the ministers or the white politicians or
the police . . . In many cases, a social worker has more authority than the
chief." Native people were trying to recover authority, to bring it back to
their communities, but it wasn't easy. "The sad reality is that the shooting
of Dudley George has now clouded the whole . . . relationship. In the last
10 years, there have been genuine efforts made . . . Not just by governments, but by the police themselves . . . The white politicians in this
country are not listening to the Indian people . . . They get the police to
do their work for them."

Mercredi said that Native people don't have a particular hatred of police, but consider that law enforcement is being carried out unfairly. "There is a selective application of the law." He noted that heavily armed police weren't called in to uphold Aboriginal treaty rights when Native people were clearly in the right, and said relations between Natives and police in Ontario took a downward turn when Premier Mike Harris came to power in June 1995. The Ontario government didn't support the tripartite process that was taking place at the time, with Native groups, the federal government, and the provincial government all participating in the discussions. Mercredi noted that he had intervened at Gustafsen Lake in British Columbia, where a standoff was taking place at about the same time as the Ipperwash crisis. In Mercredi's words, however, Gustafsen Lake was "a totally different situation than Ipperwash." At Gustafsen Lake, the Natives had picked up guns. "Our Indian movement," on the other hand, said Mercredi, " has no place for violence." All the same, despite the weapons, the situation at Gustafsen Lake had been resolved without loss of life. "It took a while . . . There was some shooting going on, but no one got killed." He said he could support land occupation, but not violence. "I support the occupation of land . . . when all other means have been exhausted."

Even if there had been a real threat of Native gunfire at Ipperwash that night, he opposed the choice of sending in the paramilitary squad under cover of darkness. "I'm questioning the methods. I'm not saying that police have no duty to maintain law and order." Then he noted that "peace and order" included Native people too.

After Mercredi's statement, the glowing testimonials about Deane started up again. Each witness seemed to be striving to top praises lavished by the previous one. David Hill, a sales supervisor for a cable TV firm, said that he had known Deane for more than two decades, going back to a high school friendship. "He always worried about other people," Hill said. Deane worked extremely hard to stay in shape and was "more dedicated to his career than I could be . . . I admire the guy."

Hill spoke of one day when he dropped by the fifteen-year-old Deane's home and found him scrubbing floors.

"Ken, what are you doing?" Hill had asked.

"I want to help my mom" was Deane's reply.

"He went back to help his mom even when he was working. You have to admire Ken Deane for what he does."

As the tributes went on, it was impossible not to get the feeling that Deane really was someone who tried very hard to do the right thing. If not for the night of September 6, 1995, it would have been easy to envision him having a productive, decorated police career. But that night had taken place, and Dudley George was dead, and so the courtroom accolades continued.

The court heard more of how Deane always stressed safety as he trained younger officers in high-risk takedowns. "The thing that we try to have on our side is time," OPP Detective Inspector Robin Shrive said, noting that Deane had always taught younger officers to "Slow it down."

The irony was impossible to ignore. What had been the rush on the night Dudley George was shot dead? Deane had taught others to take things slowly, yet he was rushed into the park at night, at the end of a fourteen-hour day, after being fed an unsubstantiated report that the Natives were armed with Russian AK-47s.

The court heard particularly emotional testimony from Myrna Chiverton, who lived on Craig Street in London. She said she'd known Deane since he was a little boy, when her son and Deane had started kindergarten together. They'd gone through cub scouts together, played on teams together, and worshipped at the Knox United Church together. Deane and her son had remained joint leaders in scouting until they were about twenty-two.

There was clearly something else she felt she had to say. She took a deep breath and told the court that her boy had killed himself about a year and a half ago, not long after the Ipperwash shooting. At the funeral, she said that she'd talked to Deane and found him "a very sad young man." She didn't sense that this deep sadness was totally related to the loss of her son. "It was almost more than he could handle. He was just very sad."

Childhood friend Tim Huff told the court that he had known Deane for some thirty years and that he considered him to be one of his best friends, something Huff said he takes very seriously. "I believe in Christian values and ethics," he said.

Huff noted that Deane's parents split up while he was in high school and that it was a hard break-up, with three children still in the home. "Ken took a role where he was a stabilizing force in the family, a bridge builder." While in high school, Deane worked midnights at a grocery store stocking shelves and, Huff added, "I know that a lot of his money went into the family budget."

Scott asked how many times they had spoken since the Ipperwash shooting, and Huff said about twenty but never about Ipperwash.

Constable John Kelsall of the OPP TRU team called Deane "firm but fair." "It was evident to me," he said, "that he was training . . . to the highest standard in the pursuit of excellence . . . Acting Sergeant Deane has the highest level of respect within the TRU program."

At the end of Kelsall's questioning, Scott asked him about Deane's nickname, "Tex."

"Do you have any idea how he got that nickname?"

"No I don't." With that, the police officer stepped down from the witness stand.

Outside the courthouse, Deane's friend Huff said that Scott had it all wrong when he'd implied that Deane's nickname, "Tex," indicated a cowboy, shoot-em-up mentality. The nickname "Tex" had come about because of nothing more sinister than Deane's fondness for Tex-Mex cooking, like Texas hogies and Texas toast. "I worry about how he's feeling," Huff added, "but I know that he's strong enough to weather the storm and come out ahead."

A little distance away outside the courthouse, Sam George also looked tense, as he often had since the shooting. "It's tiring . . . It doesn't get any easier, as the time goes on."

The judge had heard more than two dozen defence witnesses, each speaking in glowing terms about Deane, and he had been given another sixty letters of reference. No one talked about Deane feeling remorse for the shooting, but that was consistent with the argument that he thought pulling the trigger was the right thing.

"I've been waiting twenty years to meet the perfect man," one Native woman joked during a break in court proceedings. "Now, I've met him."

The judge had plenty to think about and few legal precedents to fall back upon as he determined Deane's fate. It was the first case of a Canadian police officer shooting a Native to death in a land claims dispute in the twentieth century and it was also believed to be the most serious charge ever laid by the Special Investigations Unit.

Police officers in prisons often end up in protective custody, as they are despised by other convicts, and now Mr. Justice Hugh Fraser had the option of sending Deane to prison for the rest of his life. Judge Fraser could also let him walk free from the courtroom without serving one day behind bars for knowingly shooting an unarmed man and then lying about it in court. The decision was his alone.

THE DAY FOR SENTENCING was July 3, 1997, five weeks after Deane had been pronounced guilty. As usual, Acting Sergeant Kenneth Deane was stone-faced when escorted into the courtroom by a tight phalanx of fellow TRU team members. Moments later, the judge entered. The court was almost filled with some hundred spectators, split about evenly between supporters of the Natives and supporters of the police. Sentencings are always painful, and today, no one would leave the courtroom happy.

Mr. Justice Hugh Fraser asked Acting Sergeant Deane if he had anything to say before his sentence was delivered. As the judge spoke, the rhythmic beating of drums by six young men could be heard from outside the courthouse as they played a traditional song of remembrance. Deane had to have heard this, but his thoughts must have been even farther away, with his father, who had died less than twenty-four hours before, after a lengthy illness. The judge had obviously already made his decision about the sentencing, so no words from Deane would change his fate now. He stood ramrod straight and softly told the judge that he had nothing to say.

Deane knew that Crown Attorney Ian Scott had asked for significant prison time — at least two years for the crime — and a ten-year prohibition on owning firearms. That would mean the end of Deane's career as a police officer, but the verdict remained that Deane had knowingly shot an unarmed man and then repeatedly lied about it.

Deane knew that the judge also had to consider Defence Attorney Norman Peel's call for a sentence of a year, to be served in the community.

That amounted to no time in jail and token community service — considerably less time than Dudley had served, when as a seventeen-year-old, he had pleaded guilty to being part of the group of teens who had burned down the warehouse in the town of Forest. If Deane was sentenced to community service only, he would, in effect, have to do things like cutting lawns and painting buildings as punishment for ending a man's life. Peel had also told the judge that he opposed any lengthy ban on firearms possession, saying this would amount to a "professional life sentence" for the career police officer.

Mr. Justice Hugh Fraser cleared his throat to begin reading his sentence. He opened his remarks by saying that he had reviewed about eighty-five cases of criminal negligence causing death, most of which involved drunk driving. In the end, they told him nothing, except that he was alone in making his decision. "There is not one case that has a similarity to the case before me . . . The word 'unique' . . . cannot be used too often in this case."

Judge Fraser told the court that the public relies upon police for protection and needs to be able to trust them, so it was a "significant aggravating factor" that the acting sergeant was an on-duty police officer at the time of the fatal shooting. He noted, however, that Deane was also "a devoted son, brother, committed neighbour . . . and highly competent officer" and that he had no previous record of crime. He was lawfully doing his duty as a police officer until the fatal gun blast, the judge said.

The judge continued to note that Deane and other members of the TRU team had relied on intelligence information that the Native protestors in the park were armed, even though those reports proved to be grossly wrong. "It is not for this tribunal to decide where that intelligence originated, or why it was so inaccurate."

The judge seemed to be signalling here that many important outstanding questions still remained — questions that could not be resolved within the constraints of this court case alone. Judge Fraser continued by saying that he was moved by the victim-impact statements about how Dudley George's death had affected his family and relations between Natives and police, but added that responsibility for the late-night tragedy in the park "cannot be brought to rest solely on the shoulders of Ken Deane."

The judge continued his difficult task. Whatever the sentence he eventually read, his decision would surely make good people weep. There is prestige and power in being a judge, but sometimes it is just a lousy, joyless job, and this must have been one of those times. Fraser drew a deep breath, then took what seemed to be a swipe at those whose decisions resulted in Deane and his fellow officers marching toward the park that insane night of September 6, 1995. "The decision to embark on this ill-fated mission was not Sergeant Deane's," he said. It was clear that the judge agreed with the George family that Acting Sergeant Deane should not be the scapegoat.

Fraser then also noted that Deane had expressed no remorse and speculated that he may have lied under oath "because of his intense pride and abilities as . . . [a tactics and rescue unit] officer."

Fraser took yet another deep breath before he finally said what everyone had been waiting to hear: the sentence. Once he pronounced it, no one would hear another word from him in this court. Quickly, he said that Deane would be receiving a conditional sentence of two years less a day, to be served in the community and not behind bars. That came to 180 hours of community service, and no house arrest. He could begin possessing firearms again, as soon as his sentence was completed. There was a little sobbing from the Native side of the courtroom now, and intense looks of relief from the police side as the judge noted that, before that night at Ipperwash, Deane had never been found to use a gun inappropriately.

It took a second for the sentence to really sink in. Natives who had been shocked and elated at the pronouncement of the guilty verdict were now mortified. After a couple of seconds of silence, there were shouts of "Murderer!" "Rotten Cop!" and "He's still a murderer" as police officers smiled in relief and the judge quickly packed up his papers and left the courtroom. "May he [Deane] rot in hell!" Dudley George's cousin Cathryn yelled after the judge left the courtroom.

Outside the courthouse, the Native people hugged and cried and voiced their disbelief and anger.

"What justice has been served?" Dudley George's sister Carolyn asked. "It's okay to go out and kill a Native? Is that what they're saying . . . Because you won't end up in jail for it . . . ? If we did something like that, think how long we'd be in jail. I said he'd never serve a day in jail. . . . Now they're going to really come after us. I wouldn't doubt that there'd be more of our people die."

"My brother's life comes too cheap to these people," Dudley George's brother Pierre said. "My brother gets laid in his grave and this guy gets sent home."

"The jails are full of Indian people who stole a carton of cigarettes, but if you kill a Native, you're free," said Sheila Hippern of Stoney Point.

However, some of the Natives were more subdued. They could see there were many shades of interpretation of what the judge had done in court. Dudley George's sister Pam hugged a friend and cried a little, then said that while she was naturally saddened by the sentencing, she was also relieved that the judge had ruled that the Natives had been unarmed. "It cleared my brother's name. We're happy with that."

Dudley George's brother Sam said he was more sad than angry about the sentence, but he realized the judge had a "very tough job to do." And he pointed out that the judge's comment about Deane not being totally to blame highlighted the need for a public inquiry into everything that had happened that night in September 1995.

There was no direct comment to the media from Deane's family, just a statement released through Ontario Provincial Police Association President Brian Adkin, which expressed their thanks for "all the love and continuing support that we have received throughout the trial. . . . [We] will continue to support our son and brother with the express confidence that justice will prevail."

The OPP responded only on paper, issuing a press release saying that Deane would be relieved of operational duties and assigned to administrative work. Inspector Mike Shard of the OPP Professional Standards Bureau said that under the *Police Services Act*, the force was permitted to suspend an officer's pay only if he or she was sentenced to a period of incarceration. The force was going to look at transcripts of the trial and perhaps pursue charges of misconduct against Deane. If he was found guilty, it would cost him his job.

11

LEGAL
BEATING

"I felt I had a right to be there, in a public parking lot ...
If you were there, your heart would have been broken also, sir."
— CECIL BERNARD "SLIPPERY" GEORGE TESTIFIES AFTER HIS BEATING.

The few minutes of violence in the parking lot outside Ipperwash Provincial
Park brought a seemingly interminable string of court cases. There were
trials set to run from October 21 to November 1, 1996, for twenty-three
Natives facing the rarely used charge of "forcible detainer" — to wit,
detaining the park. It was an odd-sounding charge, as if the park itself was
being held hostage by the Natives. However, those charges were eventually
withdrawn because, in the words of Henry Van Drunen, assistant Crown
attorney in the Attorney General's office, London Region, "there is no
reasonable prospect of conviction."

As Van Drunen explained, "With respect to the Forcible Detainer
charges, the Crown is required to establish that the detention or 'holding'
of Ipperwash Provincial Park was done by the accused persons 'without
colour of right.' 'Colour of right' is defined as an honest belief in the

existence of a state of facts which, if it actually existed, would, at law, justify or excuse the act done," Van Drunen continued. "The accused have raised the defence of colour of right on the basis that there is a Chippewa burial ground within Ipperwash Provincial Park and that therefore they were justified in being in the Park during the time set out in the charges.

"Whether or not there is, in actual fact, a burial ground within Ipperwash Provincial Park and whether or not there is in actual fact a valid right of ownership, possession or occupation by the accused persons — these are considerations which are *not* [emphasis added] relevant in determining whether the defence of colour of right is valid. In this criminal proceeding, the issue is whether this belief by the accused persons is honestly held.

"The Crown has confirmed the existence of correspondence made in 1937 between the Federal Indian Affairs Branch and the Ontario Department of Lands and Forests which refers to 'the old Indian cemetery which . . . is located within the territory now being developed as a park' [referring to what is now Ipperwash Provincial Park]. This documentation gives objective support for the reasonableness and the honesty of the accused's belief."

In effect, the Crown was admitting that someone on its side had screwed up, big-time. The existence of the 1937 papers referring to the old Indian cemetery wasn't the result of any great provincial government soul searching. Federal Minister of Indian Affairs Ron Irwin had waved them in front of the media during the days after the shooting, then passed out copies to anyone who was interested. Irwin made it impossible for Ontario to deny the existence of the burial ground any longer. From the provincial point of view, Irwin's gesture was an infuriating one.

Now, Van Drunen was saying that he knew he had no real chance of winning on the "forcible detainer" charges, and so he wasn't going to waste the court's time for what could only be a humiliating string of losses. Also, he was conceding that the Natives' best argument came from documents in the provincial government's own files, something the government side should have known about before Slippery George was beaten, Dudley George was shot, or these charges were ever laid.

There were also charges against twenty-three Natives for forcible entry of the park. This time, the Crown had the onus of proving that the accused had entered Ipperwash Provincial Park in a manner "likely to cause a breach of the peace or reasonable apprehension of breach of the peace." In other words, the Crown had to prove the nature of the conduct of the people at the time they entered the park.

The problem this time for the Crown was obvious. How do you breach the peace of an empty park? Those charges were dropped against twenty of the accused, although they remained against three who were considered community leaders: Glenn Morris George, David Abraham George, and Roderick Abraham "Judas" George. When it came time for their day in court, on May 9, 1997, they each smiled when Mr. Justice A.M. Graham acquitted them, saying the Crown had failed to prove how and when any of them had entered the park. However, Judas George was found guilty of smashing the window of a police cruiser and ordered to pay a $500 fine and $692.33 to fix the window. It wasn't much of a victory for the Crown, considering the time and money and bloodshed put into the operation.

THE NIGHT OF THE SHOOTING, police had talked on their portable radios about a mob of out-of-control Natives attacking a private citizen's car with stones and baseball bats. However, when it finally got to court, the case of Stewart "Worm" George wasn't horrifying or even really much of anything. Laid bare for what it really was, the incident involved one stone thrown by one man at a car that was driving away. That was it. No blood. No tears. No great escape. Not even a big dent.

Now, in court, the stone throwing seemed nothing more than a nuisance. It wasn't even a whodunnit, as Worm George freely admitted having thrown the rock at Gerald "Booper" George's sister's car hours before the fatal shooting. The police didn't have to go hunting for Worm George either. He heard somehow that they were looking for him and simply turned himself in to find out what the problem was.

Worm George was fined three hundred dollars and walked out of the courthouse a free man. The stone throwing had been used as the legal justification for the march of the riot squad and the TRU team snipers on the park that night, and this had led to one death, a severe beating, millions of dollars in police costs, millions more in legal costs, and the derailing of the career of Ken Deane, an extremely accomplished police officer. However, when the case was finally settled, it was too small even to merit a press release by the OPP.

CECIL BERNARD "SLIPPERY" GEORGE still hadn't fully recovered from his beating when he went on trial in July 1996 to face a charge of assaulting police. The testimony of police officers worked in his favour, as Constable James Root told the court that he had seen a Native struck with batons during a confrontation with about ten officers. Other officers told the court that they had not seen the protestors doing anything illegal but were ordered anyway to move them off the public roadway and back into the park.

Judge Douglas Walker ruled that the Crown's own case pointed to Slippery George's innocence, not his guilt, saying, "The evidence was consistent with the intention to avoid being struck and run over, not to commit an assault."

Slippery George burst into tears upon hearing the words and waved his eagle feather at the judge, then hugged his lawyer, Fletcher Dawson of London, Ontario, and shook hands with friends and family. Outside the courthouse, he said, "I told our people when this happened that there would be a day when it would be proven that what they did was wrong. This is only one day, a stepping stone toward the truth of what happened at Ipperwash."

UNDERSTANDABLY, THE POLICE WERE not eager to solve the mystery of who had beaten Slippery so severely his heart had stopped. The Ontario Provincial Police Association had successfully blocked the release of I.D. photos of the OPP officers who had been at the Ipperwash operation — which meant that Slippery George could not use them to identify who beat him.

Even the Natives who'd seen the beating could not identify the officers involved because the police were wearing visors, and Slippery George, who should have been the key witness, wasn't any help, since he had been unconscious for some of the beating.

For all of their efforts, the most the civilian Special Investigations Unit could do was to conclude that some OPP officers "apparently" used excessive force against George. However, no one could identify the officers. There had been nearly ten police officers beating him, surrounded by other police, and the police riot squad was operating in a carefully rehearsed formation, so it should have been no great mystery to identify exactly who was standing where at the time Slippery George was clubbed so badly his heart stopped. Roughly a quarter to a third of the riot squad were doing the beating, so it shouldn't have been too difficult to identify suspects.

However, the civilian investigators were able to discover little of this information from the police witnesses, and the OPP had not released any still photos or videos of the arrest, even though such visual records had been called for in the original Project Maple. The OPP were willing to mobilize snipers and the riot squad and armoured personnel carriers against a small group of loosely organized protestors in a provincial park and on a complaint of minor property damage to a car, but when a man was clubbed so hard his pulse stopped, the force was unable to provide evidence that might have helped lead to the arrest of the assaulters.

"This is extraordinary that a police force has simply clammed up," said George family lawyer Andrew Orkin. "If they had cooperated with the SIU, then the SIU would have been in a position to lay charges."

OPP Commissioner Thomas O'Grady was troubled by the matter, however, and he called for a second probe into the Slippery George beating. But true to form, the commissioner did not explain exactly why he was concerned.

On February 11, 1999, Peter Tinsley, head of the provincial Special Investigations Unit, called a news conference at the OPP headquarters in London to announce the findings of his unit's renewed investigation into the beating of Slippery George. There had been some 250 witnesses interviewed, he reported, making this one of the most extensive investigations ever undertaken by his unit. In the end, Tinsley reported, they found . . . *nothing*.

"The file has been closed," Tinsley said. "I have determined that based on the available evidence, there are no reasonable grounds to support the conclusion that the police used excessive force in all of the circumstances of this arrest."

It was a carefully worded statement, as the phrase "available evidence" clearly left open the possibility that other evidence might be found. If the police had provided only limited audio and written records and no video records, what could the SIU have hoped to find? Tinsley's explanation that there were "no reasonable grounds to support the conclusion that the police used excessive force in all of the circumstances of this arrest" was a notable turn of phrase as well. No one had ever alleged that the police had "used excessive force in *all* of the circumstances of this arrest," though the visored officers had collectively used so much force that Slippery George's heart had stopped. Tinsley pointed out that it was impossible to say which officers were involved in the incident, since they were wearing "hard tack gear" that obscured their faces. To the Stoney Pointers, the message was clear: if on-duty officers wear their peacekeeping uniforms, complete with equipment that masks their faces, they can beat Indians.

CECIL BERNARD "SLIPPERY" GEORGE HAD a sad, faraway quality in his voice during the trial of Nicholas Cottrelle, who was charged with driving the schoolbus at police officers. It was March 1997 when he told prosecutor Henry Van Drunen, "I felt I had a right to be there, in a public parking lot . . . If you were there, your heart would have been broken also, sir."

Slippery George was being respectful to Van Drunen, the same Crown who had thrown out the dozens of charges against other Natives for what happened that night, and the polite tone of his words made them all the more compelling. Van Drunen pressed on, nevertheless. Numerous Natives told the court that they had seen and heard a crowd of officers kicking Slippery George with their boots and beating him with steel batons, even as he was being dragged away. However, when the police officers were called to testify, almost all of them swore on the Bible and then said they could not recall anyone striking Cecil Bernard George. Even their police notes were of no help — including the notes of Constable Mark Beauchesne, who'd been standing on a sandy knoll overlooking the parking lot with night-vision goggles. Perhaps, Van Drunen suggested, at least some of the twenty-eight wounds had been on Slippery before he'd come to the park.

By the time his case reached court, Nicholas Cottrelle had become something of a hero at Stoney Point. He was the unarmed kid who'd braved a hail of bullets to try to help a fellow Native he didn't even know that well. By the time of his trial, the skinny, gangly kid was more than six feet tall, and the traditional blue ribbon-shirt he wore to trial was clearly small on him, with the cuff riding up his forearms. He didn't feel like a hero, just like someone who had stood up for something he knew was right. Between the time of the shooting and the trial, not a day had passed when he hadn't thought of the violence. The memories remained painfully clear, softened neither by time nor by constant reflection. Burned also in his mind was the instant in the hospital when he heard doctors pronounce his Uncle Dudley dead. He still found it hard to express the feelings that came from that night. He felt he'd aged five years in the space of a week, and at first, he was terribly bitter toward all police, but that had softened. "I can't hold it against all white people, either," he told Richard Brennan of the *Toronto Star*. "That isn't right."

Nicholas Cottrelle's lawyer, Jeffry House, was defending him with a bold offence. When Nicholas was in the hospital immediately after the shooting, he'd been coy when police had asked him what he'd done that night — but that was all gone now. Nicholas wasn't denying that he'd driven the schoolbus at officers that night. What he and House were going to argue was that Nicholas had been *justified* in doing so. If they lost, they were going to go down swinging.

IF SOMEONE WAS PLAYING Jeffry House in a movie, the perfect person for the role would be Dustin Hoffman. He was a determined little guy with a tack-sharp mind who stood up straight and refused to back down. The son of a journalist, House had worked as a night janitor at the *Milwaukee Sentinel* to help pay his way through the University of Wisconsin in Madison, a campus which was extremely politicized in the late 1960s at the height of the antiwar movement.

House had crossed the border and moved to Toronto on January 28,

1970, a day before he was to enter the draft for the Vietnam War. "I don't want to hear anything about cause and effect," he would later joke. He completed a master's degree in political theory at York University, analyzing totalitarianism as it applied to Nazism and the former Soviet Union. His thesis evolved partly from an idea in George Orwell's *1984* that he found fascinating: "the enemy of yesterday is the friend of today."

In 1972, he worked as a researcher for former Ontario NDP leader Michael Cassidy, but felt he was at a disadvantage when he tried to analyze legislation because he had no legal background. That led to a return to university to study law at Osgoode Hall law school, where his influences included a professor who encouraged his students to seek more than paycheques. He urged them to also use their training and influence to do something positive for the poor and the disadvantaged. That professor was Larry Taman, who by the time of the Dudley George shooting, had moved on to become the deputy minister in the provincial Attorney General's office. His had been a voice of caution during the meeting in the Premier's Office on September 6, 1995, against serving the Natives in the park with an *ex parte* injunction. When House graduated, he articled for lawyer Harold Levy, who went on to become a *Toronto Star* reporter, who played a key role in breaking the Ipperwash story.

By the time the Nicholas Cottrelle trial began, House was no stranger to big-issue, small-money cases. His argument for Cottrelle in Sarnia Youth Court on May 6, 1997, was that it was simply unbelievable that no OPP witnesses could recall having seen Slippery George being severely beaten. House argued that the police simply had to be lying, since the story they told couldn't possibly hold up to logical scrutiny. House accused Staff Sergeant Wade Lacroix, head of the riot squad, of testifying "absolutely falsely" that Natives had rushed police to spark a wild mêlée. House asked how Nicholas Cottrelle could stand by in good conscience and let the beating continue. Driving a bus to rescue Slippery George made sense in the circumstances. It was also the moral thing to do. "[Cottrelle] had a right to stop that beating," House argued. "What force was required to ensure that Bernard George didn't die or didn't suffer serious long-term injuries?

No other force, no lesser force, would have been effective."

Van Drunen, on the other hand, tried to portray the police as the ones who'd been under attack that night. Officers were terrified that their lives might end in the sand. "The accused simply got in the bus and drove at a line of police officers." The result was a horrifying spectacle, as Van Drunen described it. One officer dived over a fence to escape the oncoming bus, while other officers fired upwards of a dozen shots at it.

After the testimony from a parade of police and Native witnesses, many of whom had also testified in the Deane and Slippery George trials, Mr. Justice Alexander Graham was left in the same position as Judge Fraser in the Ken Deane trial: either the Natives or the police were lying. There was no middle ground. No one else had been at the park. There were no cameras and only limited audio tape or other forensic evidence. On May 26, 1997, Graham had to announce whom he believed. So far in court it was 2–0 for the Natives. The judge then read from his judgement: "It is reasonable . . . to assume that a breach of the peace was occurring and that Bernard George was being assaulted." Suddenly, the Natives in court were smiling a little. The judge had concluded that the police — the public *peacekeepers* — were the ones breaching the peace. They were the ones committing the assaults, not the Natives, like Slippery George. To reach this conclusion, Judge Graham had obviously found, as had Judge Fraser, that police officers had lied in court under oath. It was a breathtaking moment. "I find Bernard George to be a credible witness and I accept his evidence," the judge said.

In a flat, steady voice, Judge Graham explained that he accepted Nicholas Cottrelle's testimony that he had driven the bus at police in an attempt to rescue Slippery George from about eight OPP officers, who were kicking, punching, and clubbing him. The judge said Nicholas had been justified. With those words, it was confirmed that Nicholas was not a criminal because of his actions that night. He was a hero.

Nicholas quietly shook the hands of his lawyer, Jeffry House, and lawyers Peter Hatch and Bob Kellermann, who had represented dozens of other Stoney Point Natives charged at Ipperwash.

It was too much for some of the police in the room. As Sergeant George Hebblethwaite quickly left the courtroom, he muttered, to no one in particular, "Unbelievable."

ACTING SERGEANT KEN DEANE'S defence team wasn't satisfied with his sentence, even though he didn't have to serve a day in jail for knowingly shooting an unarmed man, then repeatedly lying about it. He would even be allowed to carry a gun after he had finished his community service. But Deane's legal team wanted him back on the force, with no blotch on his record. And as long as his appeals were underway, Deane could remain on the OPP payroll. The force was also quietly paying his legal bills, which seemed more than a little odd, and which was contrary to the *Police Services Act*.

The first stop for Deane and his lawyers was the Ontario Court of Appeal. By now, Deane had switched from Norman Peel to Alan Gold, a respected, brilliant lawyer who was president of the Canadian Criminal Lawyers' Association. If Deane lost this time, he couldn't blame it on his lawyer, since they didn't get much better than Alan Gold.

Gold crafted an appeal that included a raft of after-the-fact "evidence" — evidence that pushed the argument that the demonstrators at Ipperwash were armed and had fired at police. The new defence package was full of statements from neighbours and OPP officers, but still there were no credible eyewitnesses. For all of their suspicions and all of Gold's brilliance, however, no one had seen Dudley George with a gun in his hands.

There was an obvious, logical downside to this argument about dangerous, heavily armed protestors in the park that night. If the police thought the Natives were such a threat, why had they marched on them at night with absolutely no cover? If the judges were to believe the argument that the Natives were armed with firearms, they would also have to believe that the Natives in the park were spectacularly awful shots, all incapable of holding a rifle horizontal and pulling the trigger. Many of them worked as guides and hunted to supplement their diets. For this, they had to be quite handy with rifles. Yet, if what police were saying was true, on that night, when their lives were at stake, not one of them could hit any of the dozens of police officers directly in front of them and only feet away in the middle of a tiny parking lot.

The documents filed for the appeal by lawyer Michelle Fuerst of Deane's legal team stated that the thirty-two members of the Crowd Management Unit had not been told that the Natives were heavily armed. "Staff Sergeant Skinner did not brief [the unit] about weapons in the park," Deane's appeal document states. No explanation was given about why the riot squad officers were not told such obviously crucial information. If the officers had truly believed that the Natives were armed with firearms, wouldn't they have been outraged later when they learned that they had not been warned that they were marching head on into possible gunfire?

The appeal document also spoke of new information. Sounds of gunshots were mentioned. Most interesting was the argument that the trial had been unfair for Deane because Deane's comments to Skinner in the mobile command post after the shooting had been made without the benefit of counsel. Should Staff Sergeant Skinner or Acting Sergeant Deane have insisted on the presence of a lawyer in the cube van before Deane debriefed the TRU leader on the shooting?

The defence at Deane's trial was a bold one. Pretrial hearings were waived, and Deane did not even allow for the *possibility* that he might have been wrong. Deane didn't just say that he *thought* Dudley George had a gun. He said with absolute, one-hundred-per-cent certainty that Dudley George *did* have a gun, and then he went on to describe that gun, which no one else in the crowded parking lot had observed.

As was customary with the court of appeal, the judges gave no hint of when they would return with a verdict.

THE CAR WARREN GEORGE WAS driving the night of the shooting had cost one hundred dollars, and no one argued that it was a bargain. The four-door, scratched-up white 1982 New Yorker wasn't running at all when he'd bought it from a buddy he used to play ball with. Warren had been able to get the engine running again, but the steering remained problematic at best.

By the time Warren George's case of dangerous driving, criminal negligence causing bodily harm, and assault with a weapon (a car) reached the
courts, it appeared that he expected an easy ride in court. It was the last of
the trials against the Stoney Pointers. Of the sixty-two charges laid, forty-
five had been withdrawn by the Crown because there was "no reasonable
prospect of conviction." This was particularly embarrassing for the government, because the evidence that gave the Crown no reasonable chance of
conviction came from the government's own files, in the form of the letters
and reports about the old burial ground. The few cases that the Crown
actually still pursued were almost all won by the Natives, including the
major ones involving Ken Deane, Slippery George, and Nicholas Cottrelle.

On the surface, it seemed likely that twenty-four-year-old Warren
George would be in the clear. He'd driven the New Yorker out of the park
as part of the same mêlée in which Nicholas Cottrelle had driven the
schoolbus. Both men explained that they'd been trying to save Slippery
George, so how could Nicholas be innocent and a hero and Warren George
be judged guilty? Aside from their choice of vehicles, what did they do
differently?

Originally, Constable Chris Cossitt said he'd seen a gun pointed out of
the car, and this was the story that police had used in their original public
justification for the shooting of Dudley George. However, no other officers
supported this version of events, and Mr. Justice Hugh Fraser had lam-
basted Cossitt's credibility during the Deane trial. Now, on the eve of
Warren George's trial, on September 28, 1997, the Crown dropped charges
against him of discharging a firearm and possession of a dangerous weapon.
There was "no reasonable prospect of conviction," Crown Attorney Henry
Van Drunen said, not elaborating. However, the Crown retained charges of
criminal negligence causing bodily harm, assaulting a police officer with a
weapon (the car), and dangerous driving.

Crown attorneys rarely say, "I'm sorry" or "We never should have laid
these charges and put you through this expense and aggravation." "No
prospect of conviction" was about as close as it gets. The Crown was as
much as admitting that there was no evidence that Warren George had
had a gun. The importance of the move didn't escape defence lawyer Jeff

House, who said, "It's significant that after the [provincial police] announced they were responding to firearms, it turns out it's not only unproven, but the Crown isn't going to attempt to prove it."

Also in Warren George's favour was the fact that he was represented by House. Bright, committed, and articulate, House was also familiar with what had happened on the sandy parking lot at Ipperwash that night, since he had won Nicholas Cottrelle's case. House conceded that Warren George, like Cottrelle, had driven into a line of officers. House also argued that Warren George's motive, like Cottrelle's, was an honourable one: to rescue band councillor Slippery George from a horrific beating. "No one is required to stand by while police beat a citizen, much less a band councillor," House argued.

Warren George told the court that he had veered off the road to avoid being shot by a police officer who was directly in front of him with a gun raised. After swerving, the car knocked down four officers, but no one had been seriously injured. The worst of the injuries was to officer Mark Close, who'd sustained a twisted ankle and a strained knee ligament, which were treated with some Tylenol and a tensor bandage. He didn't have to stay overnight in hospital and was back on the job after five days' recuperation.

Warren George was straightforward about his motivation, telling House, "I started gatherin' rocks [when the police first approached the park] . . . In case they were goin' come and try to take us away, come in the park and take us away . . . I felt that the government desecrated a burial ground plus I felt that they had stolen the land."

He was equally frank under cross-examination by the Crown, saying he and the other protestors felt the police were trespassing.

"So you wanted to push them back?" the Crown asked.

"Yes," Warren George replied.

In re-examination, House clarified Warren George's evidence about whether the occupation was "peaceful."

"Did you see anything that wasn't peaceful prior to the arrival of the police on the scene?" House asked.

"No."

In the Ken Deane trial, the strongest witness against him came, inadvertently, from his own ranks, in the person of Sergeant George Hebblethwaite. There was a similar odd twist in the Warren George trial, with the testimony of Staff Sergeant Wade Lacroix. If this officer's shots had been more true, Warren George would have been in a grave and not sitting before a judge. Lacroix told the court that he had been standing directly in the middle of the road as Warren George's New Yorker came at him, and he'd pumped out several shots at Warren George. This account was backed up by Warren George himself, who said he'd swerved away from a police officer in the middle of the road who had his gun pointed directly at him. Finally, the Natives and the police agreed on something about what had happened that night: Wade Lacroix was standing in the middle of the road, firing at the oncoming New Yorker. If Warren George was acquitted, he would have one police officer to thank.

The verdict was delivered on February 12, 1998, in the same Sarnia courthouse where the OPP had suffered the humiliations of the Deane conviction and the Slippery George and Nicholas Cottrelle acquittals, and where the dozens of other charges against the Natives were dropped. But the Native winning streak in court ended that day with Warren George.

The judge hearing the case, Mr. Justice Greg Pockele, asserted that councillor Slippery George had assaulted OPP officers, even though he had been acquitted of those charges during his own trial and even though his testimony had also been considered credible in the related trials of Acting Sergeant Kenneth Deane and Nicholas Cottrelle. The judge then convicted Warren George of criminal negligence causing bodily harm, assaulting a police officer with a weapon (a car), and dangerous driving. Then he took things even further. He blamed the protesting Stoney Pointers for the death of Dudley George, saying that, after the riot squad had initially cleared the parking lot, "Cecil (Slippery) George, Warren George and the other occupiers then commenced a course of conduct which was extremely dangerous, violent and assaultive. Adopting a principle more frequently known at civil law, the principle of 'proximate cause,' these activities henceforward constituted the proximate cause of all the violence and injuries which occurred that night and, perhaps even, the death of a man.

"Under cross-examination [Warren George] admitted that he was not going to let the police push him back and not resist, nor would he let the police 'take him.' His evidence supports the Crown theory that the accused was engaged in an escalating course of violent conduct which culminated in criminal driving behaviour minutes later . . .

"Warren George had a vast array of excuses, beliefs and justifications for his conduct in occupying Ipperwash Provincial Park, confronting the officers, resisting and stoning police officers and driving his vehicle out of Ipperwash Park into the Crowd Management Unit officers. Upon review, these were unrealistic, illogical and unfounded . . .

"There is little logic in Cecil (Slippery) George's position that he was a peacemaker and that he approached the police with words of moderation. He was a short term visitor to Ipperwash Park. He arrived that evening and he did not indicate or testify that he had any authority to speak for the occupiers. If he was a peacemaker, why did he not speak to the occupiers first about withdrawing and attempting to dialogue with the police?

"After all, the occupiers were gathering stones, they were armed with poles and clubs and readying for violence.

"When a citizen is being arrested, our society and the *Criminal Code* demands a full and immediate submission to police authority. In Cecil (Slippery) George's own words, after he was batoned by Lacroix, he swung out at the police; he swung out at the 'shadow.' There was also evidence that he kicked out at the police. There was not evidence that he immediately submitted to arrest."

The judge continued, "Then the occupiers began to stone the Crowd Management Unit and at least ten occupiers, including Cecil George, attacked the Crowd Management Unit with bats, poles and other weapons. There was no reason known to man which would justify this violence as directed to the Crowd Management Unit."

He dismissed Warren George's testimony as "incredible, hyperbolic, illogical and unworthy of belief," and said he didn't buy his argument that he hadn't intended to hit officers with the car. He ignored the testimony by both Warren George and Staff Sergeant Wade Lacroix that Lacroix was in the middle of the road pointing a gun at him when he swerved the car away — even though that was about the only thing the Natives and the police could agree upon about the events of the night of September 6, 1995.

Outside the court, uniformed officers escorted a plainclothes officer past angry Natives, as Warren George's grandmother, Reverend Melva George, a direct descendant of Chief Tecumseh's nephew, Oshawanoo, sobbed. The world seemed upside down. Hadn't Deane been convicted of criminal negligence causing death? Hadn't police officers lied in court during Deane's trial? Weren't there a number of police officers who had gone unpunished for beating Slippery George so badly his heart had stopped?

"I felt like bawling my eyes out in there," Melva George said outside the court. "We've been denied justice again."

IN THE SENTENCING HEARING, Jeff House argued for a conditional sentence. If community service and no jail time was enough for Acting Sergeant Kenneth Deane, whom court found had knowingly shot an unarmed man and then repeatedly lied about it, then didn't Warren rate the same mercy? His actions had resulted in a twisted ankle and a strained knee ligament, not a dead man. Prosecutor Henry Van Drunen asked the judge to impose a jail sentence of up to eighteen months.

In spite of House's arguments, Judge Pockele said Warren George's actions in driving into the riot police were too serious to be considered for a conditional sentence. The judge wanted the sentence to be a deterrent to others and a loud denunciation of Warren George's behaviour. Then Judge Pockele sentenced Warren George to six months in jail, banned him from driving for two years, and prohibited him from having firearms for ten years, even though there was no evidence offered in court that he had handled a firearm at Ipperwash.

As the police started to take Warren George from court, his stepmother lost control. She jumped forward and screamed, "You're not taking him. He didn't kill anybody."

Additional officers rushed in to shuffle her aside, as Warren was led away.

12

A CALL FOR ANSWERS

"Ontario Indian's Death Is an Issue That Won't Die"
— NEW YORK TIMES HEADLINE, JUNE 26, 1996

Martin Mittelstaedt of the *Globe and Mail* correctly reasoned that the files of OPP Superintendent Ron Fox were central to the mystery of what had happened at Queen's Park the day Dudley George was shot dead. Fox had been at the crisis meetings in Toronto on the tenth floor of The Atrium on Bay the day before the fatal shooting and the morning of Dudley's death. He had likely heard much of what Mike Harris's senior aide Debbie Hutton had had to say. As the liaison between the government and the police, Fox should know pretty much everything. A couple of hours studying his computer files and there shouldn't be much mystery left. So Mittelstaedt filed a Freedom of Information request for Fox's computer files to be located, and a Freedom of Information officer looked them up and found . . . *nothing*. It wasn't that the officer found nothing of significance or nothing of interest. There were no files left at all.

In an attempt to explain the vanished files, Deputy Solicitor General

Tim Millard said in an affidavit that Fox's standing on the government's computer system had been eliminated in April 1996, when Fox had transferred jobs. Arrangements had been made for his computer records to be given to his replacement, but when the computer folders were opened, nothing was in them. "Efforts by staff of Information and Technology Division to retrieve any records which may have been located in the folders were unsuccessful," Millard said.

Once again, faulty technological support systems were cited as reasons why records of events could not be provided. No Polaroid or video record of the arrests that night had ever appeared, though they had been called for by the OPP's Project Maple. No explanation had ever been given as to why there was no photo record of that night. No audio record had ever been provided of the comments made by Deane and the other members of his paramilitary unit the night Dudley George was shot to death, because one officer had failed, according to his court testimony, to press the "Record" button on a simple tape recorder. And now it was said that Fox's hard drive had been erased and there was no hope of retrieving it. OPP officers probing Internet crime pride themselves on being able to resuscitate deleted files to save evidence, but there was no heroic forensic work here. Once again, the public had the choice of believing the premier and the police or believing the Natives who were fired upon. The police gave them no other option.

In his affidavit to the privacy commissioner, Fox said that when he changed jobs and returned to the OPP after his stint at the Solicitor General's office, he was "generally aware that the intention was to have my computer information transferred to [his replacement's] computer and that there was some technical difficulties in doing so . . . I am not aware of any destruction of documentary material related to Ipperwash and did not destroy or participate in any such destruction of Ipperwash material," Fox said.

Fox's records from the crisis would have been particularly interesting. Fox had a solid reputation for honesty and competency. Now, however, Millard said that even finding the computer that he had used during the crisis was difficult. Fox's computer and its hard drive had been declared surplus and returned to the leasing company from which they'd come in

February 1997, Millard said in his affidavit. No explanation was given as to why the hard drive hadn't been copied — something most elementary school students could easily do.

According to Millard's affidavit, the Ministry of the Solicitor General keeps information for only thirty days in its backup systems. Major firms in the private sector, like newspapers, routinely have such data copied and stored off-site so that there is a permanent record of their labours. And as for paper documents, the Ministry of the Solicitor General initially said it could find only three pages. Those who wanted to trust in the government and the police were challenged here.

After the reporter's appeal to the Privacy Commissioner, the ministry located about two hundred additional pages and released a heavily censored version of these records, saying disclosure of all the records "could reasonably be expected to be injurious to the financial interest of the government of Ontario or the ability of the government of Ontario to manage the economy of Ontario." Somehow, providing records about the Ipperwash crisis would impede the efficient running and economic well-being of the province. It was difficult to see the connection.

The Privacy Commission also argued that Fox's remaining records could not be released in their entirety because they would reveal Cabinet deliberations and advice from civil servants, undermine intergovernmental relations, and be an unjustified invasion of personal privacy. No one noted that firing a hollow-tipped, exploding submachinegun bullet into Dudley George's chest when he was unarmed might also have been deemed an unjustified invasion of his personal privacy.

MADAM JUSTICE SUSAN LANG of Ontario Court, General Division (now the Superior Court of Justice), must have had some sense of history when, three years after the George family began their lawsuit against top members of the government and the Ontario Provincial Police, she prepared to announce her ruling. It was March 3, 1999, and up to this date, no premier of Ontario had ever been required to answer questions in a lawsuit while still in office. That all changed when Judge Lang announced her ruling that Premier Mike Harris and a host of government and police officials named in the lawsuit "must proceed to the next stages of litigation of production and disclosure."

Lawyers for Harris and the others had argued that whatever the merits of the lawsuit, the George family lawyers had been three days late in serving papers to initiate the case. The George family lawyers erupted with indignation, until Lang calmed them by ruling that government records clearly backed the George family case. "It is surprising, to say the least, that the Crown would raise this issue [late service] in the face of its own correspondence of acceptance of proper service of the pleading," the judge ruled.

The government lawyers appealed, but on June 16, 1999, Mr. Justice James Southey, Divisional Court, Superior Court of Justice, kept the wheels of the lawsuit turning when he denied the government's motion for leave to appeal. Even for lawyers, it must have been getting dizzying now, to think that this latest move meant that a stay granted by Madam Justice Gloria Epstein the first week of June 1999 preventing the George family from obtaining Harris's list of Ipperwash documents was no longer in place. It was tough to understand all the details, but David appeared to be getting some good shots in against Goliath.

However, while lawyers for the George family were scoring points in court, they still had no government records in their hands to show for it. At this stage, the government documents were six months overdue for production.

Also on June 16, 1999, the provincial ombudsman called for a public inquiry into the death of Dudley George. No one thought that this in itself would be enough to bring an inquiry, but it was nice for the George family to hear, nonetheless. Some people in government were listening.

July 21, 1999, marked the Ontario government's final spasm in its drawn-out, taxpayer-funded effort to have the lawsuit against the premier et al. thrown out of court. The government lawyers announced they were no longer going to appeal the earlier decision about their argument that the statement of claim against them was filed three days too late.

It was now approaching four years from the night that Dudley had been shot dead, and the court case had been in the works for three and a half of them. The George family had argued that the strategy to have the case thrown out came despite the fact that, more than two and a half years before this, lawyers for the province had confirmed, in three separate letters, that the Crown had no limitations arguments and that the George family rights in the lawsuit were protected. The exhaustive forty-month legal marathon had all been about whether or not the George family lawyers had been three days late in filing papers, and a judge had already supported the George family here. So what was the point of all the protracted legal fighting, at taxpayers' expense? The George family thought they had a pretty good idea.

Their lawyers were working *pro bono*, while the government had a seemingly bottomless fund of tax dollars to pay its legal team. In a war of attrition, the army with the most bullets wins. In a civil suit, it's often the side with the most money to pay its lawyers.

"The Harris government has been trying to crush us with motions and appeals," Sam George said on July 21, 1999. "Their tactics of obstruction and delay have caused our family great stress. This issue and appeal should never have been pursued, at great taxpayers' expense."

IN NATIVE CULTURE, time is measured in units of four, just as there are four seasons to a year and four phases to a person's life. As the fourth anniversary of the killing passed, none of the key government players — Premier Mike Harris, former OPP commissioner Thomas O'Grady, former solicitor general Robert Runciman, or former attorney general Charles Harnick — had yet been questioned in court. So in October 1999, the George family lawyers accused Cabinet ministers of trying to duck out of being questioned under oath.

Nothing of the sort, Harris replied. He was not trying to avoid the legal process. He was more than eager to cooperate. It was simply a scheduling issue. He wasn't the only one with scheduling problems. Back on March 19, 1999, Harris, Harnick, and Runciman had all been summoned to an examination for discovery as part of the George family suit. The date of the Runciman discovery was set at September 8, 1999, with Harnick to testify October 6, 1999, and Harris on December 8 and 9, 1999.

Harnick and Runciman, the top politicians in charge of administering justice in the province, still hadn't testified. And a week before Premier Harris's opportunity to set the record straight, his high-profile lawyer, Eleanore Cronk, convinced a judge to postpone his appearance until a more "suitable" later date could be found. That suitable date wasn't specified. Then the judge, Gloria Epstein of the Superior Court of Justice, urged "co-operation" among all parties, to get the case underway.

Harris's choice of lawyers did not go unnoticed. In choosing to switch from Dennis Brown to Eleanore Cronk, perhaps the top civil litigator in Ontario, Harris had gone outside the stable of highly capable staff lawyers at his disposal. When Ian Urquhart of the *Toronto Star* asked the Premier's Office exactly how much taxpayers were paying for Cronk's services, he was told curtly that the answer would come "in due course."

It seemed clear that the government's strategy was to throw procedural roadblocks in the way of the civil suit, even though Premier Mike Harris kept saying publicly that he was more than willing to cooperate. However, a year after the George family's lawyers had filed an affidavit for the production of documents, the government had yet to produce a single page of records and the public was none the wiser about what had happened the night Dudley George was killed.

In January 2000, the government lawyers were in court again, arguing once more why they shouldn't have to produce papers about the killing just yet. This time, the argument was that the George family affidavit was too vague and ought to be replaced with one identifying the author and recipient of each document requested, "including information as to their function, role, status and relationship to the parties to the action." One might have argued that such detailed information could be discovered only by consulting the files, which is what they were asking for in the first place.

At this point, the government had already spent some $500,000 defending itself in court, while not producing a shred of paper that explained the shooting or clubbing of the Native protestors. For his part, as records obtained under the *Freedom of Information Act* show, Harris paid Cronk $123,667.97, using taxpayers' dollars, for legal work done between September 15, 1999 (when she'd taken on the case), and the end of 1999.

And he did not dispute that this bill had hit $500,000 by mid-October 2000. Pressed in the legislature about the costs to the taxpayer, Harris replied that most of the fee was covered by insurance and glibly added that it was still cheaper than holding an inquiry. He did not mention the fact that neither he nor any of his ministers had yet said one word in the lawsuit. He also did not mention what an unseemly spectacle the case presented in court, with five well-paid government lawyers doing paper battle against Klippenstein and articling student Velko Zbogar, who were working *pro bono*.

". . . The inquiry should probably cost several million dollars, and those very questions are indeed the same questions that are being dealt with in the lawsuit," the premier said under questioning by Liberal MPP Gerry Phillips in the legislature on October 19, 2000. "I have already committed, of course, that when the trials are over I would ensure the information would be made available, one way or another." Harris was saying that the lawsuit was asking the same questions as the inquiry, but meanwhile, huge sums of taxpayers' money were being used up to derail the lawsuit.

ON FEBRUARY 24, 2000, the court dismissed an application by Bill King, a communications aide to Harris at the time of the killing, to be removed as a defendant in the lawsuit. This marked the sixth time that government defendants had gone to court to try to have the lawsuit struck down and the sixth time that they had lost. King's failure in court came within a week of a ruling by the Ontario Court of Appeal, on February 18, 2000, dismissing an appeal by OPP Acting Sergeant Kenneth Deane. The province's top court stated that "Deane cannot expect a fairer trial than he has received."

When the government reversed its strategy of not producing documents, it did so with an avalanche of paper. On August 4, 2000, Queen's Park handed over nine boxes of documents containing some 34,742 pages, to the George family lawyers. Now they faced a bizarre new problem — that of a sailor dying of thirst in the middle of the ocean. The George family lawyers said they would need at least two years to study them, but the court gave them six months instead. They couldn't help but feel suspicious now.

Was the government strategy now simply to deluge them with paper?

It was a mind-numbing, time-consuming exercise to plough through the paperwork, but when the George family legal team reached Document no. 11,774, their mood brightened considerably. That document read,

> Sept. 6/95.
> Ron Fox,
> — Tim has asked for s.o. fr OPP to give vive voce evidence before J today in Sarnia
> — now OPP commissioner is involved - decisions will be made at his level.
> — he was called into Cabinet - Larry Taman was also there + was eloquent — he — cautioned abt rushing in with ex part inj — + can't interfere w police discr.
> — but Prem. + Hodgson came out strong
> — Larry, Elaine Todres were at Cabinet.
> Ron ws there for part of discussion. decision to go *ex part* appeared to have already been made.

An interpretation of the document might read as follows:

> September 6, 1995
> — I just talked with Ron Fox, the liaison between the OPP and the Solicitor General's office.
> — Tim McCabe, a lawyer with the Attorney General's office, has asked for someone from the OPP to give verbal supporting evidence before a judge today in Sarnia.
> — Now OPP Commissioner Thomas O'Grady is involved and decisions will be made at his level.
> — Larry Taman, the Deputy Minister in the Ministry of the Attorney General, was there and was eloquent. Taman cautioned about rushing in with an *ex parte* injunction which would exclude the Natives from having legal representation or even attending the court

proceeding regarding their occupation of the park and said the
government can't interfere with police discretion.
— But Premier Mike Harris and then Minister of Natural Resources
Chris Hodgson came out strong.
— Larry Taman and Deputy Solicitor General Elaine Todres were at
Cabinet.
— Ron Fox was there for part of the discussion. The decision to go
ex parte without the input of Native lawyers appeared to have already
been made.

It was nothing short of a revelation for the George team. For the first time,
Chris Hodgson, minister of natural resources at the time of the shooting,
was mentioned, and he seemed to be in the thick of things. It was also
the first indication that the operation — the so-called "isolated incident" in
the words of OPP Commissioner Thomas O'Grady — came in the midst
of a top-level government operation. It also showed conflict between senior
advisors and the Premier's Office, with the premier himself "coming out
strong," contrary to their cautions. This didn't seem to jibe with the remarks
made by the premier in the legislature on August 26, 1997, when he commented on a meeting he'd had the day of the shooting. The premier then
suggested that he'd followed the lead of the attorney general, saying, "Any
results of any of the meetings that took place were in Cabinet on Wednesday
where, as you know, the attorney general suggested and Cabinet accepted
the advice and the recommendation that we seek an injunction."

Whoever wrote the memo that was Document no. 11,774 seemed to be
referring to a meeting of Cabinet, since the memo suggests that the premier
and at least one member of his Cabinet were present and Larry Taman and
Elaine Todres were "at Cabinet." The memo also intimates that Harris
and Hodgson came out against legal advice from Larry Taman, deputy
minister in the Attorney General's office, who had "cautioned about rushing in with an *ex parte* injunction."

Instead, they sought an *ex parte* injunction, deliberately excluding the
Natives from being allowed to present their case in court. In addition,

Document no. 11,774 noted that Deputy Minister Larry Taman had argued against interfering with police discretion.

Then there was the phrase "but Premier and Hodgson came out strong." This phrase does not explicitly state what the premier and Hodgson came out strongly about. However, it suggests — by the word "but" — that the premier and Hodgson were saying something in opposition to Larry Taman's cautions against the *ex parte* injunction and interfering with police discretion.

Now Klippenstein was back in court, seeking to have Chris Hodgson, the minister of natural resources at the time of the Ipperwash crisis, added to the lawsuit. Not surprisingly, the government lawyers fought this, saying it was too late to add him on, but the George family lawyers successfully argued that they hadn't known about Hodgson's role before they'd received Document no. 11,774, and it wasn't their fault that the government had taken so long providing the records.

On December 20, 2000, the *Toronto Star* reported on Document no. 11,774 and how it suggested that Premier Mike Harris had met with former OPP Commissioner Thomas O'Grady on September 6, 1995, the day of the Ipperwash operation. That afternoon, MPP Gerry Phillips grilled Harris in the legislature about the memo and Harris replied, "It [the memo] confirms that the OPP commissioner was at a meeting that I was at, something I indicated quite freely five years ago at the time of the Ipperwash situation."

Phillips could not recall Harris having said this, and in January, he wrote a letter to Harris asking for "proof of any such statements confirming that this meeting took place." Harris did not reply to this or to a follow-up letter from Phillips. Later, he would claim that he'd never received the letters.

Things only got more confusing. On May 4, 2001, the premier told the Ontario legislature that he'd been wrong on December 20, 2000, when he'd said that he'd met with O'Grady the day Dudley George was shot. "I think I may have indicated that we did meet with the OPP commissioner. I'm told we did not meet with the OPP commissioner and I did not."

Harris then went on to say he didn't think he'd even been in Toronto that day. "I'd be pleased to check for you, but my recollection is I was not here the day of the actual shooting, and any meeting, I certainly would not have met with the OPP commissioner." However, Harris amended this comment later in the day, perhaps aware of documents obtained by Phillips under the *Freedom of Information Act*, which showed that the premier had been in Toronto on September 6, 1995, at the York Club, celebrating his election victory.

Now, the premier said that he had been in Toronto but had not met with O'Grady. That meeting came a few days later, he explained. In case things weren't confusing enough, O'Grady told the *Toronto Star* that he'd never met with the premier about Ipperwash, either before or after September 6, 1995.

The dizzying flip-flops came as the George family lawyers dealt with an odd delivery, which arrived at Murray Klippenstein's office in downtown Toronto in mid-March 2001. An additional 100,000 pages of records weighing 630 lbs. were dropped off as part of the government's disclosure. By this point, Klippenstein's law office had its own "Ipperwash Room," packed tight with papers from a government which had earlier fought their release. They couldn't complain about having no government records any longer.

On May 30, 2001, Klippenstein received more documents through the court disclosure process: notes taken by lawyer Julie Jai from September 5–6, 1995, when she was chair of the government committee on the Ipperwash crisis.

The new documents, filed in court, included an e-mail memo Jai sent to Yan Lazor, the director of legal services for the Ontario Native Affairs Secretariat, on the afternoon of September 5, after the emergency meeting that included Harris's senior advisor, Deb Hutton. That e-mail stated: "Deb Hutton had already spoken to the Premier, and MNR (ministry of natural resources) had already spoken to their minister. The Premier's views are quite hawkish on this (Deb's words) and he would like action to be taken asap to remove the occupiers."

In her September 5 notes, Jai also quoted Peter Allen, executive assistant to Ron Vrancart, the deputy minister of natural resources, as saying the occupation didn't call for drastic action. "They're just occupying an empt. park — shouldn't take overly precipitous action," Jai quotes Allen as saying.

Jai's notes mentioned other cautions, including one from government lawyer Elizabeth Christie, who told the meeting that she felt the government could apply for an injunction to remove the Natives, but only on a "non-urgent basis — wld be heard in a couple of wks."

Hutton apparently wasn't happy with the thought of a delay. "Deb — wants an emergency inj (injunction). — doesn't want to wait 2 wks." In other notes besides Hutton's name, Jai wrote, "Prem — feels the longer they occupy it, the more support they'll get — he wants them out in a day or 2."

Jai's notes from the September 6 emergency meeting stated that lawyer Tim McCabe of the Ministry of the Attorney General did not think the government had a chance for an *ex parte* emergency injunction, which would bar the Indians from court proceedings.

However, minutes for the September 6 meeting state, "(Note: Following the meeting, Cabinet directed MAG (ministry of the attorney general) lawyers to apply immediately for an ex parte injunction."

Later, yet another government memo caught the eyes of the George family lawyers. It read:

ONAS,
    Wednesday, 6 Sept.
    mtg re Ipperwash
    AG instructed by P. that he desires removal within 24 hrs — instructions
to seek injunction.

The memo came to them in mid-June 2001, more than five years after the lawsuit had been launched.

EVERY TIME THERE WAS activity in the Toronto courts, Sam George would take time off work and make the three-hour drive to the city. Sometimes, as he drove, he would think of what lessons had been learned through the whole exercise. He thought he could tell his five grandsons about how impatience had been so deadly, ending in tragedy. "As they get older, I'll talk to them about how quickly things happen. That you have to sit down and go slowly."

Those drives to Toronto were always accompanied by stress. His work as a youth counsellor was suffering and he knew it. Sam George knew he had to find a balance, but things seemed so out of line, so unfair, that it was difficult to be moderate. How can you be moderate when you feel that you're a David fighting a white Goliath? "It was like everything got put on hold. I know what I have to do, to maintain, but I can't do it," he said. Then in May 1999, Sam suffered a mild heart attack, and he was sure that stress over the court case was a factor, just as his doctor told him stress had contributed to his developing diabetes. Still, the feeling that he had to do something wouldn't go away.

Sam George's eyesight was also suffering, due to his diabetes. Aside from conventional medicine, Sam sought out traditional healers. He felt he could talk to them and say anything, and often he needed to talk. They told him to try to maintain a balance, to try to steer clear of extreme highs and lows. It was the same sort of thing he would say himself when he counselled troubled teens. "Usually, when you're calm, the other people calm down. You don't argue with them. You get over that first hump."

Throughout the troubles, Sam didn't appear that much different to outsiders. His voice was still soft. He still had a quick smile. He still looked for a joke to lighten things, just as Dudley had. Much of this was just his normal nature, but he also knew that if he was too hostile or too strident, that would only put people off, and he needed as much support as he could get. "It was hard enough for people to look at what happened."

He often marvelled about how much effort it was taking to get an explanation that would help make sense of the thirty seconds in which his younger brother had been killed, and what a high cost, in time, money, and emotion, was being paid in search of those answers. "I've lost a few years of my grandsons," he said. "I've dragged my wife across the country. It's almost like fighting a giant because he's got all of the power and the resources." He kept reminding himself that bitterness wouldn't solve anything. "If you let hatred get a hold of you, it will eat you, just eat you."

SAM GEORGE AND his lawyers weren't the only ones upset with the delays in getting answers about the death in the park.

In March 1999, questions about the government response to the death were raised on the floor of the United Nations, as about two dozen questions were posed to a Canadian government delegation. The general thrust was that Canada should live up to an international convention its leaders had signed on political and civil rights. The UN Human Rights Committee asked the Canadian government whether an inquiry had been held "into the circumstances, including the role and responsibility of public officials, of an incident in which a police officer shot dead Mr. Dudley George . . ."

The Human Rights Committee is the official enforcement body that oversees states' compliance with the binding *International Covenant on Civil and Political Rights*, and on April 9, 1999, it sternly rebuked the Canadian and Ontario governments, arguing that they should set up a public inquiry into his death. The Human Rights Committee ruled it was "deeply concerned that the State party has so far failed to hold a thorough public inquiry." The committee "strongly urged" that Canada and Ontario establish such an inquiry, and that the inquiry specifically look into "all aspects of this matter, including the role and responsibility of public officials" in George's death.

The UN Committee was unimpressed with arguments by Ontario and Canada that they could not call an inquiry at this time. Memories weren't getting any fresher, and it had now been more than four years since the killing.

George family lawyer Joanna Birenbaum didn't use the word "hypocritical" to describe the Canadian government's stance, but she might as well have, as she said: "In signing this International Covenant in 1976, Canada agreed to be bound under international law by the findings of the Committee. Canada is sending warplanes to Kosovo to enforce international human rights. Will Canada abide by this clear legal finding in its own backyard?"

The committee's ruling came two years after Amnesty International had urged a public inquiry into Dudley George's death. The new call for an inquiry echoed earlier opinions of a coalition of senior officials of eleven Canadian church groups and the provincial ombudsman. The committee's ruling also came more than three years after a United Nations report recommended a full investigation. Those earlier calls had had the same effect on Mike Harris as shouting into an empty mine shaft, and it was doubtful the latest international rebuke would have any more impact. Such proclamations might have moral weight, but Mike Harris was the one sitting in the Premier's Office, and his government wasn't going to call any inquiries.

Ipperwash Provincial Park was once an oasis associated with summer fun and relaxation, but now it was becoming an irritant to Harris as reporters like the *Toronto Star*'s Rick Brennan persistently questioned him about what was happening in the Dudley George case. Liberal MPP Gerry Phillips also would not let go of the issue. The representative from Scarborough-Agincourt, Phillips was a former Cabinet minister himself and might well have become the Liberal leader, if not for health problems. Phillips wasn't a flashy man, but he was determined not to give up, even if the public's interest was waning at best. He had a particular interest in the problem because he felt a bond with the Ipperwash area. When he was a child growing up in London, Ontario, Phillips' family rented a cottage there for two weeks every July, and the region still had a place in his heart.

Several things about the government version of events simply didn't ring true to Phillips. The government had argued that the Natives had no land claim, but what reason would they have to occupy the park if they didn't see it as a land claims matter? How could anyone argue that the police had handled this dispute like any other? Why were key files missing? Why would police suddenly reverse their past policy for peaceful negotiation? What about local Tory MPP Marcel Beaubien's presence at the police command post?

"It didn't seem logical to me," Phillips said later. "Something didn't ring true." And so Phillips persistently dogged Harris with questions about Ipperwash in the legislature, even when some members of his own party were weary of the issue.

Phillips neatly crafted a question that found the soft underbelly of the premier's argument that it wouldn't be proper — *yet* — to call an inquiry into Ipperwash. On December 9, 1999, Phillips introduced a private member's bill that would set up a commission of inquiry into Ipperwash and also deal with Harris's argument that an inquiry couldn't be held until court cases were exhausted — because this inquiry would be held *sub judice*. "The commission," the bill read, "may defer beginning the inquiry if necessary to avoid prejudice to any person who is a party to court proceedings concerning matters which may be a subject of the inquiry." Phillips just wanted the commitment that there would be an inquiry, noting that inquiries into the 1992 Westray mine explosion in Nova Scotia and the 1993 Somalia mission had been conducted before court cases pertaining to those issues were concluded.

The government wasn't biting. Attorney General Jim Flaherty told *Toronto Star* Queen's Park columnist Ian Urquhart, "We should see what the Court of Appeal rules before we embark down one road or the other." But when the court of appeal ruled against Acting Sergeant Ken Deane, there was still no move for an inquiry. Harris was less delicate, choosing simply to ridicule Phillips as the MPP kept pushing for answers on Ipperwash. On February 5, 1997, when Phillips pressed him about the disappearance from government records of major files on Ipperwash, the premier shot back, "You have a wild imagination with no facts, and nothing's been destroyed."

On May 13, 1997, Harris said he had interfered neither with the OPP nor with the Attorney General's office, then accused Phillips of rumour mongering, saying, "I think the member is well aware that in opposition you can be irresponsible, quote rumours and draw innuendo from where ever you are. In government, unfortunately, you actually have to be responsible and you have to understand the justice system is taking its course."

Phillips simply refused to let go. "It's like a Polaroid picture," Phillips said in an interview. "At first there's nothing, and then, slowly a clear picture emerges." Phillips didn't know the George family before the tragedy, but as time passed, he also got a clearer picture of Dudley's brother Sam and his need to get answers into the shooting death. In his opinion, Sam George was "a gentle, kind, sensitive, honest guy who has been an island of dignity in a sea of mud."

One of the key points Phillips seized upon concerned the burial ground, which he continually stressed was "at the heart of the matter on

Ipperwash." The government had dismissed any suggestion that there had ever been a burial ground at the park. Under intense questioning in the legislature on June 2, 1998, Minister of Natural Resources John Snobelen referred to a 1972 provincial government report to argue that there was no burial ground near where Dudley George had lost his life.

"We . . . have an archaeological survey of Ipperwash Provincial Park in 1972," Snobelen told the legislature. "That report indicated that there were no finds made and recommended that no further archaeological work of any kind be carried out there."

What Snobelen did not mention was that his ministry had also drawn up a memo from its Aylmer office about the report he was now describing to the legislature. That memo, which was obtained by the *Toronto Star* under the *Freedom of Information Act*, cautioned strongly against taking the 1972 report too seriously. The memo was a full page, a third of the length of the entire report referred to by the minister. It stated: "A few comments concerning the value of this report: the methodology used at the time [1972] does not agree with current archaeological survey standards. This report cannot be used to say, with authority, there are no burial grounds within Ipperwash Provincial Park. The methodology as described in the report would not likely uncover possible sites."

In other words, the very department that had prepared the report about the absence of a burial ground now felt the report could not be used with authority.

Snobelen didn't bother to mention this memo or its conclusions when he stood up in the legislature and attempted to undermine the Natives' claims. The cautionary memo that Snobelen did not cite in the legislature was dated September 12, 1995, six days after Dudley George had been shot dead and a day before federal Indian Affairs Minister Ron Irwin released four federal documents from the 1930s, which supported Native claims that the park was located on a burial ground.

ON JUNE 5, 2001, Premier Mike Harris brought the level of debate in the Ontario legislature down to a new low. Liberal Gerry Phillips was calling yet again for a public inquiry into the fatal shooting of Dudley George, noting the George family would drop its lawsuit if Harris would commit to a public inquiry. Phillips had just finished his comments when, according to five Liberals and one New Democrat, Harris swore at Phillips, calling him an "asshole."

At first, Harris's office denied he'd made any crude comment. A day later, however, Harris wouldn't say whether or not he'd used profanity in the legislature. "I was having a private conversation with [Minister of Municipal Affairs and Housing] Chris Hodgson, and if any member thought they heard something they take offence to obviously I apologize, but I was not speaking to anybody in the legislature." As he walked into a Cabinet meeting, Harris told reporters he didn't understand the fuss. "I respect the legislature and I don't know why you're making such a big hassle out of this."

Harris had once more forced the Ipperwash story onto the front pages of the newspaper.

13

UNHAPPY ENDING

"For the last four and a half years, Dudley George's brothers and sisters have fought a lonely battle to uncover the truth about the involvement of the Premier of Ontario and other political leaders in the use of lethal force that led to their brother's death."
— MATTHEW COON COME SUCCESSFULLY CAMPAIGNS IN JULY 2000 TO BECOME CHIEF OF THE ASSEMBLY OF FIRST NATIONS.

There is no happy ending to this story, no triumph of David over Goliath . . . *yet.* There are individual victories and defeats but no final chapter in the story of the killing of Dudley George. Nothing has happened which makes sense of that tragic night and its aftermath.

It took just ninety minutes for the Supreme Court of Canada to hear the appeal of Acting Sergeant Ken Deane and render a decision. They didn't even bother to hear the Crown's case after reading through the defence brief. Instead, on January 26, 2000, the top judges wrote one word — "dismissed" — on the file. Mr. Justice Hugh Fraser's decision was upheld:

Acting Sergeant Kenneth Deane knowingly shot an unarmed man and then lied about it in court.

Meanwhile, Mike Harris's former top aide and troubleshooter Debbie Hutton was promoted to vice-president of governmental relations for Ontario Hydro Services Co. in February 2000, the same month that Deane lost an earlier appeal of his conviction before the Ontario Court of Appeal.

More than half of the two dozen members of the Emergency Planning for Aboriginal Issues Interministerial Committee that met to discuss Ipperwash on September 5 and 6, 1995, have left government in the more than six years since the killing.

Liberal MPP Gerry Phillips continues to file Freedom of Information requests and to question Premier Mike Harris on Ipperwash.

Relations between the OPP and the Aboriginal community have plummeted in the Ipperwash area, with OPP officers saying they are afraid to do their jobs around Stoney Point. Things have become so bad that in a May 13, 2000, editorial, the local *Sarnia Observer* newspaper called for the RCMP to step in and police the Ipperwash area.

Many of the OPP feel wrongly scapegoated as a result of the operation, and John Carson, who has been promoted to the rank of superintendent, said he would welcome a public inquiry. "That day can't come too soon," he told the *Toronto Star*. "We would all like to put it behind us. Everybody has got their lives to live and it would be nice to move on."

Even if an inquiry were called today, three witnesses to that night's madness cannot be called. Inspector Dale Linton and Sergeant Margaret Eve have since died in traffic accidents, while great-grandmother Melva George has died of old age.

The family of Dudley George are finding that their lawsuit against the premier and the Ontario Provincial Police continues to be extremely time consuming and costly. The family has also suffered a variety of stress-related health problems as a result of the shooting, including nightmares, loss of sleep, and ulcers.

War veteran Clifford George has finally moved off the old military base and into a comfortable ranch-style home at Kettle Point. He still has a bright sense of humour and sparkling eyes, and he still carves wood, although not as much as in his younger days. The old soldier, who survived the battlefields of Europe and Korea, is worried that his family homeland may be dying from the weapons of an army he used to serve. He is troubled by rumours of nuclear waste dumping at the military base at Stoney Point and canisters of nerve gas tipped into what Native people used to call a bottomless lake. He worries that someday the canisters will rust and the area will be horribly poisoned. He has also heard stories about a long mound of earth which is thought to be a burying ground for mustard gas. He's suspicious about what might have been dumped in one area of the old army base that never seems to freeze over in the winter and that was once encircled by wire. Some bushes on the base are dying at the roots, and this also makes him fearful. "It's down the line they're going to pay," he says.

Clifford George also has recurring nightmares about earth-moving machines chasing him. In these nightmares, he is not really in danger, but he has to keep moving to get away from them. Sometimes, in his dreams, he's almost totally in the dark, except for a tiny patch of light. When he looks through it, he can see a green forest and he wants to go to that land, but he is somehow blocked. In another dream, he's simply wandering, alone, with no one noticing him.

Nicholas Cottrelle, the teenager who drove the schoolbus to save Cecil Bernard "Slippery" George, has grown to manhood since that night and has been praised as a warrior by fellow Natives. He was given the honour of marching at the front of a veterans' parade in Toronto in 1997, followed by veterans of the Korean War; the Vietnam War; and Wounded Knee, an armed standoff that had lasted seventy-three days in South Dakota in 1973 between members of the Pine Ridge Indian Reservation and the FBI. Nicholas hopes someday to work recording Native music. In the meantime, he cuts lawns and does maintenance work on the former Ipperwash military base. Ironically, his employer is the Department of National Defence, whom the Stoney Pointers drove from the base.

The people of Stoney Point continue to occupy a section of the park, more than six years after the night of bloodshed that ended the life of Dudley George. Their presence lends more than a little irony to the 1995 government order to remove them "ASAP" — an order that made the

government appear ineffective as well as demonstrating what happens
when action is valued over thought, and violence over negotiation.

Ignored largely in life, the name of Dudley George has become increasingly resonant since his violent death. In July 2000, Matthew Coon Come
referred to him and the Stoney Pointers as he successfully campaigned for
the position of chief of the Assembly of First Nations. "What of our many
veterans who came back from service in the cause of freedom, only to be
denied veteran's benefits at home because they were Indians? What of those
veterans who came home to find that while they were in Europe, their land
had been taken and their families forcibly resettled?"

WE WOULD ALL like to believe the government. Not to be able to trust those
in political power leaves one feeling uncomfortable and vulnerable. It also
seems, somehow, un-Canadian. Nonetheless, it is difficult to believe much
of what the provincial government has said about Ipperwash.

To believe the government, one would have to believe that Harris has
a justification in law when he claims that his government cannot even
commit to holding an inquiry until all court cases relating to the Ipperwash
crisis are resolved — even though inquiries were called into other tragedies,
like the 1992 Westray mine disaster, the 1993 Somalia mission, and the
year 2000 Walkerton water scandal while related legal cases were still ongoing. The Walkerton water inquiry was called in the spring of 2000 by his
own government — amidst enormous public pressure and dozens of civil
suits — and no explanation has been offered as to how the legalities of
that case differed from those surrounding the Ipperwash crisis. The main
difference is that Ipperwash threatens to investigate the role, if any, that the
Premier's Office played.

The government's credibility and wisdom are also called into question
by the fact that for three and a half years, it has used taxpayers' money to
fund court battles in attempts to invalidate the lawsuit brought against it
by the George family. Their approach seems all the more wasteful and
petty, in that they argued that the George family were three days late in
serving the government with court documents. They persisted in doing
this, even though Madam Justice Susan Lang, in March 1999, had ruled

against the objection, noting that the Crown, in its own correspondence, "had accepted proper service of the pleading." Then this government, which preaches "fiscal responsibility," used even more taxpayers' dollars to appeal Lang's decision — only to have the appeal denied by Mr. Justice James Southey in June 1999.

Apparently, Mike Harris's provincial government also believes that a lawsuit brought by a family of modest means is a more appropriate means of probing what happened at Ipperwash than a public inquiry. The logic on which they base this belief is questionable, however, since lawsuits deal only with damages, while an inquiry would have the scope to cover broader public issues — such as recommending policies that could be put in place to prevent similar tragedies in the future.

To accept the government's position would also mean that church groups, organized labour, the Opposition parties, surrounding municipalities, Native groups like the Assembly of First Nations, at least one senior OPP officer, the former Ontario provincial ombudsman, Amnesty International, and the United Nations are all mistaken in calling for an inquiry.

To believe the government, one would have to assume that the government responded to the Ipperwash protest the same way it would have done for any other demonstration. That means it would send dogs and a riot squad and snipers to protests held by any unarmed citizens — small businesspeople, university students, or any other resident of Ontario. They would also confront protestors in the dead of the night, even if they could see no crimes being committed. But a belief in this type of consistency would be undermined by the fact that in the fall of 2000 the Ontario government negotiated with angry truckers — some of whom blocked exits and entrances to government weigh stations and created massive traffic tie-ups on major highways — until some solution to their dispute was found.

The government was able to negotiate with the truckers — and, interestingly, campus police successfully handled the situation when eight University of Toronto students occupied the office of the university's president earlier in 2000. They ousted the protestors by constantly playing the music of the Spice Girls, Celine Dion, and the Backstreet Boys. Only the Natives in out-of-the-way Ipperwash were met with submachineguns, batons, and dogs.

To believe the government, the public would have to believe that the Ipperwash occupation wasn't really about a land claim at all and that the Native protestors had no right to be in Ipperwash Provincial Park the night of the slaying, even though former federal Indian Affairs Minister Ron Irwin produced documents from government files that supported the Native claim to the land shortly after the shooting. To accept the province's argument, one would also have to discount advice from experts within its own Ministry of Natural Resources (who wrote the memo discounting the 1972 report that suggested there were no burial grounds in the park). One would also have to overlook the work of University of Western Ontario anthropology professors Elsie and Wilfrid Jury and Michael W. Spence, who concluded that there were one and possibly more burial grounds at the park, just as the Native people had maintained. One would also have to ignore an important statement made by Assistant Crown Attorney Henry Van Drunen of the Attorney General's office, London Region. He argued that government records gave the Natives "colour of right" to be in the park.

IN A DEMOCRATIC SOCIETY, one would also like to have faith in the police. For this to be the case at Ipperwash, one would have to assume that it made sense for the OPP to spend $121,000 a day, including $58,000 daily in overtime for some 255 officers, in an operation which had begun partly because one stone was thrown at a car, inflicting just $400 damage — at a time when the police force was cutting costs by laying off office staff. The force spent $2.12 million over a twenty-seven-day period in September 1995 and succeeded only in driving more Natives into the park and solidifying their resolve never to leave. Seen another way, the OPP spent $88,000 that month in an attempt to remove each of the two dozen protestors; yet they only made the protest stronger. That done, the government then spent millions more dollars of taxpayers' money fighting the George family lawsuit in court, a move that seems odd for a government elected on a platform of small government and fiscal responsibility.

To believe the police, one would have to assume that they somehow thought that listening to desperate pleas from Ovide Mercredi, then national chief of the Assembly of First Nations and a lawyer with much experience in mediation, would make things worse, even though he had been able to help defuse a much more tense situation, in which Natives had guns and shots were fired, at Gustafsen Lake, B.C., earlier that fall.

To believe the police, one would have to accept that they truly wanted to talk to the Natives that night, even though they didn't bring in any of the thirteen trained negotiators designated earlier for the task. One would also have to assume that they considered the Natives too hostile to talk with, even though some officers were shopping for hand-carved souvenirs from Native Clifford George hours before the shooting. It is also strange that the OPP would have gone to the trouble of drawing up their sophisticated "Project Maple" police master plan, the goal of which was to "contain and negotiate a peaceful resolution," only to suddenly set that plan aside. Even if the police decided to bypass Project Maple, it is strange that they did not call upon Dudley George's cousin, Ron George, a Native lawyer working in the area, who had been the first Native to achieve the rank of inspector in the OPP before moving into law full time.

Instead of making every conceivable effort to talk with Native protestors, the police banged on their shields as they marched on the park, and they severely beat a Native man who tried to approach them as a mediator.

A number of OPP officers noted that they had heard a rumour that the Native people occupying Ipperwash Provincial Park had firearms at their disposal. If this were true, one would have to assume that the protestors — many of whom work as guides and hunt to supplement their diets — were unable to hit any police or police vehicles, even though the entire battle was fought in an area about the size of a high school gymnasium, with no cover to protect police.

To believe the police, racism was not involved, even though, in the same week that Dudley George was buried, officers had souvenir T-shirts and coffee mugs made up and sold in a local store, with the logo "Team Ipperwash" and a broken arrow on them.

To accept the actions of the police, one would also have to accept that the Natives were the aggressors, but for some unexplained reason chose not to fight until after the police advanced toward them.

To understand the police advance on the protestors, one would have to believe that the police truly thought the Natives were heavily armed, even though the riot squad marched directly at them with no cover. If the police had reliable and verified information that the Natives had Russian AK-47 rifles, they must then have knowingly marched directly into a nest of weapons, each capable of firing six hundred bullets per minute and killing a human from a mile away.

It would be easier to believe that the Natives had firearms at their disposal if the OPP's own Native mole in the Stoney Point community, Jim Moses, who also worked for the Canadian Security Intelligence Service, had not concluded otherwise. Although he was motivated to discover illegal drugs and firearms, he reported none.

To believe the police, one would have to believe that the emergency meetings at Queen's Park attended by government and police representatives on September 6, 1995, had absolutely nothing to do with the OPP decision to march on the park late that night. To believe this, one would have to believe that — for other reasons no one has yet been able to divine — the OPP independently decided to embark on the costly, dangerous, and inefficient tactic of aggressive, physical confrontation that resulted in the death of Dudley George, even though negotiation had defused protest groups in the past.

If Acting Sergeant Kenneth Deane's version of events was correct, one would have to believe that Dudley George had some sort of suicidal impulse the night he died, since Deane said that Dudley walked out onto a roadway with absolutely no protective cover to open fire, at a time when seven officers had opened fire.

To believe Deane's court testimony, one would also have to believe that Dudley George suddenly got the urge to toss away a gun, even though he was supposedly standing in clear view of heavily armed police officers, several of whom were firing their guns. One would also have to believe that he was physically able to throw his gun, even though his collar bone and some ribs were cracked and his left lung was punctured.

As for the beating of Cecil Bernard "Slippery" George, many of the police were unable to identify the eight to ten officers who severely clubbed him, even though they were nearby. And to believe Constable Chris

Cossitt, one has to accept that he could recall swinging his baton above Slippery George, but couldn't remember if he struck him.

To believe the police, one has to accept that they wanted to keep a permanent and complete record of what happened that night, but somehow managed to botch a tape recording that was to have been made in the mobile command post. According to the police, they were also unable to produce Polaroid and video records of the evening's events. In addition, a raft of officers forgot to record key incidents in their notes, as no mention of Acting Sergeant Deane's alleged statement that night about seeing a man with a gun was recorded on paper by police. Then, as luck would have it, the Queen's Park computer files of Superintendent Ron Fox, who was working in the Solicitor General's office at the time, were also said to have been irretrievably erased, with no backup copies kept.

SAM GEORGE AND HIS FAMILY want to be able to believe the police and the government. They would rest easier if they were given believable explanations for what happened the night of September 6, 1995. Hours after the shooting, shortly after he saw his brother Dudley stretched out dead at Strathroy-Middlesex General Hospital, Sam George said he needed answers about what happened that night. His voice was soft and he wasn't accusing anyone of anything. He just needed answers. More than six years have passed, and Sam George is still waiting for those answers.

AFTERWORD
Tide of Scandal

"I know that there are spirits here with us tonight. Spirits from that land you people call Ipperwash Provincial Park. And in a way they will not rest until your society, your government, does the right thing."
— SAM GEORGE SPEAKING AT UNIVERSITY OF TORONTO'S CONVOCATION HALL

A chilling warning was delivered to Mike Harris on September 5, 2001, on the eve of the sixth anniversary of the death of Dudley George. The lead editorial in the *Globe and Mail* that day began, "Some scandals blow in like Arctic storms. Others gather inexorably, pooling in dribs and drabs. The Ipperwash scandal that threatens to engulf the government of Ontario Premier Mike Harris exemplifies the latter." The editorial went on to link Ipperwash with the Walkerton tainted-water scandal, in which seven people died and more than two thousand fell ill in May 2000 after the government cut funding that would have ensured water quality. That linkage between Ipperwash and Walkerton in the media was growing increasingly common, and it meant the Stoney Pointers weren't as isolated from mainstream residents of Ontario as they were back on the night of September 6, 1995. "Lately, the Walkerton water scandal and the erosion of the provincial health and public education systems have left Mr. Harris looking increasingly remote and imperious," the *Globe* continued. "The tide of scandal is rising, Mr. Premier. The water is lapping at your door."

It couldn't have been pleasant for the Premier if he read this, especially considering its source. The conservative *Globe* was sounding a lot like the more liberal *Toronto Star* on Ipperwash – except for the use of more commas, longer words, and less zippy verbs. The *Globe* editorial was accompanied that week by two front-page stories, each of which quoted liberally from an advance copy of *One Dead Indian*, which was due to hit the bookstores. Now, the Harris government was under siege from the centre-left and centre-right on Ipperwash.

The Premier met the new wave of criticism by clinging to his argument that a private lawsuit – which would be behind closed doors and would drain the finances of the George family – was good enough to find out the truth about the night that Dudley George was shot dead. On September 10, 2001, Harris told reporters that, as the lawsuit proceeded, all outstanding questions about his government's role in the Ipperwash affair would be answered and "free-wheeling accusations" against himself and members of his government would be proven false.

Few people paid attention to the Premier's defensive comments the day they were published – September 11, 2001. The horrors of the World Trade Center attack meant the Ipperwash story was buried deep beneath thousands of others on the terrorist attacks.

Terrorism was still foremost on everyone's mind when Acting Sergeant Ken Deane appeared in a hotel ballroom in downtown London, Ontario, before an OPP disciplinary hearing on September 17, 2001. The force was now officially seeking his removal, eight months after he had lost his appeal to the Supreme Court of Canada and more than six years after the fatal shot was fired. Deane looked far older than he had during his trial three and a half years earlier, when Mr. Justice Hugh Fraser ruled that he knowingly shot the unarmed protester and then lied about it, in a cover-up supported by some fellow officers. The athletic bounce in Deane's walk was long gone. His hair was greyer. His eyes were sadder. He looked like a man who had forever lost something that he dearly loved.

As the hearing began, Deane's lawyer, Ian Roland, made one of the few comments that everyone in the ballroom could agree upon: "Acting Sergeant Deane didn't make the decision for the OPP to be involved and cannot be held responsible for the damage that has flowed from the involvement." The words sounded much like comments made by Judge Fraser back during Deane's trial. They were intriguing, raising questions the George family had been asking for years – but they were left to hang in the air.

Then Roland raised the topic on everyone's mind: terrorism. He told adjudicator Loyall Cann that Deane had been the explosives-disposal-unit co-ordinator for the OPP since 1997 and had trained students at the Ontario Police College in Aylmer and in training academies in Orillia and Ottawa. Deane's continued membership on the force meant "Ontario is a better and safer place," Roland told the hearing.

Roland then called Inspector Robert Bruce, director of the Ontario Police Academy, as a defence witness, and Bruce quickly noted that the terrorist attacks earlier that month in New York City had heightened fears about the threat of explosives in Ontario. Bruce testified that Deane was "one of the most respected explosives technicians in the country."

Before the September 11 terrorist attacks, the province's big policing story had been the sudden expansion of the Hells Angels biker gang into Ontario, and soon Loyall Cann was hearing Deane described as a bastion against outlaw bikers as well. "When you are dealing with motorcycle gangs, there is always the threat of explosives," Inspector Brian Deevy testified.

However, when Kettle and Stoney Points Chief Tom Bressette was called by the prosecution to testify, he said that his community was also concerned about attacks from outsiders, and not necessarily from overseas or from tough-looking men in leather vests riding motorcycles. Bressette sadly noted there were just a handful of Natives at the hearing, and said this shouldn't be a surprise. "They've lost faith," he said. Dudley's cousin Cathryn George put things more bluntly outside the hearing room when she told reporters, "On September 6, 1995, there was an act of terrorism against our people."

On September 19, 2001, Deane began his testimony by pulling out a written statement. "I sincerely apologize to the family and friends of Dudley George, and to his community, for causing the terrible loss that they have been forced to endure," Deane read, in a slow, flat voice. He sounded genuinely sad as he told Cann that he would have apologized earlier, but his lawyers advised against it. "I know I could have written a personal and private letter or statement to the George family, but I felt this was the appropriate forum in which to offer this apology."

When Deane was done reading the apology, Crown Counsel Denise Dwyer asked him why several of his co-workers couldn't recall his ever expressing any remorse. Deane explained that this was because he had "compartmentalized" and "internalized" his feelings. "When you take a human life, it is a tragic, tragic incident, and it is one I will carry for the rest of my life. On the issue of remorse, I have always carried that." Deane continued that he still believed that he did the right thing when he pulled the trigger. "I was convicted in a court of law by a judge that chose to disbelieve my evidence," he said.

"Your personal belief is that you were justified in discharging your firearm?" Dwyer said.

"That is my belief that night," he said.

"And it remains that today?" Dwyer continued.

"Yes it does," he said.

Deane continued that he accepted the court's ruling, even though he still could not agree with it. "This is the court system that we as citizens must believe in."

Sam George wasn't in the hotel ballroom to hear the apology, as he hadn't been alerted that it was forthcoming. "We wanted an apology for a long time – now we weren't even there, and we hear bits of it on the radio," he said when contacted by a reporter.

ON SEPTEMBER 21, 2001, Ipperwash became the first story not related to terrorism to make the front page of the *Toronto Star* since the World Trade Center attack. The *Star* published quotations from documents in a court brief filed by the George family, which stated that the Premier's Office didn't want police to negotiate with protesters at Ipperwash Provincial Park hours before Dudley George was shot dead.

"Premier's office doesn't want to be seen to be working with Indians at all," wrote one official who attended the September 6, 1995, meeting of the Emergency Planning for Aboriginal Issues Interministerial Committee, hours before the incident. Although the police had prepared an exhaustive negotiation plan, another handwritten account of the September 6 meeting states, "Premier . . . We don't want any [illegible] form of negotiations." Handwritten notes, filed in court from September 6, 1995, also described OPP Inspector Ron Fox urging a more cautious course, other than rushing into the park. The notes read: "– appreciate Premier's concern but should we rush in step by step approach with longer term view."

Another handwritten account by a government official also refers to Fox, stating that the veteran OPP officer, then acting as a liaison with the government, didn't want confrontation, stating: "not in anyone's interest to rush in."

TORONTO STAR REPORTER Harold Levy once practised law, and thrives on complex legal stories that scare other journalists away. In September 2001, Levy pored over typed summaries of police officers' notes that were given to defence lawyers representing Natives charged at Ipperwash. Then he took a long, hard look at the original, handwritten notes prepared by police officers at the time of the operation. There was something odd here. The handwritten notes didn't match the typed summaries. Someone had edited out the political references.

The phrases "heat from political side" and "made strong comments in the House" were nowhere to be found. The typed passage simply read, "Sgt. Skinner is to attend command post meetings. Advised members that court injunction is moving along. Advised members to keep tonight quiet, keep an eye on checkpoints and advise logistics what your locations are."

Liberal MPP Gerry Phillips did his own comparison between the officers' handwritten notes and typewritten summaries prepared for lawyers representing Natives, and found even more peculiarities. The word "Premier" was also omitted from the typewritten summary. While the original notes stated, "Premier, no different treatment from anybody else. We're OK. On the right track," the summaries given to the Native defence team read, "John Carson notes that we're on the right track."

Government spokesperson Rui Brum told Harold Levy he was speaking on behalf of the government, including Attorney General David Young and the Premier's Office. Then he declined to speak at all on the OPP documents, saying only, "I am referring any questions about these OPP documents to counsel for the OPP." However, calls to the OPP failed to yield even the name of their counsel. Pressed further, Brum told Levy, "I would also say that the former OPP commissioner, Thomas O'Grady, and other senior OPP officials have stated clearly that neither the Premier nor any other government officials had any input into or participation in, or interference with, in any way, the command decisions of the OPP." Still there was no explanation for why someone had cut out the words "Premier" and "political heat."

Dudley George's cousin, Warren George, Jr., was the only person from the police or Native ranks to be locked up for the violence at Ipperwash, serving six months in jail for driving a car out of the park towards police in his bid to rescue Slippery George from his near-fatal beating. His lawyer, Jeff House, told Levy he could definitely have used that phrase, "heat from political side," when he was representing Warren Junior and Nicholas Cottrelle on their assault charges arising from the Ipperwash operation. "The information they withheld was central to the defence of my clients," House said. "Without that evidence, it became more difficult to show police misbehaviour."

Asked if he felt the OPP officer who wrote the notes did something wrong, Premier Harris curtly replied, "I don't know. Talk to him." That was far easier said than done, because the officer's name wasn't on the paper, and neither the Attorney General's nor Solicitor General's Offices would provide the name of whoever wrote the notes. The OPP was no more helpful, declining to provide to Levy the name of the person who wrote them or even the name of their lawyer dealing with the file.

Osgoode Hall law professor Dianne Martin declared it was too important an issue to shrug off, saying, "failure to disclose relevant information to the defence is a common cause of wrongful convictions and miscarriages of justice." However, out at Stoney Point, Warren George, Jr., wasn't losing any sleep. "I had no faith in their justice system before I was tried," he told Levy in a telephone interview. "I have no faith in it now."

AS PREMIER MIKE HARRIS told it, it wasn't Walkerton, Ipperwash, or any other political issue that drove him suddenly to quit what was arguably the second-most-powerful political job in the country. It was autumn leaves. Harris was just two years into his second four-year term as Premier when, on October 16, 2001, he made the stunning announcement that he was departing in mid-term. Sounding choked by emotion, Harris said he was resigning as Ontario Premier for "very personal reasons." The decision came, he said, during a visit over the Thanksgiving weekend with his wife and children in North Bay. He was trying to reconcile with his wife, Janet, after a two-year separation. "During my time at Queen's Park, I estimate that I've travelled back and forth between North Bay about a thousand times," Harris said. "Half of the time I drove, half the time I flew. But this time of year, one of the most breathtaking experiences is to fly over the miles and miles of autumn colours on a crisp fall day. That's what I did about a week ago, flying home for Thanksgiving. I saw the leaves, I saw the land, like I really had never seen it before, and I had time in the flight and I had time over Thanksgiving weekend to stop and reflect." Down on the ground at Kettle and Stoney Points, not everyone bought the autumn-leaves explanation. One band member smiled and told Sam George, "You're the guy who got rid of the Premier."

SAM GEORGE'S LEGAL TEAM in the civil suit against the government got a strange phone call in mid-November 2001. The outgoing Premier was due to testify in pre-trial examination-for-discovery hearings at 9:00 a.m. on November 21, 2001. The Premier's Office was hoping for a little favour. Would the George family please consent to moving the appearance time to 1:00 p.m.? That way Harris could still attend a weekly morning cabinet meeting. While such a question from a Premier was unprecedented, so were the court hearings. History was to be made that day in the boardroom of the Premier's lawyers at Lax, O'Sullivan on King Street West in downtown Toronto. No sitting Ontario Premier had ever before been questioned under oath in a civil lawsuit against him. And now the Premier also had to ask Sam George's permission to attend a cabinet meeting.

Inside the law office, the Premier and Sam George saw each other in person for the first time, more than six years after the violent night that had brought about the lawsuit. George's first reaction was to stand up and extend his hand to the Premier. He later explained that he felt he had to do something positive. "Part of our belief is that you never wish or ask for harm on anybody," Sam George later said. "It was a hard thing to do, but it was a point that had to be made. . . . I just tried to show, 'We're not who you say we are. So I'm totally opposite. You don't know me, really. You think you know me, but you don't. You know me only as this guy that supposedly is coming to nail your hide to the wall, when really I'm not.'"

THAT SAME DAY, a couple of hours' drive away, in London, Ontario, Acting Sergeant Kenneth Deane was back in the hotel ballroom for closing arguments in his police disciplinary hearing. In her closing statement, prosecutor Denise Dwyer acknowledged that Deane had an otherwise excellent service history, but said the enormity of his offence outweighed this. "How do you get around the fact that if he did not believe he used his weapon wrongly that day, he may do so again?" Dwyer asked adjudicator Loyall Cann.

For his part, defence attorney Roland argued that the OPP still considered Deane an asset, even though they were officially seeking to remove him from the force. If they didn't still think Deane was valuable, why hadn't he been fired years before? "The [OPP's] actions speak louder than its words and what it is trying to do here today," Roland said. Outside the hearing room, Roland was more animated as he described Deane as the OPP's leading expert in biological and nuclear warfare. "It's crazy, that they gave him more responsibilities in the past six years and now this. It's complete hypocrisy."

On January 18, 2002, Deane was called back to hear Cann's verdict. There were more than a hundred police officers present, sitting on one side of the ballroom. About fifteen George family members and supporters sat on the other side. The two groups were in the same room, but worlds apart.

Cann noted that Deane's conviction on charges of criminal negligence causing death was "the most serious conviction" that had ever been recorded against an OPP officer. She acknowledged that senior officers had testified before the hearing that he was an exemplary officer, and that his skills as a bomb-disposal expert made him a valuable resource. However, that wasn't enough. "What could possibly be more shocking to society than to have a sworn, fully trained and experienced police officer, while on duty, in full uniform, using a police-issued firearm, kill an unarmed citizen? This is further aggravated by the fact that the sworn police officer was found by the presiding criminal court justice to have concocted and fabricated his evidence.

"A whole community was traumatized and feeling as though the people they normally called for help were the ones they needed to fear," Cann said.

Cann noted that, apart from Ipperwash, Deane had had a stellar sixteen-year career with the OPP. "I find that this is one of those exceedingly tragic incidents in which one act of negligent behaviour has totally nullified an otherwise promising career." There seemed to be sadness and not anger in her voice as she ordered Acting Sergeant Deane to submit his resignation within seven days or face immediate dismissal. Deane stared straight ahead, still looking every inch a police officer.

Given the options of resigning from the force or being dismissed from it, Deane chose neither. He instead appealed to the Ontario Civilian Commission on Police Services. The dismissal order was blocked. He continued to collect full pay, pending his appeal, but he was barred from performing police duties. His legal bills were now $700,000 and rising, with the tab being covered by the Ontario Provincial Police Association. His next appeal was slated for late September, 2002, and if he lost that, he still had the option of seeking a judicial review to overturn the dismissal order.

SAM GEORGE is not given to dramatic displays of emotion, but on January 9, 2002, he suddenly stood up and walked out of a pre-trial court hearing. That abruptly halted questioning from government lawyer John Zarudny, counsel for former Attorney General Charles Harnick, former Solicitor General Robert Runciman, and former Minister of Natural Resources

Chris Hodgson. At this point, Sam George had been examined by six different government lawyers over ten days, even though he had not been a part of the protest that led to his brother's death.

What drove Sam George out of the hearing room was a comment by Zarudny. "Well, governments don't bargain with terrorists and I'm not here to bargain with the plaintiffs today," the government lawyer said.

In the post–September 11 world, there are few terms more insulting than "terrorist," and now Sam George was hearing it applied to him, his dead brother Dudley, and others in his family.

"Excuse me?" he asked.

Zarudny pressed on, saying, "No, I'm just saying, governments don't bargain with terrorists. I'm not here to bargain with the plaintiffs on these matters. I am asking questions . . ."

That was the point when Sam George stood up and walked out the door.

He later appealed to the court to halt the insulting questioning. In papers filed with the court, Sam George said he found the comments degrading, and that he personally found the September 11 terrorist attack on the World Trade Center "horrid" and "appalling."

"My brother died at the hands of an OPP sniper while trying to protect a sacred burial ground which had been desecrated over the decades by the provincial government, and now it appeared to me that Mr. Zarudny was calling him a terrorist for doing so, and that he was calling me and my family terrorists for trying to find answers about the events which led to my brother's death," Sam George stated in the court document. He added that Zarudny's comments about terrorism "hit me like an emotional explosion."

Zarudny wrote back to Sam George's lawyer, Murray Klippenstein, later that day, sounding taken aback that Sam George was somehow offended because he and his family had been compared to terrorists. "I regret that your client was offended as a result of the discussion between you and I this morning," Zarudny wrote. "[It] was never my intention to offend either him or you. I continue to be mindful of the fact that your client, Mr. George is sensitive about matters that may be raised during this discovery. . . . I am sorry if he was offended by anything I said to you."

MEANWHILE, lawyers for another government department were fighting hard with the Freedom of Information and Protection of Privacy office to keep Ipperwash records sealed. The records in dispute involved Inspector Ron Fox, who had been at that key meeting at Queen's Park the day of the fatal shooting. Fox had argued against rushing into the park, and it was his computer files that had somehow been destroyed. However, there were apparently still some printed records from his files that day, and the *Toronto Star* was pushing to obtain copies of them. Now, the Ministry of Public Safety and Security, formerly known as the Solicitor General's Office, said it would not serve the public good to make them public.

In its arguments to the Freedom of Information and Protection of Privacy office, the Ministry of Public Safety and Security took a more gentle tack than Zarudny, with his comments about "terrorists." Now, the ministry presented a sensitive public face as it argued, "The Records were prepared in a response to the Occupation, which occurred nearly seven years ago, during an emergency situation that resulted in the shooting death of an individual, and which profoundly affected and disrupted the lives of the citizens of a close knit rural area in the vicinity of the Park. These citizens are now moving on with their lives."

The government did not quote any of those citizens and did not point out that there was no "emergency situation" until the OPP marched on the park late at night, pounding on shields and flanked by snipers.

SAM GEORGE decided to hire Oraclepoll Research Limited to conduct a province-wide poll in late February, 2002. He hoped to find that at least 55 per cent of 1,025 Ontario residents interviewed backed him in his bid for a public inquiry. When results came back, he was startled. The poll indicated that 72 per cent of Ontario residents agreed with the statement "The provincial government of Mike Harris or his successor should call a public judicial inquiry into the death of Dudley George." The poll further found that close to half of Ontario residents, 47 per cent, were "strongly" of the view that such an inquiry should be held. The poll also concluded that 49 per cent of the provincial public agreed the government had refused to call a public inquiry because the Premier and senior cabinet ministers did not want their role in George's death exposed, and that 31 per cent of Ontarians agreed that the provincial government was responsible for Dudley George's death. Perhaps most tellingly, it found that 65 per cent – almost two-thirds – of provincial Progressive Conservative Party supporters favoured such an inquiry. Even members of the Premier's own party were having trouble digesting his position on Ipperwash.

"We want the people of Ontario to know that we really, really appreciate their willingness to listen to us," Sam George said. "Maybe together we can try to work this out in a better way, a way that shows the good side of all of us, not our bad side."

By now, Sam George owed his legal team some $800,000, and the pretrial phase of his lawsuit was at least a year from completion. The outgoing Premier's taxpayer-funded legal bill was more than one million dollars. Although the government still balked at an inquiry, people wanted to know about Ipperwash and, in one week that March, Sam George put almost 3,000 kilometres on "Rosie," his Rosewood-coloured 1989 Oldsmobile 98. Rosie now had some 360,000 kilometres on her in all, from carrying Sam and his wife, Veronica, to speaking engagements at churches, schools, universities, and labour halls across the province.

One of these stops was at Convocation Hall at the University of Toronto, less than five minutes' walk from the Premier's office, at an event organized by the union The Elementary Teachers of Toronto. When he took the stage, where Pierre Elliott Trudeau and Nelson Mandela had spoken in the not-so-distant past, Sam George looked out upon 1,600 people who packed the hall, leaning forward to hear him.

By now, Sam had developed into a powerful speaker in his own right: he didn't need notes and could move an audience with his soft-spoken, from-the-heart words. "I don't think the government or the police ever thought that anyone would still care about my brother or the burial grounds six years later," he said. "Our elders tell us, when the bodies are bothered or dug up or moved around, then the spirits don't rest until there is a proper ceremony done again. I know that there are spirits here with us tonight. Spirits from that land you people call Ipperwash Provincial Park. And in a way they will not rest until your society, your government, does the right thing."

The Elementary Teachers of Toronto event raised more than $47,000 for the court case. When Sam and Veronica George drove Rosie back to Kettle Point that night, it was clear they were not alone.

IN MID-MAY, 2002, Liberal MPP Gerry Phillips released a previously secret government memo from a high-level meeting of various ministerial staff just hours before Dudley George was shot. The handwritten memo said the OPP was pushing for a go-slow approach, advocating "removal later (ASAP)" or "when feasible i.e.: injunction." Under a reference to the Premier's Office are the words "removal NOW."

Once again, there were calls in the legislature for an inquiry, and once again, the government, now led by new Premier Ernie Eves, repeated the government's position that a public inquiry would be inappropriate while the civil suit from the George family was under way. Also, once again Sam George said that the family would drop the lawsuit on the promise of a full inquiry. Meanwhile, Patrick Macklem, a University of Toronto law professor and an expert in constitutional law and aboriginal rights, called the Premier's response a "cop-out" and argued that most lawyers in Canada would concur with him that there were no significant obstacles to the government calling a full inquiry despite the civil case. A raft of civil suits certainly hadn't stopped an inquiry on the Walkerton water deaths.

THAT AUGUST, the Coalition for a Public Inquiry into Ipperwash took its case overseas to the United Nations Committee on the Elimination of Racial Discrimination. During meetings with the Canadian delegation in Geneva, Dr. Kurt Herndl of Austria asked specifically why the Government of Canada claimed it "did not have the authority to conduct inquiries into allegations of misconduct by provincial officials and the province's police force."

This downloading of responsibility by Ottawa to the provinces did not sit well with the U.N. committee. The first of their "Concerns and Recommendations" for Canada reiterated "that the principal responsibility for the implementation of the Convention lies with the federal Government of Canada. The Committee is concerned that the federal Government cannot compel the provincial and territorial Governments to align their laws on the requirements of the Convention."

MEANWHILE, documents kept leaking out about Ipperwash – a reminder of the *Globe and Mail* editorial from a year before, which talked of the tide lapping at the door of the Premier's office. Now, documents filed in the court case suggested that Harris himself met with senior advisers the morning of September 5, 1995. After that meeting, one of those advisers – Debbie Hutton – told a high-ranking police officer and other police officials that Harris was "hawkish" on the Ipperwash occupation, according to the fresh documents.

The leaked paperwork tightened up the timeline for activity at Queen's Park before the operation at Ipperwash. An hour after the September 5, 1995, meeting, Hutton went to a top-level interministerial meeting attended by a police superintendent. In that meeting, she said the Premier felt the province was "being tested" on the issue, according to the documents. "Premier wants to deal with the groups as if they were non-aboriginals," Hutton is quoted as telling the meeting. "Premier is hawkish on this issue – will set the tone for how we deal with these issues over the next four years."

ON SEPTEMBER 23, 2002, the OPP issued a short press release, stating simply that Acting Sergeant Kenneth Deane had resigned from the force. The announcement came on the morning that Deane was to appeal his dismissal order. Five and a half years after he was found guilty of the worst criminal offence in the history of the force, Deane was finally no longer on the public payroll.

Sam George didn't rejoice in the news. He said he considered Deane a "scapegoat," who didn't make the decision to storm the park and didn't change police tactics from peaceful negotiations to a show of force.

IPPERWASH WAS BACK in the news in January 2004, after the CBC won the release of tape recordings and photographs of the police operation there. The corporation had fought for three years and risked $80,000 in legal fees after journalist Lynette Fortune was denied access to about 220 video and still photos of the native occupation of Ipperwash Provincial Park filmed by the Ontario Provincial Police from September 5 to 7, 1995.

At first, Fortune was told there were no tapes or photos of the operation. Eventually, she was told that there were tapes but they couldn't be released because they were sealed by a court warrant. Finally, in August 2003, a judge heard there was no court warrant sealing the tapes.

"Information originally received by the ministry of the attorney-general from the ministry of public safety and security (MPSS) was that the records in question were obtained pursuant to a sealed Criminal Code warrant," government counsel Luba Kowal wrote to CBC lawyers on August 11.

"This led to the position taken by the ministry before the commission and on the judicial review that the commissioner had no authority over these records," the letter continued. "Recently, new information from MPSS revealed this to be in error."

The newly released tapes included a conversation accidentally recorded by two OPP officers who posed as journalists and filmed Natives the day before the OPP marched on the park. In that conversation, one officer asks, "Is there still a lot of press down there?"

"No, there's no one down there. Just a big, fat f— Indian," says the other.

Later on, one officer says: "We had this plan, you know? We thought if we could get five or six cases of Labatts 50 we could bait them and we'd have this big net and a pit."

"Creative thinking," says another.

"Works in the south with watermelon."

Contacted by the media, OPP Superintendent Bill Crate called the officers' comments "disgusting." He continued, "Nobody is more outraged than the OPP concerning these remarks. We really regret the highly inappropriate comments made by these officers."

The previously secret OPP tapes also included a wiretapped conversation between Stoney Point protester David George and his girlfriend, hours after Dudley George was fatally shot. The OPP admitted in court the wiretap was made without a warrant.

David George was beside Dudley George when he was shot, and in his secretly taped conversation, he said Dudley didn't appear to know he was dying. "He got knocked down but he got back up," David George said in a trembling voice. "He didn't even know."

"We had sticks and rocks," David George continued. "They had guns, shields and clubs . . . They opened up on us. I can't believe it . . . We weren't shooting at them. We had sticks and rocks . . . I'm willing to take a lie detector and I'm sure everybody else here is."

David George told his girlfriend in the wiretapped conversation that he was convinced that police had to know the protesters didn't have guns with them. "They were taking pictures all day," he says. "They knew we were unarmed."

THE CBC WASN'T THE ONLY organization having difficulties learning about what happened at Ipperwash through the Freedom of Information Act. In September 2003, Ann Rees, a journalism instructor at Kwantlen University College in Langley, B.C., concluded a year-long study, funded by the Atkinson Foundation, of the Freedom of Information Acts across Canada, with the conclusion that "the Ontario government knew it was using questionable tactics to delay and obstruct the release of freedom-of-information records concerning the 1995 fatal police shooting of native protester Dudley George at Ipperwash Provincial Park."

Rees referred to a request from Canadian Press reporter Tom Blackwell when she concluded that "the Ministry of Natural Resources used exemptions its own internal memos say were 'weak at best' to block freedom of information (FOI) requests for records that said then-premier Mike Harris wanted the protesters out of the park 'and nothing else.'"

Rees continued, "The memos, obtained under the FOI act, show the Ministry of Natural Resources (MNR) bowed to pressure from other ministries to seek an extension it did not need."

THE GEORGE FAMILY LAWSUIT was set to go to court within days when the Liberal Party won the Ontario election in October 2003. The family dropped the suit in favour of a public inquiry, and five weeks later, Mr. Justice Sidney Linden was named commissioner of the inquiry. His credentials included being the first chief judge of the Ontario Court of Justice

(Provincial Division), the province's first information and privacy commissioner, and the first Metro Toronto police complaints commissioner.

Linden's mandate was to probe the circumstances surroundng Dudley George's death and to draft recommendations to prevent similar tragedies in the future. While Linden had the power to subpoena witnesses, he wasn't able to lay criminal charges. While the Stoney Pointers had problems with both the federal and provincial governments, the federal Liberals snubbed the inquiry, declining to send representatives to participate. Despite the constraints, Linden was hopeful that the inquiry could accomplish something positive. "I'd like to see the inquiry be a constructive force in the healing process," Linden said in an interview. "Most of the experience that I've had in the law has been constructive and positive. . . . That's my nature. I'd like to make a positive contribution that the community can use for healing."

The connection between the truth and healing was something that Sam George's spiritual adviser, Tommy White, thought about often. White lived 1,800 kilometres north of Kettle Point, near Kenora, where he ran a one-room healing centre in a cabin among the spruce and cedar trees. In an interview, White noted that the Ojibwe word *Debwewin* means "the truth," but that it's a truth based in the heart, not in harshness. "*Debwewin*, in my language, means positive words, positive ways of thinking," he said. "*Debwewin* is soft – a soft, honest way . . . That's part of healing. In our culture, the spirits tell us, 'We'll help you if you do things in a positive way.' The best advice they [spirits] gave me was, 'Don't use what we've given you in a negative way or we'll take everything back.'"

White said the inquiry would go far beyond Sam or Dudley George. "Sam doesn't know it, but he's going to make a lot of communities strong. He's going to make a lot of Native communities strong across Canada . . . It's going to make our communities strong – the truth."

THERE WERE MANY people at Kettle and Stoney Points who feared that elder Clifford George wouldn't live to see the inquiry begin in the town of Forest, about a fifteen-minute drive from where Dudley George was killed. However, eighty-four-year-old Clifford was there with his walker and broad smile when the inquiry began public hearings on July 14, 2004, in the Forest hockey arena, where Dudley was once a peewee goalie. The first witness Clifford George heard was Darlene Johnson, assistant professor and Aboriginal student adviser at the University of Toronto Faculty of Law, and originally from the Chippewas of Nawash First Nation on Georgian Bay, Ontario. She testified that Native people of southwestern Ontario have an obligation to protect the remains of their ancestors, and that it's redundant to call a native burial ground "sacred."

"It's hard to think of a non-sacred burial ground, from an aboriginal perspective," she testified, explaining that in Native culture, spirits remain with a dead person's body and can still feel cold, heat, and hunger. "They need to be cared for."

Two months later, it was Clifford George's turn to testify. He appeared wholly at ease when he swore to tell the truth on an eagle feather, a Native symbol for truth, wearing a veteran's beret and blue blazer, with medals across the chest from World War II and the Korean War.

Clifford was eager to tell the inquiry that he was warned by two local police officers hours before Dudley George was shot dead that he had better beware of a special squad of police being brought into the area. "He said, 'Watch it, Cliff, these people are coming. We're gone at six o'clock. These people are specially trained.'"

He also told of how he and his two brothers returned home from war in 1945, and how they were initially told they couldn't visit their mother's gravesite. When they finally got permission, Clifford described them as "good, hardened soldiers, crying their eyes out."

"There was trenches dug where they were playing soldier, right in our gravesite," George said under questioning from commission lawyer Don Worme, who represented the family of Neil Stonechild, a seventeen-year-old Native who froze to death in November 1990 on the outskirts of Saskatoon, Saskatchewan, after a late-night encounter with police.

Clifford continued, "That is what made it bad for us. . . . I always say, 'I found all my enemies when I got home.'"

Clifford added that he later heard how his Stoney Point schoolteacher had to be forcibly moved from her home in 1942. "She sat on her chair outside [her home] with a shotgun on her knees. . . . I don't think the gun was even loaded. But that didn't stop them. They just picked her up . . . I think that none of them went voluntarily. That was their home, their land. We had the idea that the Creator put us there."

OPP Association lawyer Ian Roland pressed Clifford on whether or not he heard automatic weapons fire inside the park from Natives before the police operation.

"You know what they look like, right?" Roland asked.

"Sure I do, sir," Clifford replied firmly, his medals from two wars shining.

After Clifford's testimony, Leland White was among the dozens of Stoney Pointers who described the trauma of the night of September 6, 1995. Leland, who was fifteen years old when he rode in the school bus fired upon by police, said he still hadn't shaken memories of his cousin Dudley lying on the sand, his shirt bloodied by a bullet wound. He had no recall of other parts of that night. "I don't want to remember. It's like a bad dream I can't remember." Eighteen months after the shooting, Leland said he started having nightmares. "I am constantly looking over my shoulder. I feel like whenever I am being pulled over [by police] they're going to throw me in jail."

Leland said his grandfather had told him about the Aboriginal burial ground in the park. "I felt like I should be there because I was a Stoney Pointer."

WHEN SAM GEORGE testified at the inquiry in April 2005, Roland pressed him on his mother's drinking habits, even though she died in 1971 – twenty-four years before her son Dudley's death. Roland also wanted to know about Dudley's drinking and marijuana usage.

"I've never claimed, in all my times that I've been seeking the truth as to what happened to him, that Dudley was an angel," Sam George told the inquiry. "But I can guarantee you one thing right now – that he is now."

CLIFFORD GEORGE REMAINED one of the dozen or so regular attendees from the public at the inquiry in May 2005, when previously secret tapes of police officers were made public. In those newly released tapes, then OPP

Inspector Ron Fox vents his frustrations with then Inspector John Carson early in the afternoon of September 6, 1995, immediately after Fox left a meeting in the Premier's private dining room with former Premier Mike Harris and senior government officials, including then Solicitor General Bob Runciman, Attorney General Charles Harnick, and Minister of Natural Resources Chris Hodgson.

"He believes he has the authority to direct the OPP," Fox says on the tape to Carson, not realizing the conversation is being recorded.

"They just want us to go and kick ass," Carson replies.

Fox continues to say that Harris made it clear that he didn't consider the park occupation to really be "an issue of Native rights." Instead, Fox says that Harris bluntly told the government meeting, "We've tried to pacify and pander to these people for too long. It's now time for swift affirmative action. . . . They should have just gone in."

Fox continued: "He [Harris] views it as a simple trespass to property. That's in his thinking. He's not getting the right advice. Or if he is getting the right advice he sure is not listening to it in any way, shape or form."

However, Carson, who was now an OPP deputy commissioner, told the inquiry that he received no political direction and did not buckle to political pressure in the operation that ended in Dudley George's death.

"What, if anything, did you do as a result of this call?" inquiry lawyer Derry Millar asked.

"Quite frankly, nothing," Carson replied.

Another tape released at the inquiry records Fox talking with both Carson and then OPP Chief Superintendent Chris Coles, who cautions Fox to "be very careful here. That's what's going to happen. We're going to lose control of it."

In that tape, Fox is clearly shaken by his first and only meeting with Harris and senior members of his government, telling his fellow officer, "We're dealing with a real redneck government. They are [expletive] barrel suckers. They just are in love with guns."

"Okay," Carson replies.

"There's no question they don't give a shit-less about Indians," Fox continues.

FOX TESTIFIED he didn't know he was being tape recorded when he made the comments picked up on tape, and apologized before the inquiry for his colourful language. In his cross-examination by Julian Falconer, a lawyer representing Aboriginal Legal Services in Toronto, Fox was asked about the death of the Archbishop of Canterbury Thomas Beckett in the year 1170. Falconer noted that King Henry II had ranted before some of his knights, "Will no one rid me of this meddlesome priest?" Within days, Beckett lay dead at the altar of Canterbury Cathedral from multiple stab wounds.

"Now throughout history, it's always been a question, Did, in fact, Henry II give an order, give a direction?" Falconer asked Fox. "But he did express an opinion, didn't he?"

"He did," Fox replied.

"And no one will ever know if the knights followed that opinion, will they?" Falconer continued.

"No sir," Fox replied.

IN HIS TWENTY DAYS on the witness stand, Carson admitted that the OPP gave false information to the media, which stated that police marched on the park because a gang of Natives threatened an area woman's car with baseball bats. He also admitted that this misinformation was never corrected. In fact, the incident that triggered the march on the park was one Stoney Pointer throwing a stone at the car driven by Gerald (Booper) George. "It was a long time after the event before I learned that," testified Carson. The errors in the press releases were honest mistakes, he said.

Peter Rosenthal, who represented some of the Stoney Pointers, suggested a police officer would have to be "superhuman" not to be affected by pressure from the Premier the day Dudley George was fatally shot. "You obviously have no concept of what we are working through as an incident commander if you believe that," Carson quickly replied.

CLIFFORD GEORGE HAD MISSED a few days of testimony for traditional and mainstream cancer treatments by the time former OPP Commissioner Thomas O'Grady testified in August 2005. When he did attend hearings that summer, Clifford continued to joke and downplay his ailments, but those around him noticed he tired more easily and shuffled about on his walker with more difficulty. When he sat in his padded grey chair at the inquiry, Clifford often appeared tired and didn't grumble "bullshit" as much to friends and family during testimony he disputed.

O'Grady testified that he was now comfortable in concluding Natives in Ipperwash Provincial Park had no guns with them when seven officers opened fire the night Dudley George was killed. "It turned out that the First Nations [people] in the park were not armed," O'Grady testified under questioning from Matthew Horner, a lawyer for the Chiefs of Ontario.

O'Grady insisted his force didn't buckle to police pressure at Ipperwash. However, in an often heated cross-examination by Falconer, the former commissioner said he could understand if people think there was political influence on the massive Ipperwash police operation. "A reasonable person might feel that there was a perception of . . . influence," replied O'Grady.

ON FRIDAY SEPTEMBER 30, 2005, surrounded by family, Clifford George died in hospital at age eighty-five, after suffering two heart attacks and a stroke while in hospital. True to his wishes, his body was buried at Kettle Point, as he did not want to be buried in the contaminated soil of Stoney Point, where chemicals from the old military base still lay underground.

Staff at the inquiry didn't have the heart to remove the grey padded chair where Clifford had held court. Instead, Clifford's chair became a makeshift shrine, with objects that included a veteran's poppy, sacred sweetgrass, and a picture of him, wearing his veteran's beret. The shrine was still up in mid-October, when the inquiry heard that a provincial government worker discovered documents supporting the Stoney Pointers' claim that there were burial grounds in the park. That discovery was made in mid-January 1975 – two decades before Dudley's death – by a ministry of natural resources researcher in the Whitney Block in Toronto, near the provincial legislature, and then forwarded to the researcher's superiors.

Then, for the next twenty years, nothing happened with those documents. Ron Vrancart, who was deputy minister of the ministry of natural resources in September 1995, testified that he was never told of their discovery. "It was never brought to my attention," Vrancart testified. "I was never aware of it."

THREE OF DUDLEY GEORGE'S sisters, a niece, and a nephew were among the twenty or so community members in the audience in late November 2005, as Debbie Hutton, former Premier Mike Harris's senior aide, swore that she never told government meetings that the Stoney Pointers occupying the park should be evicted as quickly as possible. She flatly denied saying that police should use guns if necessary.

"Absolutely not," Hutton replied under questioning from Susan Vella, a lawyer working for the commission.

Vella pressed on, asking for details on interministerial meetings on Ipperwash on September 5 and 6, 1995, and another meeting with Harris in his private dining room at Queen's Park on September 6.

"Do you recall describing the Premier's position on this issue as 'hawkish'?" asked Vella.

"It's a word that I knew," Hutton replied. "I simply don't recall using it at that time."

Hutton said that negotiating with the park occupiers was never discussed during government meetings hours before Dudley George was shot dead. "It was not an option that was put on the table," Hutton testified, adding, "I think it is prudent to say, we will not have substantive negotiations while an occupation is underway."

Appearing cool and composed, Hutton testified on November 22, 2005, that she can't recall what Harris said at a meeting in his private dining room at Queen's Park on September 6, 1995 – less than half a day before George's death. In fact, Hutton testified that she couldn't recall a word he said on Ipperwash for September 4, 5, or 6, 1995. However, Hutton said she did recall that there was no tension or urgency in Harris's voice. "I recall that he [Harris] participated in the meeting and spoke," Hutton said. "I just don't recall specifically what he said." Hutton said she also couldn't recall Harris's reaction when he received news of Dudley George's death.

Susan Vella asked Hutton if Harris appeared "frustrated in any way" during the meeting on the Ipperwash park occupation in his private dining room at Queen's Park early in the afternoon of September 6, 1995.

"I don't recall that," Hutton replied.

That evening, law clerk George Argyropoulos of the Falconer and Charney firm in Toronto tallied 134 times during Hutton's testimony on that day alone when she replied "I don't recall," "I don't specifically recall," "I don't recall specifically," "I don't have a specific recollection," "I don't have a recollection of it," "I just don't recall it," and "I don't recall the specifics." The next day, Falconer asked Hutton if she suffered from any form of memory loss that could be explained medically.

"I wish I could recall more," Hutton replied. "It was ten years ago. As I've tried to indicate to the Commission, I had – while this was an important issue, I, I had much more on my plate than this and, and I appreciate there are others who, who had this as their sole issue. So I've done the best I can to recall and I've tried not to speculate unless I had something that I felt could assist in a general nature, the fact that I couldn't recall."

Falconer pressed on, saying, "I understand that's your explanation, but my question to you was that it's regrettable that your memory is so lacking. Do you agree with me?"

"And I believe I said yes," Hutton replied.

William Horton, a lawyer representing the Chiefs of Ontario, said Hutton's memory lapses undermined her overall credibility.

"I will be submitting at the end [of the public inquiry] that she essentially is not to be believed," Horton said.

Hutton retained her composure as she testified she had done her best to be honest and precise. "I am under oath and have not at any time done anything or said anything to disrespect that oath. I have been wholly as honest as I possibly can be before this commission."

WHEN HE TOOK THE WITNESS STAND, former Attorney General Charles Harnick quickly tried to distance himself from comments made by Larry Taman, his former deputy attorney general. Taman had testified that Harris instructed Harnick before 9:30 a.m. that day that he wanted Harnick to obtain an injunction so the Stoney Pointers could be removed from the park within twenty-four hours.

"He [Harris] was ordering the attorney general to get the injunction," testified Taman, who wrote a note at the time that states, "AG instructed by P that he desires removal within 24 hrs – instruction to seek injunction."

Harnick dismissed this scenario as "absolutely absurd."

"I can tell you that I was never instructed by the Premier," Harnick testified. "I never heard from the Premier . . . And certainly I would remember a phone call where the Premier was instructing me to remove the occupiers within twenty-four hours.

"I mean, did people actually think that I had some magical way of removing people from the park within twenty-four hours?"

AS THE INQUIRY ground on, the Stoney Pointers remained in the park, more than ten years after Dudley George's death. Provincial government maps and literature now described Ipperwash Provincial Park as "temporarily closed," while the privately produced MapArt guide to southwestern Ontario erased Ipperwash Provincial Park from its publications altogether. It was now a First Nations meeting place, just as it had been, years before the birth of Anthony (Dudley) George.

INDEX